SEMIOTEXT(E) FOREIGN AGENTS SERIES

Published by Semiotext(e)
2007 Wilshire Blvd., Suite 427, Los Angeles, CA 90057
www.semiotexte.com

Special thanks to Robert Dewhurst, Emmanuelle Guattari, Benjamin Meyers, Frorence Petri, and Danielle Sivadon.

The Index was prepared by Andrew Lopez.

Cover Art by Pauline Stella Sanchez.
Gone Mad Blue/Color Vaccine Architecture or 3 state sculpture: before the event, during the event, and after the event, #4. (Seen here during the event stage.) 2004. Temperature, cartoon colour, neo-plastic memories, glue, dominant cinema notes, colour balls, wood, resin, meta-allegory of architecture as body. 9 x 29 1/4 x 18"

Design by Hedi El Kholti

ISBN: 978-1-58435-060-6

Distributed by The MIT Press, Cambridge, Mass. and London, England
Printed in the United States of America

10 9 8 7 6

CHAOSOPHY

TEXTS AND INTERVIEWS 1972–1977

Félix Guattari

Edited by Sylvère Lotringer

Introduction by François Dosse

Translated by David L. Sweet, Jarred Becker, and Taylor Adkins

\<e\>

Contents

François Dosse

INTRODUCTION TO *CHAOSOPHY*

Chaosophy gathers a series of scattered texts by Félix Guattari according to several themes accessible to an Anglo-Saxon readership: first, there are clarifications on the singularity of the writing machine assembled with Gilles Deleuze, which lasted from 1969, when they met, to the publication in 1991 of *What Is Philosophy?* Second, the texts from 1977 give an idea of what the private La Borde clinic, in which Guattari worked, was like, and of his ambivalent relationship with antipsychiatry. Third, the texts collected in subsequent volumes (1977–1985 and 1986–1992) will allow us to better understand his important role in the Italian autonomists' movement, and his relationship with a triumphant modernity. Guattari never allowed himself to lament a world which we have lost. Rather, always displaying a critical spirit, he tried to bounce back in order to chart innovative paths leading to the most creative processes of subjectification possible: "I'm hyperpessimistic and hyperoptimistic at the same time."[1]

D&G: A Writing Machine

After May 1968, Deleuze intended to bring a philosophical answer to the questions raised by Lacanian psychoanalysis. His meeting with Guattari offered him a magnificent opportunity. Moreover, in 1969 his health already was seriously impaired by the operation he had the year before. More than one of his lungs had to be removed. As a result, his tuberculosis worsened and chronically weakened his respiratory system until he died. He was exhausted in the full sense of the term by which he will later characterize the work of Samuel Beckett—an exhaustion which offered an opening and allowed for a true meeting, a presence for the other and a fruitful relationship. Meeting Guattari would be crucial for reviving his vital forces.

As for Guattari, he disclosed his own weaknesses to his new friend, revealing aspects of the inhibition which led to his "extremist misfiring."[2] The basis for this writing disorder, he admitted, was a lack of consistent work and theoretical readings, and a fear of diving back into what he had left fallow for too long. To these failings he added a complicated personal history with an upcoming divorce, three children, the clinic, conflicts of all kinds, militant groups, the FGERI ...[3] As for the theoretical elaboration itself, Guattari considered "concepts mere utensils, gadgets."[4] For example, he used the concept of "vacuolar group" as a way of bringing out something less oppressive within militant organizations, also more conducive to rethinking singular phenomena. Guattari invented his concept of "transversality" in order to unsettle so-called "democratic centralism"[5] in favor of "effectiveness and a breathing."[6]

From their first encounter, both of them immediately identified their critical target: "the Oedipal triangle" and the familial reduction brought about by psychoanalytical discourse, the critique of which became the core of *Anti-Oedipus*, published in 1972. From the beginning their relation was located at the heart of theoretical stakes, based on an immediate friendship and intellectual affinity with an equal rigor on both sides. However, this friendship would never be fusional, and the use of *vous* would always be *de rigueur* between them, although they otherwise readily used the *tu* form. Coming from two different galaxies, each respected in their difference the other and his singular network of relations. What made the success of their joint intellectual endeavor possible was the mobilization of everything that made their personalities different, sharpening contrasts rather looking for an artificial osmosis. Both had a very high idea of friendship. Guattari had admittedly been apprehensive of meeting with Deleuze face-to-face. He was more at ease working with groups, and would rather have involved his friends from the CERFI[7] and integrated them in their collaboration. Putting their first book together, especially, mostly involved an exchange of letters.[8] This writing protocol upset Guattari's everyday life, and he had to immerse himself in a kind of solitary work he wasn't used to. Deleuze expected him to go to his work table as soon as he woke up, jot his ideas down on a piece of paper (he had three ideas a minute) and, without even rereading it, send him the products of his reflections in their rough state. Deleuze thus subjected Guattari to a kind of asceticism which he believed necessary for him to overcome his writing problems. Guattari fully went along and locked himself up into his office, working like a horse to the point of getting writers' cramp. Instead of spending his time directing his groups, he found himself confined to his lonely study every day until 4 p.m. He only went to La Borde in the late afternoon, always in a rush because he always had to be back to his house in Dhuizon around 6 p.m. The director of the clinic, Jean Oury, experienced this change as an intolerable desertion. Usually omnipresent in the daily life of La Borde, Guattari had to remove himself from all the activities at the clinic and devote himself to his work with Deleuze.

According to the writing arrangement they adopted for *Anti-Oedipus*, Guattari would send preparatory texts which Deleuze would rework and polish into their final versions: "Deleuze said that Félix discovered the diamonds and he was cutting them for him. Guattari only had to send him the texts as he wrote them and

Deleuze would arrange them. That's how it all came about."[9] Their joint task therefore involved the mediation of texts far more so than dialogue or live exchanges, even though Guattari occasionally met with Deleuze in Paris on Tuesday afternoons, after Deleuze gave his class at the Vincennes University in the morning. In the summer months, it is Deleuze who went to Guattari's in order to work with him.

On several occasions, Deleuze and Guattari described their joint work and its singularity. After the publication of *Anti-Oedipus*, Guattari said of their writing duo: "Initially it was less a question of pooling knowledge than of accumulating our uncertainties, and even a certain distress regarding the turn of events after May '68."[10] Deleuze also commented: "Oddly, if we tried to go beyond this traditional duality, it is precisely because we wrote in tandem. Neither one of us was the madman or the psychiatrist, it was necessary to be two to release a process ... The process is what we call a flux."[11]

From this exchange, a genuine work machine was born, and from then on it was impossible to identify what belonged to one or to the other because this machine was not a simple sum of two individuals. It only seemed to reside in a "two of us" that the cosignature of the book evokes, yet it functions more profoundly in a "between-two" capable of creating of a new collective subjectivity.

In their machinic bifurcation, the true sense of these notions lies in the interval of their respective personality. To try and identify the father of such and such concept, as Stephan Nadaud wrote, would be "to completely disregard an essential concept in their work: that of assemblage."[12] Their entire writing machine relies on positioning a collective assemblage of enunciation as the true father of the concepts invented. Does it, for all that, lead to the creation of a third man who would result from the coalescence of both, a Félix-Gilles, or a "Guattareuze" as the cartoonist Lauzier has coined?

This idea of assemblage is fundamental for understanding the singularity of the Deleuze-Guattari mode of writing. Deleuze explained this to his Japanese translator Kuniichi Uno: "What is enunciated does not refer to a subject. There is no enunciating subject, only assemblages. This means that, in any assemblage, there are "processes of subjectification" which will assign various subjects, some as images and others as signs."[13] It is with Uno, a former student turned friend, that Deleuze would open up most explicitly about the specificity of their joint work. He presents Guattari as a group "star" and offers a beautiful metaphor to express the nature of their bond, that of the sea sinking on a hillside: "Félix could be compared to a sea outwardly in constant movement, with continuous flashes of light. He jumps from one activity to another, he sleeps little, he travels, and he never stops. He never *pauses*. He moves at extraordinary speeds. As to me, I would be rather like a hill: I move very little, am unable to carry out two projects at once, my ideas are *idees fixes* and the few movements which I do have are internal ... Together, Félix and I would have made a good Sumo wrestler."[14]

Deleuze and Guattari's different personalities induced two rhythms of temporality, a sort of two-stroke engine: "We never had the same rhythm. Félix reproached me for not reacting to the letters he sent to me: it's simply that I was not in step at the time. I was only capable of making something out of them later, one or two months afterwards, when Félix already had moved somewhere else."[15] On the other hand, in their wrestling-match work sessions, each challenged the other to go as far as he could until they both had totally exhausted their strength or until the debated and disputed concept could take-off, leaving its shell behind and gaining its independence not through a work of standardization, but through proliferation, dissemination: "In my opinion, Félix had true flashes, while I was a kind of lightning conductor, I hid in the ground.

Whatever I grounded would leap up again, transformed, and Félix would pick it up again, etc., and thus we kept going ahead."[16]

Together, Deleuze and Guattari conceived of their writing enterprise: "Scrambling all the codes is not an easy task, even on the simplest level of writing and language."[17] The two authors sought ways of escaping any form of coding by exposing themselves to the forces of the outside so as to demolish the established forms. In this sense, the nomad horizon already defined as an ideal would be fully carried out in the second volume published in 1980, with *A Thousand Plateaus*. As for *Anti-Oedipus*, in 1972 it had been an extraordinary editorial success. The first printing of the book soon ran out and it had to be quickly reprinted and reedited with the addition of an appendix.[18] On the other hand, Deleuze and Guattari's theses never were truly debated at La Borde,[19] and they kept being ignored by the corporation of psychoanalysts, with the notable exception of Serge Leclaire.

1977: Molecular Revolution

Prior to its association with Guatarri,[20] the "molecular revolution" was Gramsci's creation, and 1977, the publication date of Guattari's book, was a key period in Italian history during which a movement developed whose radicality and violence almost relegated France's May '68 to the rank of students' pranks. Guattari was very strongly impelled and involved with these events as they were taking place. He and his friends experienced the "Italian Spring" as a veritable fountain of youth. Ten years after being deeply involved with the May '68 movement, they found themselves in the streets of Bologna looking on, nonplussed, stupefied, as the molecular revolution of their desires unfurled, a movement against bureaucracies of all kinds, expressed in a completely new language and with methods unheard-of until then.

The Italy of 1977 underwent an unprecedented crisis. Economic indicators were bleak. Each month the country was breaking down a little more. Paradoxically, it was in this country which was losing its jobs and its bearings that a broad protest movement exploded. It didn't ask for a better distribution of employment, work for all, and wages indexed to inflation, but far less traditionally strove to sap the foundations of the system by frontally attacking labor value, property, and the delegation of power and speech.

If the economic and social crisis was in full force, the political situation was completely blocked. The Andreotti government was leading the country erratically. As for the very influential and powerful alternative force represented by the PCI (the Italian Communist Party), directed by Berlinguer, it was calling for national recovery, moral order, and a politics of austerity. Invoking the necessity of a "historical compromise," the PCI was turning itself from an oppositional party to a governing party. Under Berlinguer's rule, the Italian Communists were simultaneously on the forefront in Italy and breaking new grounds outside by taking their distance from the Soviet Big Brother. They were the prestigious vanguard of European communism, while their alignment behind the Italian authorities and their willingness to ally themselves with a party as compromised as the Christian Democrats had the dramatic effect of cutting off any escape route, not even dreams or Utopia, for the great mass of the excluded (*emarginati*) hit head-on by the crisis and deprived of any hope.

This blocked situation encouraged extreme reactions, spontaneous explosions, and the violence of confrontations. Whereas in May 1968 the movement was expressed in a traditional language, a Marxism-Leninism of either the Maoist, Troskyist, or Spartakist type, ten years later the Italian protest was searching for new inspirations. A whole series of Italian currents on the extreme left found in the Deleuzo-Guattarian theses, and particularly in *Anti-Oedipus* a new language and new paths for hope, especially around the concept of the "desiring-machine." The Italian translation of *Anti-Oedipus* was published in 1975, and the movement of 1977 made its honey from it. The Glorious Thirty Days of May '68 by then had become a distant memory, and the students no longer even had the slightest hope of doing something with their diplomas. Since there was no longer a future, the alternative, autonomous currents set out to change life in the present. They hoped to be able to invent the new here-and-now in convivial collective spaces, self-managed places, communities conducive to the liberation from the self. Compared to 1968, what one could witness was a generational change.

Another component of the Italian situation was contributing to the radicality of the confrontations: it was the persistence in Italy of a fascist party, the MSI, which was not only capable of mobilizing active troops, but also entertained networks of complicity at a higher level of the State apparatus ready to be used as supplementary forces and stifle the seeds of any eventual social subversion. To this already explosive situation was added the strategy of embattled Christian Democrats who relied on the manipulation of fascistic violence as a means of intimidating the social movement and justifying the all-out repression of protest movements on the extreme left. The division of tasks was played out like a ballet: the fascists made repeated attacks, and the police went after the militants of the extreme left designated as the culprits, delivering them to a vengeful popular justice led by a consenting PCI actually enjoying the repression which befell its rivals on the left.

As for the extreme Italian left, between 1968 and 1977 it had undergone a veritable mutation which had been experienced by some as a creative search and others as a relapse into the worst kind of terrorism. Organizations of the Leninist type resulting from 1968 had essentially disappeared from the political scene.[21] A whole movement calling for worker autonomy sprouted from the debris of Leninism. This movement gathered together many collectives, some of which were particularly powerful within several large Italian companies like Fiat, Pirelli, Alfa Romeo, and Policlinico ... What was original about them was that it challenged—on principle—the traditional forms of the delegation of power and speech. Many militants of the old organization *Potere Operario* could be found there. And then, in 1977 there were the "metropolitan Indians," representing the most creative wing of the movement. They insisted more on the need for transforming the relations between individuals, and practiced as their major weapon a sort of derision or irony vis-à-vis the system. They organized themselves in tribes of "Redskins" moving within big Italian cities and fought for the liberalization of drugs, for the requisition of empty buildings, for the creation of antifamilial patrols meant to remove minors from their parents' control, and to claim one square kilometer of greenery per inhabitant.

Unlike 1968, these protest movements had no reason to claim the need for a student-worker alliance; it was a *de facto* development between the students, the young workers, the many "lumpen" and unemployed workers who came to recognize themselves in this emerging movement which claimed its autonomy against all forms of manipulation. Leading up to 1977, the actions of the Worker Autonomy movement had multiplied, many of which took place in an "in-between" zone, at once close to common criminality in terms of deeds and to political action in terms of intentions: these included occupations of private houses and auto-reductions of bills in public services, as well as the expropriation from and hold-ups of banks. 1977 was the high point of this agitation.

One aggravating factor was added to this situation, which had been spared to the France of May '68 and onwards: terrorism. It was increasingly practiced by a number of organizations on the extreme Italian left. Established in 1970, there were the "Red Brigades," the BR, who benefited from a real implantation within the factories, particularly within the strongholds of Agnelli and the Fiat factory in Turin. In 1972, the Red Brigades played an important role in the wild strikes which disturbed the industrial group. They sowed seeds of panic among foremen and strikebreakers by launching the movement of the "red scarves." But this was only a beginning and all through the '70s, the Red Brigades moved towards terrorism and kidnappings aimed especially at lawyers and politicians. In 1977, not a month went by without kidnappings, explosions, and assassinations.

Others chose speech and dialogue rather than the P. 38. Taking advantage of the end of the monopoly of the RAI[22] decided in 1976, a profusion of free radio stations seized the airwaves, opening the medium up to the possibility of countercultural expression. Among these various poles of cultural agitation, *Radio Popolare* broadcast from Milan and unified the components of the Movement with a wide audience and an impressive capacity for mobilization. In December 1976, it directly broadcasted the riots at the time of the opening of La Scala,[23] and in March 1977 "it announced the death of a woman who had been denied a medically necessary abortion; in the minutes which followed, 5000 women went down to the streets."[24]

Among all these countercultural radio stations, *Radio Alice* was not the least important. It was launched by a former leader of Bologna's *Potere Operario*, Franco Berardi, also known as "Bifo." In a city managed by the PCI, this radio station broadcasted from Bologna, showcase of the "historical compromise," to a very wide audience and impassioned public strongly committed to his dissenting voice. At 23, doing his military service, Bifo discovered Guattari's *Psychanalyse et transversalité*. Politically militant, Guattari's reflection on psychoanalysis and the way in which it affects politics inspired great enthusiasm in Bifo. Bologna is a medium-size city with a strong student component, and therefore very receptive to the themes that Radio Alice developed: "*Radio Alice* homes on the eye of the cultural storm with a subversion of language, the publication of a journal called *A/Traverso*, but it also directly plunges into political action with the idea of 'transversalizing' it."[25] As early as 1976, Bifo was arrested for "moral instigation to revolt."

On March 13, Bologna was in a state of siege. Three thousand carabinieri, police officers, and armored tanks occupied the university zone at the behest of the Christian-Democratic prefect. Zanghari, the communist mayor of the city, encouraged the police force to use the most severe repression. Between the 11th and the 16th of March, a sort of insurrection occured in Bologna. Bifo was wanted by the police as the instigator of these insurrectionary events, and the police roundup led to the arrest of 300 people in Bologna. On May 13, the Minister of the Interior took antiterrorist measures; from now on violators would be condemned to life in prison.

A fugitive, Bifo left for Milan, then Turin, and crossed over the French border. On May 30, he arrived in Paris with the ardent desire to meet Guattari whose writings he had appreciated so much. The painter Gianmarco Montesano, a friend of Bifo and Toni Negri, introduced the two. Bifo met Guattari and instantly became his friend. On July 7, Bifo was arrested and imprisoned in La Santé prison, then at Fresnes. Guattari immediately organized a support network for his release. On this occasion, he and some of his friends created the CINEL (Collective of Initiatives for New Spaces of Liberty),[26] whose primary goal was to ensure the defense of militants persecuted by the justice system. The collective published a journal, established a headquarters on rue de Vaugirard, and immediately mobilized itself on behalf of Bifo's release.

On July 11, Bifo was considered unsuitable for extradition and recognized in France as a political refugee. Guattari and Bifo wrote an appeal which condemned the repression of the movement in Italy. This text also openly accused and condemned both the Christian-Democratic power's and the PCI's politics of "historical compromise." The initiative first generated a veritable defense mechanism of national exasperation from the Italian side, where intellectuals and politicians violently accused the French for meddling with questions that they didn't understand and denying them the right to emit a judgment. After his release from prison, Bifo moved in with Guattari on the rue de Condé.

To counteract the politics of repression and to regain the initiative, all the alternative and workers' autonomy collectives and the entire extreme Italian left decided to meet for a large gathering, a big conference in the city of Bologna from September 22–24, 1977. The PCI in charge of the city accused them of provocation, and Enrico Berlinguer, its secretary general, publicly denounced the "plague carriers" (*Untorelli*). They were expecting predators, and instead they witnessed a three-day gathering of Dantesque dimensions for a middle-sized city like Bologna occupied by 80,000 people showing the greatest restraint, with no looting or violence. Given the tense atmosphere and the size of the crowd gathered there, it was quite a feat. Bifo spent these three days on the phone keeping appraised of what was happening in his city of Bologna where he could not go without risking imprisonment. But the entire Guattari gang was present in September 1977, stunned, on the streets of Bologna. All the shades of the extreme Italian left were there. Guattari had become a hero in Bologna. Considered as one of the main inspirations of Italian leftism, he attended these processions with the exhilarating feeling of watching his theses take on social and political force. The following day, the daily press and weekly magazines posted his photograph on their covers, calling him the initiator and originator of the mobilization. Suddenly Guattari had become an international figure, the Daniel Cohn-Bendit of Italy. He had been made into not just a star, but a superstar.

However, this gathering did not offer any clear outlook to a movement which fell back on its own after September, confronted anew with repression and isolation. For lack of prospects, the entire protest movement in Europe was being subjected to an increased repression, and the various governments gave themselves an adequate legal arsenal to impose their politics of oppression more efficiently. In France, it was the "antiriot" law; in Italy, a law promulgated by the President of the Republic in August 1977 carrying new "provisions in matters of law and order" reinforced the central juridical instrument of Italian repression: the Reale law, dating back to 1975, which already allowed police custody for an unlimited duration. It became necessary to organize vigilance with respect to the violations of freedoms, and the CINEL, equipped to instantly alert the intellectuals, kept watching the situation.

Close to but Distinct from Antipsychiatry

La Borde and antipsychiatry have often been wrongly associated together, with the clinic in Loir-et-Cher (sixty miles South of Paris) presented as a landmark of this movement, French style. But listening to its director, Jean Oury, is enough to convince the most reticent that a wide gulf separated the institutional psychotherapy enforced at La Borde, inspired by the teachings of François Tosquelles, from the theses of antipsychiatry. La Borde unashamedly practiced psychiatry.[27] In fact, the positions taken by Guattari in this debate manifested a proximity to every current aiming at subverting psychiatry. He was much more receptive than Oury to the theses of antipsychiatry, in particular to the political questioning of the system. This current started in Italy with Franco Basaglia who, beginning in 1961, gave a very different direction to his hospital in Gorizia. Basaglia challenged the principle of keeping mental patients under surveillance and decided to open all the services of his hospital. He called into question every compartmentalization and substituted for them general meetings open to all.

In a climate of political radicalization favorable to the emergence of alternative and protest movements in Italy in the 1960s, the brand of antipsychiatry practiced by Basaglia assumed a noticeable role. Its explicit objective was to destroy the institution. Guattari did not follow Basaglia's most extreme positions and wondered in 1970 if they were not a "headlong rush" or a "desperate sort"[28] of attempt. Guattari in addition criticized as exaggerated and irresponsible some of Basaglia's positions, like his refusal to give medicines to his patients, alleging that it would inhibit himself from entering a true relation with them. Guattari wondered even if one didn't end up, with these best intentions, refusing the mad the right to be mad. Basaglia's institutional negation would prove to be a denial, in the Freudian sense, of the singularity of mental illnesses. The movement Basaglia launched later on, called "Psichiatria Democratica," would go as far as calling for the outright suppression of psychiatric hospitals.

The other large branch of antipsychiatry, represented by Ronald Laing and David Cooper, is British.[29] Guattari met them during a conference called "Journées de l'enfance aliénée" organized in 1967 by Maud Mannoni and featuring Jacques Lacan. The proceedings of these two days were published in two issues of the journal *Recherches* directed by Guattari.[30] But he was not convinced by their antipsychiatric practice either. He considered them to be trapped in the Oedipal schema which he tried to surpass with Deleuze by publishing *Anti-Oedipus*. Soon after, he did his best to deconstruct the Anglo-Saxon experiment of antipsychiatry.[31]

The British Antipsychiatric movement all started in 1965 with Ronald Laing in Kingsley Hall in the London suburbs. The attempt to abolish the boundaries and hierarchies between psychiatrists, nurses, and patients happened in a place well known as part of the history of the English labor movement. This project was distinct from that of La Borde's, because what was at stake was not a dismissal of the institution altogether, but rather a transformation of it from the inside. Among their group of psychiatrists responsible for the life of Kingsley Hall, besides Laing himself, were David Cooper and Maxwell Jones. This experiment provoked such strong reactions of rejection from the entourage that it occasionally turned this "free territory" into a besieged fortress. To base his criticism, Guattari examined the case of the most famous boarder of Kingsley Hall, Mary Barnes, who wrote with her psychiatrist, Joseph Becke, a book describing her experience. Guattari saw in this account the "hidden side of Anglo-Saxon antipsychiatry,"[32] a mixture of neo-behaviorist dogmatism, familialism, and the most traditional Puritanism. Mary Barnes, a nurse herself, undertook the "journey" of schizophrenia and began a freefall regression into childhood that took her to the threshold of death. The familialism in which Mary Barnes locked herself up led her to deny the surrounding social reality. What was the contribution of antipsychiatry in this case? Instead of framing this familialist drift within the patient-psychiatrist dual relation, it pushed it to the extreme, allowing the eventual deployment of a collective and theatrical formation exacerbating all its effects. According to Guattari, the cure was wrongly directed because what Mary Barnes needed was not more family, but more society.

In 1974–75, Mony Elkaïm, whom Guattari met in the United States, returned to Europe to practice psychiatry in a poor district of Brussels. In 1975 he and Guattari decided to band together alternative experiments, to gather all the dissident psychiatric schools into an international network. At this time, Elkaïm occupied an important position in the field of family therapy. As for Guattari, he was very receptive to Elkaïm's systemist theses, which had the merit of envisaging therapy in terms of groups and not of desocialized individuals. As a result, in January of 1975 they decided to create an international network together in Brussels meant to circulate information on experiments in progress. They named it "Alternative Network to psychiatry." Through this engagement, Guattari expressed his desire to go beyond the theses of institutional psychotherapy towards a depsychiatrization of madness, taking the most innovative currents available as his starting points.

In order to create this network, in 1975 Mony Elkaïm managed to gather together Robert Castel and Franco Basaglia, in spite of the latter's disagreements with Guattari. Robert Castel helped create a friendly complicity between the two despite their divergences. The initial title "Alternative to the Sector" was quickly dismissed as too limited, and Basaglia's propoed "Alternative Network to Psychiatry" was adopted instead.[33] Guattari fully involved himself in this network, which actively defended Franco Basaglia as well as the German antipsychiatrists.

The Alternative Network served as a junction for various dissident psychiatric practices. After the inaugural assembly in Brussels, it sponsored many international meetings, for example in Paris (March 1976), Trieste (September 1977), Cuernavaca, Mexico (September 1978), and San Francisco (September 1980) ... The purpose of these gatherings was not to instill a new orthodoxy, but to be aware of what was being done elsewhere. In his interventions within the Network, Guattari insisted on this nonproselytizing attitude. In this domain, science could not set itself up as a unifying authority, because successful practices could only arise from a micropolitics whose singular nature was not limited in scale to analyzing small groups, but instead implied a permanent dialogue and a continuous process connecting it to the macro scale of the surrounding society. It was clearly out of the question to set up isolated cells cut off from the remainder of society in the name of some kind of alternative logic.

Modernity and New Processes of Subjectification

In the 80s, Guattari would above all become involved with ecological movements, seeing in them the site for a possible restoration of the relationship between politics and the citizen. Guattari found among the ecologists a milieu simultaneously receptive to the imperative of working towards a profound change of society and critical towards current policy, including that of the left. He immediately found himself in the left, alternative wing of the "Greens." After the major student protest movement in France of 1986 and the exit of a small group of militants from an endlessly moribond PSU (Unified Socialist Party),[34] a "call for Rainbow" was issued as a proclamation in favor of reorganizing a pole which would be alternative to the parties on the traditional left. This initiative was supported at the same time by René Dumont and by Daniel Cohn-Bendit, and Guattari was a signatory with certain Green leaders, like Didier Anger, Yves Cochet, and Dominique Voynet, but also with non-Greens like Alain Lipietz and some militants from the PSU. Their model was the powerful movement of the German Greens, *Grünen*, who succeeded in creating true associative enclaves within German society and in embodying a political hope. Joint meetings were organized through Cohn-Bendit, leader of the German Greens. The signatories of the call for a "Rainbow" were hoping "to join the transformative forces of society together in the Rainbow of their diversity."

In 1989, Guattari would be integrated into another ecologically sensitive membership group, coming out from the Group of Ten, the "Science and Culture" group, animated, among others, by

René Passet, Jacques Robin, and Anne-Brigitte Kern, all intent on imagining another left. In 1989, their first meeting took place in Guattari's apartment to debate the informational mutation. Guattari thus was part of the orientation Group for the review. He integrated this ecological dimension in its multiple interventions, emphasizing the North/South imbalance and its disastrous consequences, as well as the ethical dimension of the environmental problem.

In 1990, Brice Lalonde created a new pole of attraction called *Génération Ecologie*, which meant to be on the left of the French Socialist Party and allowed a dual membership. Quite a few political personalities gave their support to this initiative, even Guattari who nonetheless belonged to the "Greens." In fact, Guattari got involved in the two concurrent organizations, being as dissatisfied with Waechter as he was with Lalonde, but eager to promote this new pole as a way of crystallizing a political alternative. In the beginning of 1992, as the regional elections got closer, Guattari still wrote in *Le Monde*, pointing out to what degree the Waechter/Lalonde quarrels were unimportant with regard to this "vague aspiration, but indicative of an opening towards 'something else' … It behooves the plural movement of political ecology to uphold this aspiration."[35] During his last year in 1992, Guattari made an effort to bring together the Greens militants with those of *Génération Ecologie* and other ecological associations. After the success of several ecologists in the elections of March 22, 1992, he also succeeded in making a number of these militants who belonged to rival organizations adopt a common text. Deploring the division among these groups and their sterile polemics, he called for a General Assembly of Ecologists capable of exerting a unifying and mobilizing function.

The last of the many battles fought by Guattari was to be on this ecological front. In his handwritten notes, there is a text dating back to a month before his death entitled "Vers une nouvelle démocratie écologique"[36] ("Towards a New Ecological Democracy") in which he noted with satisfaction that an increasing majority of public opinion now perceived the ecologists as the only ones capable of problematizing the crucial questions of the time in an innovative way. Ecologists potentially incarnated another way of doing politics, more in touch with daily realities and at the same time connected to global issues. He regretted that the two components of this current, still known for their probity, were overly patterned on the model of traditional political parties: "It appears necessary that the living components which exist within each one of these movements organize among themselves in connection with the associative movement."[37]

In the work Guattari published in 1989, he defined ecosophy[38] as the necessary articulation between the political and ethical dimensions of three registers: the questions of the environment, of social relations, and of the subjective dimension. All through his life can be found a concern to account for modes of subjectification in relation to their points of insertion in modernity. Acknowledging that technological advancements were making it possible to free time for humanity, he wondered how this freedom could be used. He also insisted, in the era of the worldwide market, that the scale of analysis be global. A new ethico-aesthetic paradigm would have for ambition to think through the three registers of mental ecology, social ecology, and environmental ecology. As always, his method remained transversal and bent on highlighting in each case which potential vectors of subjectification would allow the blossoming of various forms of singularization. Thanks to data processing revolutions and the rise of biotechnologies, Guattari believed that "new methods of subjectification were about to be born."[39] He kept avoiding any type of Cassandra complex and predicting the worst catastrophes to come, or writing a jeremiad on this world that we leave behind; quite the contrary, he was pleased with the construction sites to come which would increasingly call upon intelligence and human initiative.[40] This is what justified his fascination with Japan who had managed "to graft advanced technological industries onto a collective subjectivity still connected to a very remote past (going back to shinto-Buddhism for Japan)."[41] This is the kind of tension that this new discipline would have to interrogate, what Guattari wished to call into being by the name of ecosophy. It would make it possible to simultaneously support solidarity between people and the processes of singularization capable of bringing out modes of subjectification.

The title of the present book, first published in the United States, of course echoes that of Guattari's last work *Chaosmosis*, published in 1992.[42] He borrowed this title, *Chaosmosis*, from his favorite literary author, James Joyce, who had invented the term "chaosmos," already used by both Deleuze and Guattari. With this final book, his swan song, Guattari undoubtedly signed his most readable text, the most accomplished that he ever wrote alone. It is an intellectual testament that he bequeathed in what was to be his final year.

Guattari's argument in *Chaosmosis* consisted in defining a new aesthetic paradigm at the end of a process which revisits subjectivity while passing through the machinic. He reaffirmed the plural, polyphonic character of his conception of the subject, and the importance of the subjective question which he had always encountered as a practicing psychotherapist. According to him, the transversalist method was more effective for giving an account of the often explosive cocktail of contemporary subjectivities preyed upon by a tension between technological modernity and archaizing attachment. Guattari reminded us of the criticism formulated against structuralism and its reductionism: "It was a grave error on the part of the structuralist current to pretend that everything about the psyche could be brought under the sole crook of the linguistic signifier."[43] He based this criticism on Daniel Stern's work on infants[44] that allowed one to perceive the emergent and heterogenetic character of subjectivity. At the end of his journey, we can note the discrete return of the one who had left his imprint on Guattari from the very beginning: Jean-Paul Sartre, and his insistence on the existential dimension.

Guattari didn't deny Freudianism its historical contribution, but he was eager to promote a different approach which would no longer revolve around the opposition between conscious and unconscious, but would envisage the unconscious as an overlay of diverse heterogeneous strata of subjectification, each of variable consistency and productive of flows—the thing he tried to identify in his schizoanalytic cartographies.[45]

This precedence given to subjectification led him to reject closed-off modelizations which denied the new and were only concerned with regularities and meaningful averages. Quite to the contrary, Guattari privileged the processual, the irreversible, and the singular. And to avoid binary oppositions, he proposed "the concept of ontological intensity. It implies an ethico-aesthetic engagement of the enunciative assemblage."[46] Freudianism had taken neurosis for its model whereas, according to Guattari, schizo-analysis would take psychosis for a model, because it is in psychosis that the other appears beyond personal identity, and because this fracture makes it possible to build a true heterogenesis.

Following the work of Pierre Lévy, Guattari showed that we cannot reduce the concept of the machine to the idea of a mechanical operation. On the one hand, all machines are crossed by "abstract machines," but today, with robotics and data processing, they increasingly involve human intelligence.[47] Like Lévy, Guattari considered that the "ontological iron curtain," which the philo-sophical tradition had built between the spirit and matter, should be dismantled. He even found in this once again the very sense of the metaphysical other which he had constructed with Deleuze in their joint works.

Guattari also proposed to rework Francisco Varela's notion of autopoiesis which designates organisms generating their own operation and their specific limits. However, by broadening this biological application to social systems, Guattari also included technical machines and the entire evolving human entity inasmuch as these elements are initially caught within singular assemblages in a process of becoming. Having reevaluated the Saussurian rupture between language and speech in a new light, and demonstrated that the two dimensions are totally intertwined, Guattari defined, in conclusion to this book which synthesizes all his reflections, what he meant by this new aesthetic paradigm he was hoping to bring about. He started from the idea that technical or social imperatives inherent to societies of the past now were perceived as so many aesthetic manifestations; they attested to the rise in power of this relation of aesthetization that our society maintains with the world. This testified to a modern civilization which could only survive through the continual creation of the new and through innovation in every domain. And yet, this process of transformation never ceased raising the question of subjectivity from different angles.

Guattari went through the great upheaval of 1989 and the fall of the Berlin Wall, the collapse of Communism and the end of the Cold War, with the same analytical acuity. He remained aware of the danger that the multiplication of archaizing outbursts represented, of the regression to sectarian and fundamentalist identity, but his optimism and his desire for better becomings, however, went unabated. Quite to the contrary, he realized that there was no better time "to reinvent politics."[48] The world that used to be bipolarized through the opposition between the Eastern and Western blocs now was on the way to becoming integrated along the lines of what Guattari, since 1980, had defined as CMI (World Integrated Capitalism). In *Libération* in 1987, Guattari presented what he conceived as "the new worlds of capitalism":[49] one of the main features of postindustrialist capitalism, also called CMI, was to transfer the productive structures of commodities and services onto structures productive of signs and subjectivity, though the media, surveys, and advertisements.

From these reflections on a world which had been shifting momentously after the fractures of 1989, Guattari would provide one last synthesis, written just a few weeks before his death. It was a published posthumously by *Le Monde diplomatique* in its October 1992 issue.[50] With this contribution, Guattari meant to shake the increasing passivity of a world busy looking at its destiny flickering on the screen as if it had no more grip on it. And yet current mutations would make it possible to set up new collective assemblages of enunciation affecting the entire social fabric, family, school, districts … He reasserted on this occasion a conception which he hoped to never cease elaborating on until it became an accepted truth, that of plural humanity—an expression from Bernard Lahire—of a humanity pertaining to a multiplicity of cities, to borrow the model from Luc Boltanski and Laurent Thévenot. "What I intend to stress is the fundamentally pluralist, multicentered, heterogeneous character of contemporary subjectivity, in spite of the homogenization which objectifies through mass-mediatization. In this respect, an individual is already a 'collective' of heterogeneous components."[51] Fordist and Taylorist conceptions were increasingly being surpassed by postindustrial society, whereas new collective assemblages of labor could be thought anew based on the transversalities still accessible through the remainder of the city activities. Guattari warned us about the urgency of answering these new challenges, as otherwise the repercussions of inertia could be cruel and destructive: "Absent the promotion of such a subjectivity of difference, of the atypical, of utopia, our epoch could topple into atrocious conflicts of identity, like those which the people of ex-Yugoslavia have undergone."[52]

The disastrous implosion which ex-Yugoslavia experienced, as well as the dangers of generalized warlike violence on a planetary scale seen in the war against Iraq, led Guattari in the '90s to oppose such logics of vicious oppositions with the greatest rigor and to debate this topic further with Paul Virilio. Guattari was radically opposed to the first war against Iraq in the early '90s, and saw it as the manifestation of an American hegemony bent on imposing its own solutions on the international community: "The conflict against Iraq is beginning under the worst possible conditions. The United States above all defends its interest as a great power: since the beginning of the crisis, it had never stopped manipulating the United Nations."[53] Without denying the major role assumed by the Iraqi dictator in the beginning of the war, Guattari invoked the perversion of the international order which has led to this disastrous situation: the complicity among the great powers in the Iraq-Iran conflict, the nonresolution of the questions of Lebanon and the Palestinians, the politics of large oil companies, and "more generally, the relationship between the North and, the South which never stops evolving in a catastrophic way."[54] This war against Iraq was rejected by Guattari at least as violently as Deleuze, who signed with his colleague at Paris VIII, René Schérer, a strongly worded text: "La guerre immonde"[55] ("The Abject War"). In it the two denounced the destruction of a nation, the Iraqi nation, under the pretext of the liberation of Kuwait, by a Pentagon presented as the "organ of a State terrorism busy trying out its weapons."[56] They also condemned what they considered a simple alignment of the French government: "Our government never stops disavowing its own declarations and increasingly throws itself into a war which it had the power oppose. Bush congratulates us as one thanks a servant."[57]

It is on this very topic of the war that Guattari's course was brutally cut short by his death. At the instigation of his friend Sacha Goldman, in the aftermath of the Gulf War, while the ex-Yugoslavia was tearing itself apart, Guattari began a dialogue in several stages with Paul Virilio. These three sessions took place on May 4, June 22, and August 4, 1992: "The Spanish War was a laboratory ... The Gulf War and the war in Yugoslavia are laboratories of something to come ... What has just happened in the '90s is the end of the weapons of mass destruction replaced by the weapon of communication."[58] In this dialogue, Guattari never stopped coming back to what remained for him the major question: the transformation of subjectivity, binding new military technologies and new strategies to the "conditions of the production of subjectivity to which they are adjacent."[59] Sacha Goldman sent the transcription of this dialogue to both partners in August. As Virilio was correcting the text he got a telephone call from Antoine de Gaudemar: "Gaudemar told me: 'Paul, did you hear what happened to Félix?' I answered: no, is he cross? Because he was a little miffed after we had an argument and I thought that he didn't want to do this book with me any more. And Gaudemar said: 'No, he's dead.'"[60]

— Translated by Taylor Adkins

I

DELEUZE/GUATTARI ON

ANTI-OEDIPUS

1

CAPITALISM: A VERY SPECIAL DELIRIUM

Actuel: *When you describe capitalism, you say:*

> *"There isn't the slightest operation, the slightest industrial or financial mechanism that does not reveal the dementia of the capitalist machine and the pathological character of its rationality (not at all a false rationality, but a true rationality of this pathology, of this madness, for the machine does work, be sure of it). There is no danger of this machine going mad; it has been mad from the beginning, and that's where its rationality comes from."*

Does this mean that after this "abnormal" society, or outside of it, there can be a "normal" society?

Gilles Deleuze: We do not use the terms "normal" or "abnormal." All societies are rational and irrational at the same time. They are perforce rational in their mechanisms, their cogs and wheels, their connecting systems, and even by the place they assign to the irrational. Yet all this presupposes codes or axioms which are not the products of chance, but which are not intrinsically rational either. It's like theology: everything about it is rational if you accept sin, immaculate conception, incarnation. Reason is always a region cut out of the irrational—not sheltered from the irrational at all, but a region traversed by the irrational and defined only by a certain type of relation between irrational factors. Underneath all reason lies delirium, drift. Everything is rational in capitalism, except capital or capitalism itself. The stock market is certainly rational; one can understand it, study it, the capitalists know how to use it, and yet it is completely delirious, it's mad. It is in this sense that we say: the rational is always the rationality of an irrational. Something that hasn't been adequately discussed about Marx's *Capital* is the extent to which he is fascinated by capitalist mechanisms, precisely because the system is demented, yet works very well at the same time. So what is rational in a society? It is—the interests being defined in the framework of this society—the way people pursue those interests, their realization. But down below, there are desires, investments of desire that cannot be confused with the investments of interest, and on which interests depend in their determination and distribution: an enormous flux, all kinds of libidinal-unconscious flows that make up the delirium of this society. The true history is the history of desire. A capitalist, or today's technocrat, does not desire in the same way a slave merchant or official of the ancient Chinese empire would. That people in a society desire repression, both for others and *for themselves*, that there are always people who want to bug others and who have the opportunity to do so, the "right" to do so, it is this that reveals the problem of a deep link between libidinal desire and the social domain. A "disinterested" love for the oppressive machine: Nietzsche said some beautiful things about this permanent triumph of slaves, on how the embittered, the depressed, and the weak, impose their mode of life upon us all.

So what is specific to capitalism in all this?

Gilles Deleuze: Are delirium and interest, or rather desire and reason, distributed in a completely new, particularly "abnormal" way in capitalism? I believe so. Capital, or money, is at such a level of insanity that psychiatry has but one clinical equivalent: the terminal stage. It is too complicated to describe here, but one detail should be mentioned. In other societies, there is exploitation, there are also scandals and secrets, but that is part of the "code," there are even explicitly secret codes. With capitalism, it is very different: nothing is secret, at least in principle and according to the code (this is why capitalism is "democratic" and can "publicize" itself, even in a juridical sense). And yet nothing is admissible. Legality itself is inadmissible. By contrast to other societies, it is a regime both of the public *and* the inadmissible. A very special delirium inherent to the regime of money. Take what are called scandals today: newspapers talk a lot about them, some people pretend to defend themselves, others go on the attack, yet it would be hard to find anything illegal in terms of the capitalist regime. The prime minister's tax returns, real estate deals, pressure groups, and more generally the economic and financial mechanisms of capital—in sum, everything is legal, except for little blunders; what is more, everything is public, yet nothing is admissible. If the left was "reasonable," it would content itself with vulgarizing economic and financial mechanisms. There's no need to publicize what is private, just make sure that what is already public is being admitted publicly. One would find oneself in a state of dementia without equivalent in the hospitals. Instead, one talks of "ideology." But ideology has no importance whatsoever: what matters is not ideology, not even the "economico-ideological" distinction or opposition, but the organization of power. Because organization of power—that is, the manner in which desire is already in the economic, in which libido invests the economic—haunts the economic and nourishes political forms of repression.

So is ideology a trompe l'oeil?

Gilles Deleuze: Not at all. To say "ideology is a trompe l'oeil," that's still the traditional thesis. One puts the infrastructure on one side—the economic, the serious—and on the other, the superstructure, of which ideology is a part, thus rejecting the phenomena of desire in ideology. It's a perfect way to ignore how desire works within the infrastructure, how it invests it, how it takes part in it, how, in this respect, it organizes power and the repressive system. We do not say: ideology is a trompe l'oeil (or a concept that refers to certain illusions). We say: there is no ideology, it is an illusion. That's why it suits orthodox Marxism and the Communist Party so well. Marxism has put so much emphasis on the theme of ideology to better conceal what was happening in the USSR: a new organization of repressive power. There is no ideology, there are only organizations of power once it is admitted that the organization of power is the unity of desire and the economic infrastructure. Take two examples. Education: in May 1968 the leftists lost a lot of time insisting that professors engage in public self-criticism as agents of bourgeois ideology. It's stupid, and simply fuels the masochistic impulses of academics. The struggle against the competitive examination was abandoned for the benefit of the controversy, or the great anti-ideological public confession. In the meantime, the more conservative professors had no difficulty reorganizing their power. The problem of education is not an ideological problem, but a problem of the organization of power: it is the specificity of educational power that makes it appear to be an ideology, but it's pure illusion. Power in the primary schools, that means something, it affects all children. Second example: Christianity. The church is perfectly pleased to be treated as an ideology. This can be argued; it feeds ecumenism. But Christianity has never been an ideology; it's a very original, very specific organization of power that has assumed diverse forms since the Roman Empire and the Middle Ages, and which was able to invent the idea of international power. It's far more important than ideology.

Félix Guattari: It's the same thing in traditional political structures. One finds the old trick being played everywhere again and again: a big ideological debate in the general assembly and questions of organization reserved for special commissions. These questions appear secondary, determined by political options. While on the contrary, the real problems are those of organization, never specified or rationalized, but projected afterwards in ideological terms. There the real divisions show up: a treatment of desire and power, of investments, of group Oedipus, of group "superegos," of perverse phenomena, etc. And then political oppositions are built up: the individual takes such a position against another one, because in the scheme of organization of power, he has already chosen and hates his adversary.

Your analysis is convincing in the case of the Soviet Union and of capitalism. But in the particulars? If all ideological oppositions mask, by definition, the conflicts of desire, how would you analyze, for example, the divergences of three Trotskyite groupuscules? Of what conflict of desire can this be the result? Despite the political quarrels, each group seems to fulfill the same function vis-à-vis its militants: a reassuring hierarchy, the reconstitution of a small social milieu, a final explanation of the world ... I don't see the difference.

Félix Guattari: Because any resemblance to existing groups is merely fortuitous, one can well imagine one of these groups defining itself first by its fidelity to hardened positions of the communist left after the creation of the Third International. It's a whole axiomatics, down to the phonological level—the way of articulating certain words, the gesture that accompanies them—and then the structures of organization, the conception of what sort of relationships to maintain with the allies, the centrists, the adversaries ... This may correspond to a certain figure of Oedipalization, a reassuring, intangible universe like that of the obsessive who loses his sense of security if one shifts the position of a single, familiar object. It's a question of reaching, through this kind of identification with recurrent figures and images, a certain type of efficiency that characterized Stalinism—except for its ideology, precisely. In other respects, one keeps the general framework of the method, but adapts oneself to it very carefully: "The enemy is the same, comrades, but the conditions have changed." Then one has a more open groupuscule. It's a compromise: one has crossed out the first image, whilst maintaining it, and injected other notions. One multiplies meetings and training sessions, but also the external interventions. For the desiring will, there is—as Zazie says—a certain way of bugging students and militants, among others.

In the final analysis, all these groupuscules say basically the same thing. But they are radically opposed in their *style*: the definition of the leader, of propaganda, a conception of discipline, loyalty, modesty, and the asceticism of the militant. How does one account for these polarities without rummaging in the economy of desire of the social machine? From anarchists to Maoists the spread is very wide, politically as much as analytically. Without even considering the mass of people, outside the limited range of the groupuscules, who do not quite know how to distinguish between the leftist élan, the appeal of union action, revolt, hesitation, or indifference. One must explain the role of these machines—these groupuscules and their work of stacking and sifting—in crushing desire. It's a dilemma: to be broken by the social system or to be integrated in the preestablished structure of these little churches. In a way, May 1968 was an astonishing revelation. The desiring power became so accelerated that it broke up the groupuscules. These later pulled themselves together; they participated in the reordering business with the other repressive forces, the CGT [Communist workers' union], the PC, the CRS [riot police]. I don't say this to be provocative. Of course, the militants courageously fought the police. But if one leaves the sphere of struggle to consider the function of desire, one must recognize that certain groupuscules approached the youth in a spirit of repression: to contain liberated desire in order to rechannel it.

What is a liberated desire? I certainly see how this can be translated at the level of an individual or small group: an artistic creation, or breaking windows, burning things, or even simply an orgy or letting things go to hell through laziness or vegetating. But then what? What could a collectively liberated desire be at the level of a social group? And what does this signify in relation to "the totality of society," if you do not reject this term as Michel Foucault does.

Félix Guattari: We have taken desire in one of its most critical, most acute stages: that of the schizophrenic—and the schizo that can produce something within or beyond the scope of the confined schizo, battered down with drugs and social repression. It appears to us that certain schizophrenics directly express a free deciphering of desire. But how does one conceive a collective form of the economy of desire? Certainly not at the local level. I would have a lot of difficulty imagining a small, liberated community maintaining itself against the flows of a repressive society, like the addition of individuals emancipated one by one. If, on the contrary, desire constitutes the very texture of society in its entirety, including in its mechanisms of reproduction, a movement of liberation can "crystallize" in the whole of society. In May 1968, from the first sparks to local clashes, the shake-up was brutally transmitted to the whole of society, including some groups that had nothing remotely to do with the revolutionary movement—doctors, lawyers, grocers. Yet it was vested interests that carried the day, but only after a month of burning. We are moving toward explosions of this type, yet more profound.

Might there have already been a vigorous and durable liberation of desire in history, apart from brief periods of celebration, carnage, war or revolutionary upheavals? Or do you really believe in an end to history: after millennia of alienation, social evolution will suddenly turn around in a final revolution that will liberate desire forever?

Félix Guattari: Neither the one nor the other. Neither a final end to history, nor provisional excess. All civilizations, all periods have known ends of history—this is not necessarily convincing and not necessarily liberating. As for excess, or moments of celebration, this is no more reassuring. There are militant revolutionaries who feel a sense of responsibility and say: Yes, excess "at the first stage of revolution," but there is a second stage, of organization, functioning, serious things ... For desire is not liberated in simple moments of celebration. See the discussion between Victor and Foucault in the issue of *Les Temps Modernes* on the Maoists. Victor consents to excess, but at the "first stage." As for the rest, as for the real thing, Victor calls for a new apparatus of state, new norms, a popular justice with a tribunal, a legal process external to the masses, a third party capable of resolving contradictions among the masses. One always finds the old schema: the detachment of a pseudo-avant-garde capable of bringing about syntheses, of forming a party as an embryo of state apparatus, of drawing out a well brought-up, well educated working class; and the rest is a residue, a lumpen-proletariat one should always mistrust (the same old condemnation of desire). But these distinctions themselves are another way of trapping desire for the advantage of a bureaucratic caste. Foucault reacts by denouncing the third party, saying that if there is popular justice, it does not issue from a tribunal. He shows very well that the distinction "avant-garde-lumpen-proletariat" is first of all a distinction introduced by the bourgeoisie to the masses, and therefore serves to crush the phenomena of desire, to *marginalize* desire. The whole question is that of state apparatus. It would be strange to rely on a party or state apparatus for the liberation of desire. To want better justice is like wanting better judges, better cops, better bosses, a cleaner France, etc. And then we are told: how would you unify isolated struggles without a party? How do you make the machine work without a state apparatus? It is evident that a revolution requires a war machine, but this is not a state apparatus. It is also certain that it requires an instance of analysis, an analysis of the desires of the masses, yet this is not an apparatus external to the synthesis. Liberated desire means that desire escapes the impasse of private fantasy: it is not a question of adapting it, socializing it, disciplining it, but of plugging it in in such a way that its process not be interrupted in the social body, and that its expression be collective. What counts is not the authoritarian unification, but rather a sort of infinite spreading: desire in the schools, the factories, the neighborhoods, the nursery schools, the prisons, etc. It is not a question of directing, of totalizing, but of plugging into the same plane of oscillation. As long as one alternates between the impotent spontaneity of anarchy and the bureaucratic and hierarchic coding of a party organization, there is no liberation of desire.

In the beginning, was capitalism able to assume the social desires?

Gilles Deleuze: Of course, capitalism was and remains a formidable desiring-machine. The monetary flux, the means of production, of manpower, of new markets, all that is the flow of desire. It's enough to consider the sum of contingencies at the origin of capitalism to see to what degree it has been a crossroads of desires, and that its infrastructure, even its economy, was inseparable from the phenomena of desire. And fascism too—one must say that it has "assumed the social desires," including the desires of repression and death. People got hard-ons for Hitler, for the beautiful fascist machine. But if your question means: was capitalism revolutionary in its beginnings, has the industrial revolution ever coincided with a social revolution? No, I don't think so. Capitalism has been tied from its birth to a savage repressiveness; it had its organization of power and its state apparatus from the start. Did capitalism imply a dissolution of the previous social codes and powers? Certainly. But it had already established its wheels of power, including its power of state, in the fissures of previous regimes. It is always like that: things are not so progressive; even before a social formation is established, its instruments of exploitation and repression are already there, still turning in the vacuum, but ready to work at full capacity. The first capitalists are like waiting birds of prey. They wait for their meeting with the worker, the one who drops through the cracks of the preceding system. It is even, in every sense, what one calls primitive accumulation.

On the contrary, I think that the rising bourgeoisie imagined and prepared its revolution throughout the Enlightenment. From its point of view, it was a revolutionary class "to the bitter end," since it had shaken up the ancien régime *and swept into power. Whatever parallel movements took place among the peasantry and in the suburbs, the bourgeois revolution is a revolution made by the bourgeoisie—the terms are hardly distinguishable—and to judge it in the name of 19th or 20th century socialist utopias introduces, by anachronism, a category that did not exist.*

Gilles Deleuze: Here again, what you say fits a certain Marxist schema. 'At one point in history, the bourgeoisie was revolutionary, it was even necessary—necessary to pass through a stage of capitalism, through a bourgeois revolutionary stage.' It's a Stalinist point of view, but you can't take that seriously. When a social formation exhausts itself, draining out of every gap, all sorts of things decode themselves, all sorts of uncontrolled flows start pouring out, like the peasant migrations in feudal Europe, the phenomena of "deterritorialization." The bourgeoisie imposes a new code, both economic and political, so that one can believe it was a revolution. Not at all. Daniel Guérin has said some profound things about the revolution of 1789. The bourgeoisie never had any illusions about who its real enemy was. Its real enemy was not the previous system, but what escaped the previous system's control, and what the bourgeoisie strove to master in its turn. It too owed its power to the ruin of the old system, but this power could only be exercised insofar as it opposed everything else that was in rebellion against the old system. The bourgeoisie has never been revolutionary. It simply made sure others pulled off the revolution for it. It manipulated, channeled, and repressed an enormous surge of popular desire. The people were finally beaten down at Valmy.

They were certainly beaten down at Verdun.

Félix Guattari: Exactly. And that's what interests us. Where do these eruptions, these uprisings, these enthusiasms come from that cannot be explained by a social rationality and that are diverted, captured by the power at the moment they are born? One cannot account for a revolutionary situation by a simple analysis of the interests of the time. In 1903 the Russian Social Democratic Party debated the alliances and organization of the proletariat, and the role of the avant-garde. While pretending to prepare for the revolution, it was suddenly shaken up by the events of 1905 and had to jump on board a moving train. There was a crystallization of desire on a wide social scale created by a yet incomprehensible situation. Same thing in 1917. And there too, the politicians climbed on board a moving train, finally getting control of it. Yet no revolutionary tendency was able or willing to assume the need for a

Soviet-style organization that could permit the masses to take real charge of their interests and their desire. Instead, one put machines in circulation, so-called political organizations, that functioned on the model elaborated by Dimitrov at the Seventh International Congress—alternating between popular fronts and sectarian retractions—and that always led to the same repressive results. We saw it in 1936, in 1945, in 1968. By their very axiomatic, these mass machines refuse to liberate revolutionary energy. It is, in an underhanded way, a politics comparable to that of the President of the Republic or of the clergy, but with red flag in hand. And we think that this corresponds to a certain position vis-à-vis desire, a profound way of envisioning the ego, the individual, the family. This raises a simple dilemma: either one finds a new type of structure that finally moves toward the fusion of collective desire and revolutionary organization, or one continues on the present path and, going from repression to repression, heads for a new fascism that makes Hitler and Mussolini look like a joke.

But then what is the nature of this profound, fundamental desire which one sees as being constitutive of man and social man, but which is constantly betrayed? Why does it always invest itself in antinomic machines of the dominant machine, and yet remain so similar to it? Could this mean that desire is condemned to a pure explosion without consequence or to perpetual betrayal? I have to insist: can there ever be, one fine day in history, a collective and enduring expression of liberated desire, and how?

Gilles Deleuze: If one knew, one wouldn't talk about it, one would do it. Anyway. Félix just said it: revolutionary organization must be that of the war machine and not of the state apparatus, of an analyzer of desire and not an external synthesis. In every social system, there have always been lines of flight, and then also a rigidification to block off escape or certainty (which is not the same thing), embryonic apparatuses that integrate them, that deflect or arrest them in a new system in preparation. The crusades should be analyzed from this point of view. But in every respect, capitalism has a very particular character: its lines of flight are not just difficulties that arise, they are the conditions of its own operation. It is constituted by a generalized decoding of all flux, fluctuations of wealth, fluctuations of work, fluctuations of language, fluctuations of art, etc. It did not create any code, it has set up a sort of accountability, an axiomatic of decoded fluxes as the basis of its economy. It ligatures the points of escape and leaps forward. It expands its own boundaries endlessly and finds itself having to seal new leaks at every limit. It doesn't resolve any of its fundamental problems, it can't even foresee the monetary increase in a country over a single year. It never stops crossing its own limits which keep reappearing farther away. It puts itself in alarming situations with respect to its own production, its social life, its demographics, its borders with the Third World, its internal regions, etc. Its gaps are everywhere, forever giving rise to the displaced limits of capitalism. And doubtless, the revolutionary way out (the active escape of which Jackson spoke when he said: "I don't stop running, but while running, I look for weapons") is not at all the same thing as other kinds of escape, the schizo-escape, the drug-escape. But it is certainly the problem of the marginalized: to plug all these lines of flight into a revolutionary plateau. In capitalism, then, these lines of flight take on a new character, a new type of revolutionary potential. You see, there is hope.

You spoke just now of the crusades. For you, this is one of the first manifestations of collective schizophrenia in the West.

Félix Guattari: This was, in fact, an extraordinary schizophrenic movement. Basically, in an already schismatic and troubled world, thousands and thousands of people got fed up with the life they led, makeshift preachers rose up, people deserted entire villages. It's only later that the shocked papacy tried to give direction to the movement by leading it off to the Holy Land. A double advantage: to be rid of errant bands and to reinforce Christian outposts in the Near East threatened by the Turks. This didn't always work: the Venetian Crusade wound up in Constantinople, the Children's Crusade veered off toward the South of France and very quickly lost all sympathy: there were entire villages taken and burned by these "crossed" children, who the regular armies finally had to round up. They were killed or sold into slavery.

Can one find parallels with contemporary movements: communities and by-roads to escape the factory and the office? And would there be any pope to co-opt them? A Jesus Revolution?

Félix Guattari: A recuperation by Christianity is not inconceivable. It is, up to a certain point, a reality in the United States, but much less so in Europe or in France. But there is already a latent return to it in the form of a Naturist tendency, the idea that one can retire from production and reconstruct a little society at a remove, as if one were not branded and hemmed in by the capitalist system.

What role can still be attributed to the church in a country like ours? The church was at the center of power in Western civilization until the 18th Century, the bond and structure of the social machine until the emergence of the nation-state. Today, deprived by the technocracy of this essential function, it seems to have gone adrift, without a point of anchorage, and to have split up. One can only wonder if the church, pressured by the currents of Catholic progressivism, might not become less confessional than certain political organizations.

Félix Guattari: And ecumenism? Isn't it a way of falling back on one's feet? The church has never been stronger. There is no reason to oppose church and technocracy, there is a technocracy of the church. Historically, Christianity and positivism have always been good partners. The development of positive sciences has a Christian motor. One cannot say that the psychiatrist has replaced the priest. Nor can one say the cop has replaced the priest. There is always a use for everyone in repression. What has aged about Christianity is its ideology, not its organization of power.

Let's get to this other aspect of your book: the critique of psychiatry. Can one say that France is already covered by the psychiatry of Secteur— *and how far does this influence spread?*

Félix Guattari: The structure of psychiatric hospitals essentially depends on the state and the psychiatrists are mere functionaries. For a long time the state was content to practice a politics of coercion and didn't do anything for almost a century. One had to wait for the Liberation for any signs of anxiety to appear: the first psychiatric revolution, the opening of the hospitals, the free services, institutional psychotherapy. All that has led to the great utopian politics of "Sectorization," which consisted in limiting the number of internments and of sending teams of psychiatrists out into the population like missionaries in the bush. Due to lack of credit and will, the reform got bogged down: a few model services for official visits, and here or there a hospital in the most underdeveloped regions. We are now moving toward a major crisis, comparable in size to the university crisis, a disaster at all levels: facilities, training of personnel, therapy, etc.

The institutional charting of childhood is, on the contrary, undertaken with better results. In this case, the initiative has escaped the state framework and its financing to return to all sorts of associations—childhood protection or parental associations ... The establishments have proliferated, subsidized by Social Security. The child is immediately taken charge of by a network of psychologists, tagged at the age of three, and followed for life. One can expect to see solutions of this type for adult psychiatry. In the face of the present impasse, the state will try to denationalize institutions in favor of other institutions ruled by the law of 1901 and most certainly manipulated by political powers and reactionary family groups. We are moving toward a psychiatric surveillance of France, if the present crises fail to liberate its revolutionary potentialities. Everywhere, the most conservative ideology is in bloom, a flat transposition of the concepts of Oedipalism. In the children's wards, one calls the director "uncle," the nurse, "mother." I have even heard distinctions like the following: group games obey a maternal principle, the workshops, a paternal one. The psychiatry of *Secteur* seems progressive because it opens the hospital. But if this means imposing a grid over the neighborhood, we will soon regret the loss of the closed asylums of yesterday. It's like psychoanalysis, it functions openly, so it is all the worse, much more dangerous as a repressive force.

Gilles Deleuze: Here's a case. A woman arrives at a consultation. She explains that she takes tranquilizers. She asks for a glass of water. Then she speaks: "You understand I have a certain amount of culture. I have studied, I love to read, and there you have it. Now I spend all my time crying. I can't bear the subway. And the minute I read something, I start to cry. I watch television, I see images of Vietnam: I can't stand it ..." The doctor doesn't say much. The woman continues: "I was in the Resistance ... a bit. I was a go-between." The doctor asks her to explain. "Well, yes, don't you understand, doctor? I went to a café and I asked, for example, is there something for René? I would be given a letter to pass on."

The doctor hears "René"; he wakes up: "Why do you say 'René'?" It's the first time he asks a question. Up to that point, she was speaking about the metro, Hiroshima, Vietnam, of the effect all that had on her body, the need to cry about it. But the doctor only asks: "Wait, wait, 'René ... what does 'René' mean to you?" René—someone who is reborn (*re-né*)? The renaissance? The Resistance means nothing to the doctor; but renaissance, this fits into a universal schema, the archetype: "You want to be reborn." The doctor gets his bearings: at last he's on track. And he gets her to talk about her mother and father.

It's an essential aspect of our book, and it's very concrete. The psychiatrists and psychoanalysts have never paid any attention to delirium. It's enough just to listen to someone who is delirious: it's the Russians that worry him, the Chinese; my mouth is dry; somebody buggered me in the metro; there are germs and spermatozoa swimming everywhere; it's Franco's fault, the Jews, the Maoists ... all a delirium of the social field. Why shouldn't this concern the sexuality of the subject—the relations it has with the Chinese, the whites, the blacks? With civilization, the crusades, the metro? Psychiatrists and psychoanalysts hear nothing of this, on the defensive as much as they are indefensible. They crush the contents of the unconscious under prefab statements: "You speak to me of the Chinese, but what about your father? No, he isn't Chinese? Then, do you have a Chinese lover?" It's at the same level of repressive work as the judge in the Angela Davis case who affirmed: "Her behavior can only be explained by her being in love." And what if, on the contrary, Angela Davis's libido was a social, revolutionary libido? What if she were in love because she was a revolutionary?

That is what we want to say to psychiatrists and psychoanalysts: you don't know what delirium is; you haven't understood anything. If our book has a meaning, it is that we have reached a stage where many people feel the psychoanalytic machine no longer works, where a whole generation is getting fed up with all-purpose schemas—Oedipus and castration, imaginary and symbolic—which systematically efface the social, political, and cultural contents of any psychic disturbance.

You associate schizophrenia with capitalism; it is the very foundation of your book. Are there cases of schizophrenia in other societies?

Félix Guattari: Schizophrenia is indissociable from the capitalist system, itself conceived as primary leakage (*fuite*): an exclusive malady. In other societies, escape and marginalization take on other aspects. The asocial individual of so-called primitive societies is not locked up. The prison and the asylum are recent notions. One chases him, he is exiled at the edge of the village and dies of it, unless he is integrated into a neighboring village. Besides, each system has its particular sickness: the hysteric of so-called primitive societies, the manic-depressive paranoiacs of the great empires ... The capitalist economy proceeds by decoding and deterritorialization: it has its extreme cases, i.e., schizophrenics who decode and deterritorialize themselves to the limit; but also it has its extreme consequences—revolutionaries.

2

CAPITALISM AND SCHIZOPHRENIA

Vittorio Marchetti: *Your book* Anti-Oedipus *has as its subtitle* Capitalism and Schizophrenia. *Why? What were the basic ideas that furnished your starting point?*

Gilles Deleuze: Perhaps the basic idea is this: the unconscious is "productive." To say that it produces means that we must cease to treat it, as we have up till now, as a kind of theater in which a very special drama, the drama of Oedipus, is enacted. We believe that the unconscious is not a theater, but a factory. Artaud said something very nice on this topic. He said that the body, especially the sick body, is like an overheated factory. Not a theater at any rate. To say that the unconscious "produces" means that it is a kind of mechanism that produces other mechanisms. Which is to say that according to us the unconscious has nothing to do with a theatrical presentation, but rather with what we could define as "desiring-machines." We must also be clear about the word "mechanism." Mechanistic theory in biology has never known how to understand desire, and basically ignores it because it cannot incorporate desire into its models. When we talk about desiring-machines, about the unconscious as a mechanism of desire, we mean something quite different. To desire consists of this: to make cuts, to let certain contrary flows run, to take samplings of the flows, to cut the chains that are wedded to the flows. This whole system of the unconscious or of desire which lets flow, which cuts, which lets move, this system of the unconscious, contrary to what traditional psychoanalysis believes, means nothing. There is no meaning, no interpretation to be given, no significance. The problem is to recognize how the unconscious functions. It's a problem that concerns the use of machines, the functioning of "desiring-machines."

Guattari and I began with the idea that desire could be understood only by reference to the category of "production." And it was necessary to recognize production as being within desire itself. Desire does not depend on a lack, to desire is not to be lacking something, and desire does not refer to any law; desire produces. So it's the contrary of a theater. An idea like that of Oedipus, the theatrical representation of Oedipus, distorts the meaning of the unconscious, expresses nothing about desire. Oedipus is the effect of social repression on desiring-production. Even on the level of the child desire is not Oedipal, but instead functions as a mechanism, produces little machines, establishes connections among things. In other words, perhaps all of this means that desire is revolutionary. Not to say that it wishes for the revolution. It's better than that. It's revolutionary by nature because it builds machines capable—when inserted into the social structure—of exploding things, of disrupting the social fabric. Traditional psychoanalysis, on the other hand, pushed all of this into a kind of theater. It's as though one were to transform into a spectacle at the Comédie Francaise something that belongs to human beings, to the factory, to production. So there's our point of departure: the unconscious as a producer of little machines of desire, desiring-machines.

Why speak of capitalism and schizophrenia?

Félix Guattari: In order to emphasize the extremes. All aspects of human existence are related to the most abstract categories. Capital in the first place and then, at the other extreme, or rather at another pole of non-sense, madness and, more precisely within the category of madness, schizophrenia. It seemed to us that these two poles have a connection in their common feature of non-sense. Not only a contingent relationship which would lead to the affirmation that modern society induces madness in human beings. Beyond that was the recognition that, in order to account for alienation, for the repression experienced by the individual in the grip of the capitalist system, and, further, in order to understand the true meaning of the politics of the appropriation of surplus value, we would have to bring into play the same concepts that one relies upon to interpret schizophrenia. We scrutinized these two poles, but it's clear that all the intermediate terms must be examined as well, whether we're talking about ways of dealing with neuroses, of studying childhood, of examining primitive societies. All the themes dealt with by social sciences are under scrutiny. But rather than establish a coexistence among the social sciences, connecting one to the other, we set out to relate capitalism and schizophrenia. So we were seeking to embrace the whole system of fields and not merely pass from one field to the next.

What were the concrete experiences at the base of your research, and in what fields and by what means do you see practical results deriving from this research?

Félix Guattari: The basis is the practice of psychiatry and psychoanalysis, and more particularly, the study of psychosis. Our impression is that the links, the descriptions, Freudian theory, and psychiatry are all rather inadequate for dealing with what really occurs in mental illness. This inadequacy has been discernible recently, as a certain way of listening to mental illness has become available.

Freud, if you will, developed his concepts, at least initially, on the basis of the type of access he had to neuroses, particularly hysteria. Freud himself, at the end of his life, lamented that he had not had any other method, any other means, at his disposal in approaching psychoses. It was only in a completely incidental and external way that he could approach psychotics. And we ought to add that one has no access to schizophrenia within the framework of repressive systems of hospitalization. One only has access to mad people who are caught within a system that prevents them from expressing the essence of their madness. They express only a reaction to the repression to which they are subjected, which they are forced to endure. It follows that psychoanalysis is nearly impossible when directed toward psychoses. And the situation cannot change as long as psychotics are held within the repressive system of the hospital. Rather than applying the descriptions of neurosis to the case of psychosis, we sought to reverse the procedure. That is, we sought to reexamine the concepts describing neurosis in light of indications derived from contact with psychosis.

Gilles Deleuze: We began with an impression, and I really mean an impression, not a piece of knowledge, that something was amiss with psychoanalysis, which had become an interminable narrative revolving around itself. Take as an example psychoanalytical treatment. Well, this treatment had become an endless process in which both patient and doctor went around in a circle which, whatever adjustments were added, was still the Oedipal circle. It was always: "Go ahead, speak ... " and the subject was always the father and the mother. The reference was always to an Oedipal axis. And in vain it was said that the subject was not a real father and a real mother, that instead a higher structure, let's say a symbolic order, was being invoked, which was not just a figment of the imagination. Patients nonetheless kept coming in to speak about a mother and a father, and the doctor kept listening to them talk about a mother and a father. These were problems that Freud put to himself with much anguish at the end of his life: something is amiss in psychoanalysis, something is stalled. Psychoanalysis is becoming, Freud thought, an endless narrative, an endless treatment that leads nowhere. And Jacques Lacan was the first to suggest to what extent things had to be reconsidered. He undertook to resolve the problem through a profound return to Freud. But we began from the impression that psychoanalysis was endlessly revolving around what we could call the family circle as represented by the figure of Oedipus. At this point something very worrisome occurs, because no matter how much psychoanalysis has changed its methods, it still must follow the lines of the most classic psychiatry.

Michel Foucault admirably demonstrated this point. It was in the nineteenth century that psychiatry connected in a fundamental way madness with the family. Now psychoanalysis has reinterpreted this connection, but what's striking is that the connection remains. And even antipsychiatry, which takes such novel and revolutionary pathways, maintains this madness-family connection. People speak of family psychotherapy. That is, people continue to look for the basic references of mental disturbances in family structures of the mother-father sort; and even when these structures are interpreted in a symbolic way, as the symbolic father function and the symbolic mother function, things haven't changed much.

I imagine everyone is acquainted with that exemplary text by the madman—as we are accustomed to call him—Schreber. The memoirs of this Schreber, and it hardly matters whether we call him a paranoid or a schizophrenic, contain a kind of racial, racist, historical raving. Schreber raves about continents, cultures, races. It's a surprising delirium, with a political, historical, cultural content.

Then we read Freud's commentary and all this aspect of the delirium disappears, it's obliterated by the reference to a father never mentioned by Schreber. The psychoanalysts tell us that the father is important precisely because Schreber doesn't talk about him. We reply that we have never seen a schizophrenic delirium that is not firstly about race, racism, politics, that does not begin in all directions from history, that does not involve culture, that does not speak of continents, kingdoms, and so forth. We state that the problem of delirium is not connected to the family, and concerns the father and the mother only in a very secondary way, if it concerns them at all. The real problem of delirium lies in the extraordinary transitions from a pole which we could define as reactionary or even fascist—statements like "I belong to a superior race" appear in all paranoid deliriums—to a revolutionary pole. Consider Rimbaud's affirmation: "I belong eternally to an inferior race." There are no deliriums that do not first involve history before they involve some sort of ridiculous Mommy-Daddy. And it's the same story on the level of treatment and therapy—assuming that it is a question of mental illness. If we don't recognize the historical references of the delirium, if we continue to go around in circles between a symbolic father and an imaginary father, then we're only talking family affairs and we remain within the bounds of the most traditional psychiatry.

Are linguistic studies useful for interpreting schizophrenic language?

Félix Guattari: Linguistics is a science in development, still largely in search of itself. There is the possibility of an illegitimate, perhaps too hasty, use of concepts that are still being shaped. In particular, there is a notion about which we have been led to reflect, namely that of the signifier. We believe that this notion offers many problems for the various sorts of linguistics. Perhaps it offers fewer problems for psychoanalysts, but we believe that a certain maturation is still called for. Confronted with the problems of our contemporary society, we believe that the traditional cultural divisions, let us say among social sciences, science, scientism (this last word in fashion in the last couple years) and political responsibility need to be called into question. Especially after May '68 it is important and necessary to revise these separations. You see, up to this point the various disciplines have gotten along by relying on a kind of respect for one another's autonomy. Psychoanalysts have their recipes, politicians theirs, and so forth. The need to revise this division does not grow out of eclecticism, nor does it have to lead to confusion. Likewise it's not out of confusion that a schizophrenic switches from one register to another. It's the reality with which he is faced that leads him to do this. The schizophrenic follows, let us say without any epistemological certitudes, this reality as it pulls him along from one level to another, from a questioning of semantics and syntax to a revision of themes related to history, races, etc. So in a certain sense people who are operating on the level of social sciences or on the level of politics ought to "make themselves schizophrenic." And I'm not speaking of that illusory image of schizophrenics, caught in the grip of a repression which would have us believe that they are "autistic," turned inward on themselves, and so forth. I mean that we should have the schizophrenic's capacity to range across fields. Very precisely, after May '68, the question is posed in these terms: will we seek to unify our comprehension of phenomena like bureaucratization in political organizations, bureaucratization in state capitalism, together with such remote and disparate phenomena as for example obsessive behavior and automatic repetitions? If we don't, if we remain attached to the idea that such things are separate and that we are all specialists who should remain in our respective corners working on our individual studies, then we will soon witness in our world explosions that will elude the comprehension of politicians and social scientists alike. So calling into question the division of fields of study, questioning as well the self-satisfied air of psychoanalysts, linguists, ethnologists, pedagogues, all of this means not dissolving their various sciences, but rather deepening them, making them worthy of their objects. A whole series of research projects conducted before May '68 by small, privileged groups have been brought to bear on these questions, have been placed at the top of the agenda in the wake of the institutional revolution of that Spring. Psychoanalysts are more and more inserted into various debates, they must enlarge their scope more and more, and the same applies to psychiatrists. It's a completely new phenomenon. What does it mean? Is it a question of fashion, or, as certain political currents assert, is it a way of deflecting militant revolutionaries from their goals? Or is it rather a call, albeit confused, for a profound revision of our conceptual system of today?

Could psychiatry take on the role of the new human science, the human science par excellence, so to speak?

Félix Guattari: Rather than psychiatry why not schizophrenics, the mad people themselves? I don't believe that those who work in the field of psychiatry, at least at this moment, are really the ones in the avant-garde.

Gilles Deleuze: Furthermore, there's no reason why psychiatry rather than another discipline should become the human science par excellence. The notion of a "human science par excellence" is not a good one. Bibliophilia could be the human science par excellence, or—why not?—the science of texts could take that position. The fact is that too many sciences would wish to have the role. The problem is not to figure out which is supposed to be the human science par excellence. The problem is to know how a number of "machines" equipped with revolutionary possibilities will be connected. For example, the literary machine, the psychoanalytic machine, political machines. They will either find a point of contact, as they have up till now within a certain system of adaptation to capitalist regimes, or they will find a boisterous unity directed toward revolutionary ends. We shouldn't put the question in terms of the primacy of this or that discipline, but in terms of their use or utility. What use are they? Up till now psychiatry has clothed itself in family affairs, a family orientation, which amounts to a decisively reactionary use of its energy—even if people working in the field of psychiatry may be revolutionary by inclination.

While philosophic or scientific thought proceeds by manipulating and contrasting various concepts, mythic thought draws on images derived from the world of the senses. That's how Levi-Strauss puts it. In his book The Interpretation of Schizophrenia[1] *Silvano Arieti maintains that the mentally ill rely on an intelligible logic, a "coherent logical system"—even if it has nothing to do with the logic which is based on concepts. Arieti speaks of "paleo-logic" and says that in fact this "coherent logical system" recalls mythic thought, the thought of so-called primitive societies, in that it proceeds by the "association of sensible qualities." How can we explain this phenomenon? Is schizophrenia a defensive strategy that pushes one to refuse even our system of logic? And if this is this case, doesn't the analysis of schizophrenic language provide an instrument of incomparable value for social sciences, for the study of our society?*

Gilles Deleuze: I understand the question very well: it's a very technical question. I'd like to hear what Guattari thinks.

Félix Guattari: I don't like that word "paleo-logic" very much because it sounds too much like "prelogical mentality" and other such phrases which have represented an invitation to the literal segregation of both children and the mentally ill. So I don't know how to approach a "paleo-logic."

Gilles Deleuze: Besides, logic is not a concept that interests us. It's such a vague term; everything is logic and nothing is logic. But as for the question, as for what I would call its technical aspect, I really wonder if what you have with schizophrenia, with so-called primitive peoples, with children, is really a logic of sensible qualities.

Maybe we are losing track of our point. It's striking that we should fail to see that the logic of sensible qualities is already too theoretical a formula. We're neglecting something which is "pure lived experience." Maybe it's the lived experience of the child, or of the so-called primitive, or of the schizophrenic. But lived experience does not mean sensible qualities, it means "intensification," it requires an "I feel that ... " "I feel that" means that something is happening inside me, which I am living intensely, and the intensity is not the same thing as sensible qualities; in fact it's quite different. It happens all the time with schizophrenics. A schizophrenic says, "I feel that I'm becoming a woman" or "I feel that I'm becoming God." Sensible qualities aren't the question here. I suspect that Arieti in fact remains stuck at the level of a logic of sensible qualities, but that doesn't really help in dealing with the words of a schizophrenic. When a schizophrenic says "I feel that I'm becoming a woman" or "I feel that I'm becoming God" or "I feel that I'm becoming Joan of Arc," what does he really mean? Schizophrenia is an involuntary and stupefying experience, something very, very acute, very intense, with high levels of intensity. When a schizophrenic says "I feel that I'm becoming a woman, I feel that I'm becoming God," it's as though he were passing beyond a threshold of intensity with his very body. Biologists speak of the egg, and the body of the schizophrenic is a kind of egg; it is a catatonic body, in all respects like an egg. So when a schizophrenic says "I'm becoming God, I'm becoming a woman" it's as though he were crossing what biologists call a gradient, a threshold of intensity, he's going beyond it, above it, etc. And traditional analysis takes into account none of this experience. Meanwhile the experimental pharmaceutical treatments relating to schizophrenia— treatments which are so badly applied today— could be very productive. These pharmaceutical studies, after all, this research on drugs, puts the problem in terms of a variation in the metabolism of intensity. The schizophrenic's "I feel that" has to be seen as reflecting transitions, gradations of intensity. So the difference between our conception and Arieti's, with all due respect for Arieti's work, lies in the fact that we interpret schizophrenia as the experience of intensification.

But what is meant by the "intelligibility" of schizophrenic discourse?

Félix Guattari: We have to see whether the coherence derives from the level of rational expression, or from a semantic level, or from a level that we could call "mechanical" (machine-like).

After all, for purposes of representation we all get by as best we can. Whether it's the scientist attempting to reconstitute something on the level of expression, or the schizophrenic. But the latter, with the means that he has within himself, with the means that he has available, doesn't have the possibility of rendering intelligible that which he's trying to reconstitute. In this sense, we can say that the descriptions furnished to us by psychoanalysis— descriptions which for simplicity's sake we will call Oedipal— constitute a repressive representation. Even some important authors, including some that have gone far in their exploration of childhood psychoses, including some that have focused on transitions in the intensity of experience, even they have ended by once again describing things according to the Oedipal model. Someone, and I'm talking of someone very important, has spoken of the "micro-Oedipal," and has done so despite having recognized in a case of psychosis that on the level of functioning, on the level of the patient's urges, there could be found only a landscape in the manner of Bosch, composed of an infinitude of fragments, pieces, in which there was not a trace of the father or the mother or the holy trinity. So the representation of the patient was simply translated wholesale from the dominant ideology.

There are certain typical transformations in schizophrenic language. Are there analogous transformations in the language of those who belong to certain social categories, such as military people, politicians, etc?

Félix Guattari: Of course. We can even speak of a kind of paraphrenization of military language, or, at the present moment, of the language of political militants. But we ought to generalize. Groups like psychiatrists, psychoanalysts, and researchers resort to a language that demands the closure of representation. To the point where everything excessive in the production of desiring-machines (the production of the unconscious) is always reduced to limiting and exclusionary syntheses, with a perennial return to dualistic categories and a constant separating of levels. This is a problem which cannot be resolved by an epistemological reform. All of this calls into question the very system of forces at play in the class struggle. It's not going to do any good just to try to engage a certain group of psychoanalysts, or this or that researcher. What has been called into question here is not one isolated system, but rather the whole dynamic of social mechanisms, whether related to desire or to revolutionary struggle or to science or to industry. And since this whole dynamic is at stake, it will have to develop its own new models, its social groups, and various agreed-upon expressions. We might ask whether the discourse of the military, of politicians, of scientists isn't really a kind of anti-production, a labor of repression on the level of discourse, which has as its goal to stop this labor of questioning. But the questioning is unstoppable, it overflows boundaries, it reflects the real movement of things.

Nietzsche, Artaud, Van Gogh. Roussel, Campana: what does mental illness mean in these cases?

Gilles Deleuze: Many things. Jaspers and more recently Laing have said something very powerful about this question, even if they haven't been well understood yet. In brief, they have maintained that in this phenomenon crudely referred to as madness there are two things: a breaking through, which is to say a sudden light, a wall that is superseded; and then there's a rather different dimension which could be called a collapse. So a breaking through, and a collapse. I'm reminded of a letter of Van Gogh. "It's a question," he wrote, "of breaking through a wall." But breaking through a wall is very, very difficult, and if it's done too brutally then you crumble, you fall, you collapse. Van Gogh continued by saying, "I am trying to breach the wall with a file and with patience." So we have the "breakthrough" and possibly a collapse as well. When Jaspers speaks of the schizophrenic process, he stresses the coexistence of two elements: a kind of intrusion, the arrival of something which is not even expressible, something which is so formidable that it can only be spoken of with difficulty, because it is something repressed in our societies—and therefore it comes close to coinciding with (here's the second element) a collapse. So we end up with the autistic schizophrenic, the kind that stops moving, can remain immobile for years and years. In the cases of Nietzsche, Van Gogh, Artaud, Roussel, Campana, etc., there is doubtless a coexistence of the two elements. First there's an amazing "breakthrough," a breaching of the wall. Van Gogh. Nerval—and we could cite so many others!—have broken through the wall of the signifier, the wall of the "Mommy-Daddy" system, have traveled far beyond that point, and speak to us with a voice that is the voice of our future. But the second element is still present in this process: the risk of collapse. No one should treat lightly the risk that the "breakthrough," the breaking apart, may coincide with or degenerate into a kind of collapse. We need to consider this danger as fundamental. The two elements are connected. And there's no point in saying that Artaud was not schizophrenic. Actually it's worse: it's shameful, it's idiotic to say so. Obviously Artaud was schizophrenic. He accomplished his brilliant "breakthrough," he broke through the wall, but at what risk? The price exacted is a collapse that must be defined as schizophrenic. The two things are not identical; the "breakthrough" and the collapse are two different moments. But it would be irresponsible to ignore the danger of collapse in these processes. Even if the risk is perhaps worthwhile.

In a psychiatric hospital the doctors defy a prohibition from the director of the clinic and make it a habit of playing cards in the room of a patient who has been for years in a state of profound catatonia. He's become an object, without words, without gestures, without movement. One day the doctors are playing as usual. Suddenly the patient, whose face had been pointed toward the window by the nurse that morning, cries out, "The director is coming!" Then he falls back into silence. A few years later, without ever speaking again, he dies. So that's his message to the world: "The director is coming!"

Gilles Deleuze: It's a very beautiful story. As we develop a new schizoanalysis—something that we fervently hope for—the task will not be to ask the meaning of the phrase "The director is coming," but to ask ourselves what has occurred to allow this autistic patient, so completely turned inward on his own body, to create, even for a very short time, this little machine connected with the arrival of the director. What purpose did the creation serve?

Félix Guattari: It seems to me that it's not clear from the story whether the patient actually saw the director. The story would in fact be more pungent if he had not. Just the fact that there was a modification, a change of habits due to the presence of the young interns in the room and their transgression of the director's rule, this could have induced the patient to evoke the hierarchical figure of the director and provide an analytical interpretation of the situation. In this episode his cry presents a fine illustration of transference, a transfer of the analytical function. It's not a psycho-analyst or a psychosociologist, let's say, who is interpreting the structure of the situation. It's literally a cry, a kind of verbal slip, which interprets the alienation, not of the schizophrenic himself, but of the card players who must take special precautions just in order to play their game in the presence of a patient.

Yes, but the patient is aware of himself at the moment when he emits his cry, even if he hasn't seen the director at all ...

Félix Guattari: Aware of himself? I'm not at all sure of that. He might have seen a cat or something else go by. It's a given in the practice of institutional psychotherapy that the schizophrenic who is most lost in himself will suddenly burst out with the most incredible details about your private life, things that you would never imagine anyone could know, and that he will tell you in the most abrupt way truths that you believed to be absolutely secret. It's not a mystery.

The schizophrenic has lightning-like access to you; he is focused, so to speak, directly on those links that constitute a series in his subjective system. He's in the position of a "seer"—let's use quotation marks—whereas individuals who are frozen in their logic, in their syntax, in their interests, are totally blind.

3

IN FLUX

Maurice Nadeau: Could you briefly explain how your collaboration came into being?*

Félix Guattari: This collaboration is not the product of a simple meeting of two individuals. Aside from a combination of circumstances, we were also led to it by a whole political context. Initially it was less a question of pooling knowledge than the accumulation of our uncertainties, and even a certain distress in the face of the turn of events after May '68.

We are part of a generation whose political consciousness was born in the enthusiasm and naïveté of the Liberation, with its conspiratorial mythology of fascism. And the questions left hanging by the other failed revolution that was May '68 were developed for us based on a counterpoint that was all the more troubling because, like many others, we were worried about the future being readied for us, one that could make you miss the fascism of yore.

Our starting point was to consider that during these crucial periods something along the order of desire manifested itself on the

---

* Maurice Nadeau is the editor of La "Quinzaine Littéraire," in which this interview was published. François Châtelet is a philosopher; Roger Dadoun, a Reichian critic; Serge Leclaire, a psychoanalyst of the Freudian (Lacanian) school; Henri Torrubia, a psychiatrist; Raphaël Pividal, a writer and sociologist; Pierre Clastres, a political anthropologist; Pierre Rose, a student.

scale of society as a whole, then was repressed, liquidated, as much by the forces of power as by political parties and so-called worker unions and, to a certain extent, by leftist organizations themselves.

And we would no doubt have to go back in time even further. The history of betrayed revolutions, the history of the betrayal of the desire of the masses is becoming identified with the history of the Workers' Movement plain and simple. Whose fault is that? Beria's, Stalin's, Khrushchev's! It was not the right program, the right organization, the right alliance. We did not re-read Marx in the original text ... there is no doubt about that! But the raw evidence remains: the revolution was possible, the socialist revolution was within reach, it really exists, it is not a myth weakened by the transformations of industrial societies.

Under certain conditions the masses express their revolutionary will, their desires sweep aside all obstacles, open unheard-of horizons, but the last to notice it are the organizations and men who are supposed to represent them. Leaders betray, it's obvious. But why do those who are led continue to listen to them? Wouldn't that be the result of an unconscious complicity, of an interiorization of the repression, operating on several levels, from power to bureaucrats, from bureaucrats to militants and from militants to the masses themselves? We certainly saw this after May '68.

Fortunately, the recouping and the brainwashing spared tens of thousands—maybe more—who are now immune to the ravages of bureaucracies of all categories, and who intend to retaliate against the dirty tricks of power and bosses as well as against their maneuvers of dialogue, participation, integration, which rely on the complicity of traditional workers' organizations.

We have to recognize that current attempts to renew forms of popular struggle are still hard to extricate from tedium and revolutionary boy-scoutism, which, to say the least, is not too concerned about the systematic liberation of desire. "Desire, that's all you ever say!" That ends up irritating serious people, the responsible militants. So we are certainly not going to recommend that desire be taken seriously. It is rather urgent to undermine the spirit of seriousness. A theory of desire in history should not strive to be serious. And, from this point of view, perhaps *Anti-Oedipus* is still too serious a book, too intimidating. Theoretical work shouldn't be reserved for specialists. A theory's desire and its statements should stick as closely as possible to the event and to the collective enunciation of the masses. In order to come to that, it will be necessary to forge another breed of intellectuals, another breed of analysts, another breed of militants, with the different types blending and melting into each other.

We started with the idea that one should not consider desire as a subjective superstructure which phases in and out. Desire never stops shaping history, even in its worst periods. The German masses had come to desire Nazism. After Wilhelm Reich, one cannot avoid facing that truth. Under certain conditions, the desire of the masses can turn against their own interests. What are those conditions? That's the whole question.

In order to answer that, we realized that one cannot simply attach a Freudian wagon to the Marxist-Leninist train. First one must get rid of a stereotyped hierarchy between an opaque economic infrastructure and social and ideological superstructures conceived of in such a way that they repress questions of sex and expression on the side of representation, as far away as possible from production. The relations of production and the relations of reproduction participate in the same pairing of productive forces and antiproductive structures. We should move desire on the side of the infrastructure, on the side of production, and the family, the ego and the person on the side of antiproduction. This is the only way to prevent the sexual from remaining permanently cut off from the economic.

There exists, according to us, a desiring-production which, before all actualization in the familial division of sexes and persons as well as the social division of work, invests the various forms of production of jouissance and the existing structures in order to repress them. Under different regimes, it is the same desiring energy that we find on the revolutionary face of history, with the working class, science and the arts, and that we find on the face of relations of exploitation and of state power insofar as they both presuppose the unconscious participation of the oppressed.

If it is true that social revolution is inseparable from a revolution of desire, then the question shifts: under what conditions will the revolutionary avant-garde be able to free itself from its unconscious complicity with repressive structures and elude power's manipulation of the masses' desire that makes them "fight for their servitude as though it were their salvation"? If the family and family ideologies assume a nodal role, as we think they do, then how should one assess the function of psychoanalysis which, the first to raise these questions, was also the first to abandon them again by promoting a modern myth of familial repression with Oedipus and castration?

In order to move in this direction, we think it necessary to stop approaching the unconscious through neurosis and the family, in order to adopt the more specific approach of the schizophrenic process of desiring-machines—which has little to do with institutional madness.

A militant struggle is necessary against reductive explanations and adaptive techniques of suggestion based on Oedipal triangulation. Refusing to grasp compulsively a complete object, symbolic of all despotism. Drifting towards real multiplicities. Ceasing to dismiss both man and machine whose relationship, on the contrary, constitutes desire itself. Promoting another logic, a logic of real desire, establishing the primacy of history over structure; another analysis, extricated from symbolism and interpretation; and another militancy, with the means to free itself from fantasies of the dominant order.

Gilles Deleuze: As for the technique of this book, writing it between the two of us did not create any particular problem, but had a specific function, of which we gradually became aware. One thing is very startling in books on psychiatry or even on psychoanalysis, and that is the pervasive duality between what an alleged mental patient says and what the doctor reports. Between the "case" and the commentary or the analysis of the case. Logos versus pathos: the mental patient is supposed to say something, and the doctor to say what it means in terms of symptom or meaning. This allows for the complete distortion of what the mental patient says, a hypocritical selection.

We don't claim to have written a madman's book, just a book in which one no longer knows—and there is no reason to know—who exactly is speaking, a doctor, a patient, an untreated patient, a present, past, or future patient. That's why we used so many writers and poets; who is to say if they are speaking as patients or doctors—patients or doctors of civilization. Now, strangely, if we have tried to go beyond this traditional duality, it's precisely because we were writing together. Neither of us was the madman, neither of us the psychiatrist; there had to be two of us in order to find a process that was not reduced either to the psychiatrist or his madman, or to a madman and his psychiatrist.

The process is what we call a flux. Now, once again, the flux is a notion that we wanted to remain ordinary and undefined. This could be a flux of words, ideas, shit, money, it could be a financial mechanism or a schizophrenic machine: it goes beyond all dualities. We dreamed of this book as a flux-book.

Maurice Nadeau: Precisely, starting in your first chapter, there is this notion of "desiring-machine" which remains obscure for the layman and that we would like to see defined. All the more so that it answers everything, suffices for everything …

Gilles Deleuze: Yes, we give the machine its greatest extension: in relation to the fluxes. We define the machine as any system that cuts the fluxes. Thus, sometimes we speak of technical machines, in the ordinary sense of the word, sometimes of social machines, sometimes of desiring-machines.

Because, for us, the machine does not in any way conflict with either man or nature (to argue that forms and relations of production are not related to the machine would really require a lot of convincing). On the other hand, the machine is not in any way reduced to mechanics. Mechanics refers to the protocol of some technical machines; or else the particular organization of an organism. But machinism is something else entirely: it designates every system that cuts off fluxes going beyond both the mechanics of technology and the organization of the organism, whether it be in nature, society, or man.

For example, the desiring-machine is a nonorganic system of the body; it is in this sense that we speak of molecular machines or micro-machines. More precisely in relation to psychoanalysis: we hold two things against psychoanalysis—not understanding what delirium is, because it does not see that delirium invests the entire social field; and not understanding what desire is, because it does not see that the unconscious is a factory and not a stage.

What is left if psychoanalysis understands nothing about either delirium or desire? These two reproaches really make one: what interests us is the presence of machines of desire, molecular micro-machines in the great molar social machines. How they operate and function within one another.

Raphaël Pividal: If you had to define your book in terms of desire, I'd like to ask: how does this book respond to desire? What desire? Whose desire?

Gilles Deleuze: It's not as a book that it can respond to desire, but according to what surrounds it. A book cannot be worth anything on its own. Still the fluxes: there are a lot of people working in similar directions, in other fields. And then there are the younger generations: it's unlikely they'll buy a certain type of discourse, now epistemological, now psychoanalytical, now ideological. It's beginning to tire everyone out.

We say: Oedipus and castration, make the best of them, because it's not going to last. Until now psychoanalysis has been left alone: there have been attacks on psychiatry, the psychiatric hospital, but psychoanalysis seemed untouchable, uncompromised. We are trying to show that psychoanalysis is worse than the hospital, precisely because it operates through all the pores of capitalist society and not in special places of confinement. And because it is profoundly reactionary in its practice and theory, not only in its ideology. And because it fulfills specific functions.

Félix says that our book is addressed to people who are now between 7 and 15 years old. Ideally, because in fact it is still too difficult, too cultivated, and makes too many compromises. We have not been able to be direct enough, clear enough. Nevertheless, I must say that the first chapter, which has seemed difficult to many favorable readers, does not require any prior knowledge. In any case, if a book responds to a desire, it is insofar as there are already a lot of people who can't stand a current type of discourse. It helps refocus a number of efforts, and make works or desires resonate. In short, a book can only respond to a desire politically, outside the book. For example, an association of angry users of psychoanalysis wouldn't be a bad place to start.

François Châtelet: What seems important to me is the irruption of such a text amidst books of philosophy (for this book is thought of as a book of philosophy). Now *Anti-Oedipus* smashes everything.

In its appearance, first, through the "form" of the text itself: 'curse words' are used starting with the second line, as though a provocation. One believes, at first, that this won't go on, and then it does. That's all they talk about: "coupled machines," and "coupled machines" are singularly obscene, or scatalogical.

Moreover, I experienced it as a materialist irruption. It's been a long time since this happened. One has to admit that methodology is becoming a pain in the ass. With the imperialism of methodology, any research work or deepening of a subject is ruined. I've fallen into that trap so I know what I'm talking about. In short, I evoke a materialist irruption because I'm thinking of Lucretius. I don't know if that will please you. Too much or not enough.

Gilles Deleuze: If that's true, that's perfect. That would be wonderful. In any case, there is no methodological problem in our book. Nor any problem of interpretation. Because the unconscious doesn't mean anything; because machines don't mean anything. They merely work, produce and break down, because all we're looking for is how something functions in the real.

There is no epistemological problem either: we couldn't care less about returning to Freud or Marx. If someone tells us that we have misunderstood Freud, we won't argue about it, we'll say too bad, there is so much to do. It's curious that epistemology has always hidden an imposition of power, an organization of power. As far as we're concerned, we don't believe in any specificity of writing or even of thought.

Roger Dadoun: Up until now, the discussion has taken place on a "molar" level—to use a dichotomy that is fundamental in your interpretation—that is, on the level of great conceptual ensembles. We have not managed to take the plunge that would lead us to the "molecular" level, that is, to microanalyses that would help us understand how you have "engineered" your work. This would be particularly valuable for the analysis—the schizoanalysis, perhaps?—of the political cogs of the text. It would be particularly interesting to know how fascism and May '68, the dominant "note" of the book, intervened, not "molarly," that would be too banal, but "molecularly," in the fabrication of the text.

Serge Leclaire: Actually I get the impression that this book is engineered so that every intervention "on the molecular level" will be digested by the machine of the book.

I think that, by your own admission, your intention to come up with "a book where all possible duality would be suppressed" was achieved beyond your wildest hopes. That puts your readers, if they are somewhat perceptive, in a situation that leaves them only the prospect of being absorbed, digested, tied up and quashed in the admirable operationality of this machine.

So there is a dimension here that I question, and that I would be willing to ask you about, namely, what is the function of such a book-contraption [*livre-machin*]?[1] Because at first it seems to be perfectly totalizing, absorbing, liable to integrate and absorb all the questions one might attempt to raise, by backing the interlocutor into a corner by the very fact that he is speaking and asking a question.

Let's do this experiment right away, if you will, and let's see what happens.

One of the major parts of the desiring-machines, if I have understood you properly, is "the partial object," which, for someone who has not yet managed to get rid altogether of the psychoanalytic uniform, calls to mind a psychoanalytical concept, namely, the Kleinian one of the "partial object." Even if one claims, as you do, not without humor, to "make fun of concepts."

In this use of the partial object as an essential part of the desiring-machine, one thing seems to me very significant: you still try to "define" it. You say: the partial object can only be defined positively. That's what surprises me. First of all, how does the positive description differ essentially from the negative imputation that you denounce?

Above all: the slightest psychoanalytical experience makes it clear that the partial object can only be defined "differently" and "in relation to the signifier."

Here, your "contraption," if I may say so, can only be "lacking" its object (the banished lack pops up again!). Even though it is written, as a book is, it claims to be a text without a signifier, a text that would tell the truth about the truth, keeping close to an alleged reality, quite simply. As though that were possible without distance or intention of all duality. Very well. A contraption of this sort can have its use; the future will tell. But as for desire, the good news of which it claims to bring to society more effectively than psychoanalysis, I repeat, it can only be lacking its object.

I believe that your desiring-machine which should only work by breaking down, that is, skipping and backfiring, happens to be disarmed: a "positive" object, devoid of any duality as well as of any "lack," it ends up working … like a Swiss clock!

Félix Guattari: I don't think that one should situate the partial object either positively or negatively, but rather as a participant of nontotalizable multiplicities. It is only in an illusory fashion that it is inscribed in reference to a complete object such as the body proper, or even the fragmented body. By opening the series of partial objects, beyond the breast and the feces, to the voice and the gaze, Jacques Lacan signified his refusal to close them off and reduce them to the body. The voice and the gaze escape the body, for example, by becoming more and more adjacent to audio-visual machines.

I'll leave aside the question of how, according to Lacan, the phallic function, insofar as it overcodes each of the partial objects, does not give them back a certain identity, and, by assigning them a lack, does not call for another form of totalization, this time in the symbolic order. Whatever the case, it seems to me that Lacan has always tried to extricate the object of desire from all the totalizing references that could threaten it: beginning with the mirror stage, libido escaped the "substantialist hypothesis" and symbolic identification supplanted an exclusive reference to the organism; tied down to the function of speech (*parole*) and to the field of language, the drive shattered the framework of topics that were closed in on themselves; whereas the theory of the "a" object perhaps contains the seed that allows to liquidate the totalitarianism of the signifier.

By becoming an "a" object, the partial object detotalized, deterritorialized, and permanently distanced itself from an individuated corporeity; it is in a position to swing over to real multiplicities and to open itself up to the molecular machinisms of every kind that are shaping history.

Gilles Deleuze: Yes, it's curious that Leclaire would be saying that our machine works too well, and is capable of digesting everything. That's exactly what we held against psychoanalysis. It's curious that a psychoanalyst would reproach us with that in turn. I'm saying this because we have a special relationship with Leclaire: he wrote a text called "the reality of desire," which, before we did, goes in the direction of a machine-unconscious and uncovers final elements of the unconscious which are no longer either figurative or structural.

It seems our agreement does not go all the way, since Leclaire reproaches us for not understanding what a partial object is. He says it's not important to define it positively or negatively, because, in any case, it's something else, it's "different." But we are not really interested in categories of objects, even partial ones. It's not certain that desire has to do with objects, even partial ones. We are talking about machines, flux, sampling, detachments, residue. We are doing a critique of the partial object. And surely Leclaire is right to say that it doesn't really matter if the partial object is defined positively or negatively. But he is only right theoretically. For if we consider the way it functions, if we ask what psychoanalysis does with the partial object, how it makes it work, then knowing whether it enters a negative or positive function is no longer inconsequential.

Is it true or not that psychoanalysis uses the partial object to base its ideas of lack, absence, or signifier of absence, and to legitimate its use of castration? Even when it invokes the notions of difference or the different, it's psychoanalysis that uses the partial object in a negative way in order to fuse desire to a fundamental lack. What we hold against psychoanalysis is that it resorts to a pious conception, based on lack and castration, a sort of negative theology that involves infinite resignation (the Law, the impossible, etc.). It is against this that we propose a positive conception of desire, desire that produces, not desire that is lacking in something. Psychoanalysts are still pious.

Serge Leclaire: I won't challenge your criticism any more than I acknowledge its pertinence. I'll simply emphasize that it seems based on the hypothesis of a somewhat … totalitarian reality. Without signifiers, without flaw, splitting, or castration. Ultimately, one wonders what makes the "true difference" you invoke. It should be situated, you say, not between … let's see …

Gilles Deleuze: Between the imaginary and the symbolic …

Serge Leclaire: …between the real on one hand, which you present as the ground, the underlying element, and something like the superstructures that would be the imaginary and the symbolic.

Now, I think the question of "true difference" is, in fact, the question raised in the problem of the object. Just now, Félix, in referring to Lacan's teachings (and you came back to them), situated the "a" object in relation to the "ego," to the person, etc.

Félix Guattari: ... the person and the family...

Serge Leclaire: Now, the concept of the "a" object in Lacan is part of a quaternary which includes the signifier, which is dual (S1 and S2), and the subject (the crossed out S). True difference, if this expression were to be used, would be situated between the signifier on the one hand and the "a" object on the other.

I don't mind that at no moment it would be advisable, for either pious or impious reasons, to use the term of signifier. Whatever the case, I don't see how you can challenge some duality and promote the "a" object as self-sufficient, like some substitute for an impious God. I don't think you can support a thesis, a project, an action, a "contraption," without introducing somewhere a duality, and all it entails.

Félix Guattari: I'm not at all sure that the concept of the "a" object in Lacan is anything but a vanishing point, an escape, precisely, from the despotic character of signifying chains.

Serge Leclaire: What interests me most, and what I am trying to articulate in a way quite obviously different from yours, is how desire is deployed in the social machine. I don't think we can go without a precise clarification of the object's function. Then it will be necessary to specify its relationship with other elements at work in the machine, "signifying" elements (symbolic and imaginary ones, if you prefer). These relationships don't operate in a single direction, that is, the "signifying" elements have a backlash effect on the object.

If we want to understand something about what is happening in terms of desire in the social machine, we have to go through that narrow pass that the object constitutes right now. It's not enough to assert that everything is desire, but show how that happens. I will add a final question: what do you use your "contraption" for?

What relation can there be between the fascination of a flawless machine and the true excitement of a revolutionary project? That's the question I'm asking you, on the level of action.

Roger Dadoun: In any case, your "machine"—or your "contraption" [*machin*]—works. It works very well in literature, for example, for capturing the flow or the "schizo" circulation in Artaud's *Heliogabalus*; it works for entering more deeply into the bipolar schizoid/paranoid oscillation of an author like Romain Rolland; it works for a psychoanalysis of dreams—for Freud's dream, known as "Irma's injection," which is theatrical in an almost technical sense, with its staging, close-ups, etc., it's like a film. It remains to be seen how this works for the child ...

Henri Torrubia: Working in a psychiatric ward, I would especially like to emphasize one of the nodal points of your theses on schizo-analysis. You assert—with arguments that, to me, are very illuminating—the primacy of social investment and the productive and revolutionary essence of desire. This raises such theoretical, ideological, and practical problems that you should expect a general outcry.

We know, in any case, that to undertake an analytical psychology in a psychiatric establishment, without the possibility for "each" person to keep questioning the institutional network itself, is either a waste of time or, in the best of cases, won't go very far. In the current climate, moreover, nothing can go very far. That being the case, when an essential conflict emerges somewhere, when something goes wrong, which is precisely the sign that something like the desiring-production is liable to emerge, and which, of course, questions the social and its institutions, we immediately see reactions of panic and formations of resistance. This resistance takes various forms: meetings of synthesis, coordination, declarations, etc., and, more subtly, classic psychoanalytical interpretation with its usual effect of exterminating desire as you conceive of it.

Raphaël Pividal: Serge Leclaire, you have made several remarks, most of them in discrepancy with what Guattari says. Because the book, in a fundamental way, examines the analytical practice, your profession in a sense, and you have taken the problem in a partial way. You've only accepted it by submerging it in your own language, with theories that you've developed, where you give greater importance to fetishism, that is to say, precisely, to the partial object. You take refuge in this sort of language to reduce Deleuze and Guattari to details. Everything in *Anti-Oedipus* that concerns the birth of the state, the role of the state, schizophrenia, you say nothing about. You say nothing about your daily practice. You say nothing about the true problem of psychoanalysis, that of the patient. Of course, you, Serge Leclaire, are not being put on trial, but this is the point to which you should respond: the relationship of psychoanalysis to the state, to capitalism, to History, to schizophrenia.

Serge Leclaire: I agree with the aim you propose. When I emphasize the precise point of the object, I mean to highlight, through an example, the type of operation the contraption produced can perform.

Granted that the criticism of Deleuze and Guattari concerning the change of direction, the thwarting of psychoanalytic discovery, the fact that nothing or scarcely anything was said concerning the relations of the analytical practice or schizophrenia with the political world, or the social, I do not object entirely. It is not enough to signal one's intention to do it, it has to be done pertinently.

Our two authors have tried, and it's their attempt that we are discussing here.

I simply said, and will say again, that the proper approach to the problem seems to me to go through an extremely specific pass: the place of the object, the function of the drive in a social formation.

Just a remark in regard to the "it works" which is put forward as an argument in favor of the pertinence of the machine, or the book in question. Of course it works. And I was going to say that for me, too, in a certain sense, it works. One may note that any theoretically invested practice initially has a good chance of working. This is not a criterion in itself.

Roger Dadoun: The main problem that your book raises is no doubt this: how will it work politically, since you acknowledge the political as a principal "machination." Witness the scope or the meticulousness with which you dealt with the "*socius*" and, notably, its ethnographic, anthropological aspects.

Pierre Clastres: Deleuze and Guattari, the former a philosopher, the latter a psychoanalyst, are reflecting together on capitalism. In order to conceive capitalism, they go through schizophrenia, in which they see the effects and limits of our society. And in order to conceive schizophrenia, they go through Oedipal psychoanalysis, but like Attila: in their wake, nothing much is left standing. Between the two, between the description of familialism (the Oedipal triangle) and the project of schizoanalysis, there is the biggest chapter in *Anti-Oedipus*, the third, "Savages, Barbarians, Civilized Men." This essentially concerns societies that are usually the ethnologists' object of study. What is ethnology doing here?

It ensures the consistency of Deleuze and Guattari's undertaking, which is very strong, by shoring up their argument with non-Western examples (an examination of primitive societies and barbaric empires). If the authors were merely saying: in capitalism, things work this way, and in other types of societies, they work differently, we would not have left the realm of the most tedious comparatism. It isn't that at all, because they show "how things work differently." *Anti-Oedipus* is also a general theory of society and of societies. In other words, Deleuze and Guattari write about Savages and Barbarians what until now ethnologists have not written.

It is certainly true (we didn't write it, but we knew it) that the world of Savages relies on an encoding of fluxes: nothing escapes the control of primitive societies, and if there is a slip—it happens—the society always finds a way to block it. It's also quite true that the imperial formations impose an overencoding on the savage elements integrated into the Empire, without necessarily destroying the encoding of the flux that persists on the local level of each element. The example of the Incan Empire illustrates Deleuze and Guattari's point of view perfectly. They say impressive things about the systems of cruelty such as writing on the body among the Savages, about writing's place in the system of terror among the Barbarians. It seems to me that ethnologists should feel at home in *Anti-Oedipus*. That does not mean that everything will be accepted right away. One should expect a certain reticence (to say the least) in the face of a theory that asserts the primacy of the genealogy of debt, replacing the structuralism of exchange. One might also wonder whether the idea of Earth does not somewhat crush that of territory. But all of this means that Deleuze and Guattari are not taking ethnologists lightly: they ask them real questions, questions that require reflection.

Is this a return to an evolutionist interpretation of history? A return to Marx, beyond Morgan? Not at all. Marxism kind of found its way to the Barbarians (the Asiatic mode of production) but never quite knew what to do with the Savages. Why? Because if, in the Marxist perspective, the passage from barbarism (Oriental despotism or feudalism) to civilization (capitalism) is thinkable, on the other hand nothing allows one to think of the passage from savagery to barbarism. There is nothing in territorial machines (primitive societies) that would allow one to say that it anticipates what will come after: no caste system, no class system, no exploitation, not even work (if work, by essence, is alienated). So where does History, class struggle, deterritorialization, etc., come from?

Deleuze and Guattari answer this question, for they do know what to make of the Savages. And their answer is, in my view, the most vigorous, most rigorous discovery in *Anti-Oedipus*: it concerns the theory of the "*Urstaat,*" the cold monster, the nightmare, the state, which is the same everywhere and "which has always existed." Yes, the state exists in primitive societies, even in the tiniest band of nomad-hunters. It exists, but it is constantly being warded off, it is constantly being prevented from becoming a reality. A primitive society is a society that devotes all its efforts to preventing the chief from becoming a chief (and that can go as far as murder). If history is the history of class struggles (in societies where there are classes, of course) then one can say that the history of classless societies is the history of their struggle against the latent state, it's the history of their effort to encode the flux of power.

Certainly, *Anti-Oedipus* does not tell us why the primitive machine has, here or there, failed to encode the flux of power, this death which keeps rising from within. There is indeed not the slightest reason for a tribe to let its chief act the chief (we could demonstrate this through ethnographic examples). So where does the *Urstaat* so completely and suddenly come from? It comes from the outside, necessarily, and one might hope that the follow-up to *Anti-Oedipus* will tell us more about this.

Encoding, overcoding, decoding and flux: these categories establish the theory of society, whereas the idea of *Urstaat*, whether warded off or triumphant, establishes the theory of History. This is radically new thought, a revolutionary way of thinking.

Pierre Rose: To me, what proves the practical importance of Deleuze and Guattari's book is that it challenges the virtue of commentary. It is a book that wages war. It concerns the situation of the working classes and Power. The angle is the critique of the analytical institution, but the question is not reduced to that.

"The unconscious is the political," Lacan said in '67. Analysis made its claim to universality through that. It is when it gets close to the political that it legitimates oppression most blatantly. It is the trick by which the subversion of the Subject who allegedly knows, turns into submission in the face of a new transcendental trinity of Law, Signifier, Castration: "Death is the life of the Spirit, what use is there in rebelling?" The question of Power was erased by the conservative irony of tightest Hegelianism which undermines the question of the unconscious, from Kojève to Lacan.

This legacy, at least, had high standards. We're also done with the more sordid tradition of the theory of ideologies, which has haunted Marxist theory since the Second International, that is, since Jules Guesde's thought crushed Fourier's thought.

What the Marxists did not manage to break down was the theory of reflection, or what has been done with it. Yet the Leninist metaphor of the "little screw" in the "big machine" is radiant: the overthrow of Power in people's minds is a transformation that is produced in all the cogs and wheels of the social machine.

The way in which the Maoist concept of "ideological revolution" breaks with the mechanistic opposition of ideology and the politicoeconomic sweeps aside the reduction of desire to the "political" (Parliament and party struggles) and politics to the speeches (of the leader) in order to restore the reality of multiple wars on multiple fronts. This method is the only one to come near to the critique of the state in *Anti-Oedipus*. It is impossible for a critical work that starts with *Anti-Oedipus* to become a university operation, a lucrative activity for the whirling dervishes of *Being and Time.* It takes back its effect, conquered against the instruments of Power, in the real, it will help all the assaults against the police, the courts, the army, the power of the state in the factory, and outside.

Gilles Deleuze: What Pividal said earlier, what Clastres just said seems absolutely right to me. The essential thing for us is the problem of the relationships between machines of desire and social machines, their different gears, their immanence in regard to each other. That is: how unconscious desire is an investment in social, economic and political fields. How sexuality, or what Leclaire perhaps would call the choice of sexual objects, only expresses such investments, which are in fact investments of flux. How our loves are derived from universal History and not from mommy and daddy. Through a beloved woman or man, a whole social space is invested, and can be in different ways. So we are trying to show how the fluxes flow into different social fields, what they flow on, what they are invested with, encoding, overcoding, decoding.

Can one say that psychoanalysis has touched upon all this in the slightest way, for example with its ridiculous explanations of fascism, when it makes everything stem from images of father and mother, or familialist and pious signifiers like the Name of the Father? Serge Leclaire says that if our system works, that's not a proof, because everything works. That's certainly true. We say so as well: Oedipus, castration, that works very well. But what are their effects, at what cost do they work? That psychoanalysis appeases, relieves, that it teaches us resignation we can live with, that is certain. But we are saying that it has usurped its reputation of promoting, or even of participating, in an effective liberation. It has crushed phenomena of desire on a familial stage, crushed the whole political and economic dimension of the libido in a conformist code. As soon as the "patient" begins to talk about politics, to rave about politics, look at what psychoanalysis does with it. Look at what Freud did with Schreber.

As for ethnography, Pierre Clastres said it all or, in any case, the best for us. What we are trying to do is to put the libido in relation with the "outside." The flux of women among primitives is connected to the fluxes of herds, flows of arrows. All of a sudden, a group becomes nomadic. All of a sudden, warriors arrive at the village square, look at the China Wall. What are the flows of a society, what are the fluxes capable of subverting it, and what is the position of desire in all of this? Something always happens to the libido, and it comes from far off on the horizon, not from inside. Shouldn't ethnology, as much as psychoanalysis, be in contact with this outside world?

Maurice Nadeau: We should perhaps stop here ... I would like to thank Gilles Deleuze and Félix Guattari for their elucidations regarding a book that is likely to revolutionize many disciplines and that seems even more significant to me in terms of the particular way in which its authors approach questions that concern us all. I also thank François Châtelet for having organized and presided over this discussion and, of course, the specialists who were kind enough to participate.

4

BALANCE-SHEET FOR "DESIRING-MACHINES"

1. How desiring-machines differ from gadgets—from phantasies or imaginary projective systems—from tools or real projective sytems—from perverse machines, which however put us on the track of desiring-machines.

Desiring-machines have nothing to do with gadgets, or little home-made inventions, or with phantasies. Or rather they are related, but from the opposite direction, because gadgets, improvised contraptions, and phantasies are the residue of desiring-machines; they have come under the sway of specific laws of the foreign market of capitalism, or of the home market of psychoanalysis (it is a function of the psychoanalytic "contract" to reduce the states lived by the patient, to translate them into phantasies). Desiring-machines cannot be equated with the adaptation of real machines, or fragments of real machines, to a symbolical process, nor can they be reduced to dreams of fantastic machines operating in the Imaginary. In both instances, one witnesses the conversion of an element of production into a mechanism of individual consumption (phantasies as psychic consumption or Psychoanalytic breast-feeding). It goes without saying that psychoanalysis feels at ease with gadgets and phantasies, an environment in which it can develop all its castrating Oedipal obsessions. But that tells us nothing of consequence about machines and their relation to desire.

The artistic and literary imagination conceives a great number of absurd machines: whether through the indeterminate character of the motor or energy source, through the physical impossibility of the organization of the working parts, or through the logical impossibility of the mechanism of transmission. For example, Man Ray's *Dancer-Danger*, subtitled "impossibility," offers two degrees of absurdity: neither the clusters of cog-wheels nor the large transmission wheel are able to function. Insofar as this machine is supposed to represent the whirl of a Spanish dancer, it can be said that it expresses mechanically, by means of the absurd, the impossibility for a machine to execute such a movement (the dancer is not a machine). But one can also say: there must be a dancer here who functions as a part of a machine; this machine component can only be a dancer; here is the machine of which the dancer is a component part. The object is no longer to compare humans and the machine in order to evaluate the correspondences, the extensions, the possible or impossible substitutions of the ones for the other, but to bring them into communication in order to show how *humans are a component part* of the machine, or combine with something else to constitute a machine. The other thing can be a tool, or even an animal, or other humans. We are not using a metaphor, however, when we speak of machines: *humans constitute a machine* as soon as this nature is communicated by recurrence to the ensemble of which they form a part under specific conditions. The human-horsebow ensemble forms a nomadic war machine under the conditions of the steppe. Men form a labor machine under the bureaucratic conditions of the great empires. The Greek foot-soldier together with his arms constitute a machine under the conditions of the phalanx. The dancer combines with the floor to compose a machine under the perilous conditions of love and death ... We do not start from a metaphorical usage of the word machine, but from a (confused) hypothesis concerning origins: the way in which heterogeneous elements are determined to constitute a machine through *recurrence and communications*; the existence of a "machinic phylum." Ergonomics comes close to this point of view when it sets the general problem, no longer in terms of adaptation or substitution—the adaptation of man to the machine, and of the machine to man—but in terms of recurrent communication within systems made up of men and machines. It is true that just as ergonomists become convinced that they are confining themselves in this way to a purely technological approach, they raise the problems of power and oppression, of revolution and desire, with an involuntary vigor that is infinitely greater than in the adaptive approaches.

There is a classic schema that is inspired by the tool: the tool as the extension and the projection of the living being, the operation by means of which man progressively emerges, the evolution from the tool to the machine, the reversal in which the machine grows more and more independent of man ... But this schema has many drawbacks. It does not offer us any means to apprehend the reality of desiring-machines and their presence throughout this circuit. It is a biological and evolutive schema, which determines the machine as an event occurring at a given moment in the mechanical lineage that begins with the tool. It is humanistic and abstract, isolating the productive forces from the social conditions of their exercise, involving a man-nature dimension common to all the social forms, to which are thus lent relations of evolution. It is imaginary, phantasmal and solipsistic, even when it is applied to real tools, to real machines, since it rests entirely on the hypothesis of projection (Róheim for example, who adopts this schema, shows the analogy between the physical projection of tools and the psychic projection of phantasies).[1] We believe on the contrary that it is necessary to posit, *from the outset*, the difference in nature between the tool and the machine: the one as an agent of contact, the other as a factor of communication; the one being projective, the other recurrent; the one referring to the possible and the impossible, the other to the probability of a less-probable; the one acting through the functional synthesis of a whole, the other through real distinctions in an ensemble. Functioning as a component part in conjunction with other parts is very different from being an extension or a projection, or being replaced (an instance where there is no communication). Pierre Auger shows that a machine is constituted from the moment there is communication between two portions of the outside world that are really distinct in a system that is possible although less probable.[2] One and the same thing can be a tool or a machine, according to whether the "machinic phylum" takes hold of it or not, passes or does not pass through it. Hoplite weapons existed as tools from early antiquity, but they became components of a machine, *along with* the men who wielded them, under the conditions of the phalanx and the Greek city-state. When one refers the tool to man, in accordance with the traditional schema, one deprives oneself of any possibility of understanding how man *and* the tool *become or already are* distinct components of a machine in relation to an actual machinic agency. And we believe moreover that there are always machines that precede tools, always phyla that determine at a given moment which tools, which men will enter as machine components in the social system being considered.

Desiring-machines are neither imaginary projections in the form of phantasies, nor real projections in the form of tools. The whole system of projections derives from machines, and not the reverse. Should the desiring-machine be defined then by a kind of introjection, by a certain perverse use of the machine? Let us take the example of the telephone exchange: by dialing an unassigned number, connected to an automatic answering device ("the number you dialed is not in service ...") one can hear the overlay of an ensemble of teeming voices, calling and answering each other, criss-crossing, fading out, passing over and under each other, inside the automatic voice, very short messages, utterances obeying rapid and monotonous codes. There is the Tiger; it is rumored that there is even an Oedipus in the network; boys calling girls, boys calling boys. One easily recognizes the very form of perverse artificial societies, or a society of Unknowns. A process of reterritorialization is connected to *a movement of deterritorialization that is ensured by the machine* (groups of ham radio transmitters afford the same perverse structure). It is certain that public institutions are not troubled by these secondary benefits of a private use of the machine, in fringe or interference phenomena. But at the same time there is something more here than a simple perverse subjectivity, be it that of a group. The normal telephone may be a machine for communication, but it functions as a tool as long as it serves to project or extend voices that are not as such a part of the machine. But in our example communication attains a higher degree, inasmuch as the voices enter into the make-up of the machine, become components of the machine, distributed and apportioned in chance fashion by the automatic device. The less probable is constructed on the basis of the entropy of the set of voices that cancel each other out. It is from this perspective that there is not only a perverse use or adaptation of a technical-social machine, but the superposing of a true objective desiring-machine, the construction of a desiring-machine within the technical social machine. It may be that desiring-machines are born in this way in the artificial margins of a society, although they develop in a completely different way and bear no resemblance to the forms of their birth.

In his commentary on this phenomenon of the telephone exchange, Jean Nadal writes: "It is, I believe, the most successful and complete desiring-machine I am aware of. It has everything: desire works freely in it, with the erotic agency of the voice as a partial object, in the sphere of chance and multiplicity, and connects up with a flow that irradiates a whole social field of communication through the unlimited expansion of a delirium or a drift." The commentator is not entirely correct: there are better and more complete desiring-machines. But as a general rule, perverse machines have the advantage of presenting us with a constant oscillation between a subjective adaptation, a diverting of a technical social machine, and the objective setting up of a desiring-machine—yet another effort, if you want to become republicans ...[3] In one of the finest texts ever written on the subject of masochism, Michel de M'Uzan shows that the perverse machines of the masochist, which are machines in the strict sense of the term, cannot be understood in terms of phantasy or imagination, just as they cannot be explained in terms of Oedipus or castration, by means of a projection. There is no phantasy, he says, but—and this is something totally different—a *programming* which is "essentially structured outside the Oedipal problem complex" (at last a little fresh air in the house of psychoanalysis, a little understanding for the perverse).[4]

2. The desiring-machine and the Oedipal apparatus: recurrence versus repression regression.

Desiring-machines constitute the non-Oedipal life of the unconscious—Oedipus being the gadget or phantasy. By way of opposition, Picabia called the machine "the daughter born without a mother." Buster Keaton introduced his house-machine, with all its rooms rolled into one, as a house without a mother, and desiring-machines determine everything that goes on inside, as in the bachelors' meal (*The Scarecrow*, 1920). Are we to understand that the machine has but a father, and that it is born like Athena fully armed from a virile brain? It takes a lot of goodwill to believe, along with René Girard, that paternalism is enough to lead us out of Oedipus, and that "mimetic rivalry" is really the complex's *other*.

Psychoanalysis has never ceased doing just that: fragmenting Oedipus, or multiplying it, or on the other hand dividing it, placing it at odds with itself, or sublimating it, making it boundless, elevating it to the level of the signifier. We have witnessed the discovery of the pre-Oedipal, the post-Oedipal, the symbolic Oedipus, none of which helps us to escape from the family any more than the squirrel from its turning cage. We are told: "But see here, Oedipus has nothing to do with daddy-mommy, it is the signifier, it is the name, it is culture, it is mortality, it is the essential lack which is life, it is castration, it is violence personified ..." All of which is enough for a good laugh, at least, but it only carries on the ancient task, by cutting all the connections of desire the better to map it back onto sublime, imaginary, symbolic, linguistic, ontological, and epistemological daddy-mommies. Actually, we haven't said a fourth, or even a hundredth of what needed to be said against psychoanalysis, its *ressentiment* towards desire, its tyranny, and its bureaucracy.

What defines desiring-machines is precisely their capacity for an unlimited number of connections, in every sense and in all directions. It is for this very reason that they are machines, crossing through and commanding several structures at the same time. For the machine possesses two characteristics or powers: the power of the continuum, the machinic phylum in which a given component connects with another, the cylinder and the piston in the steam engine, or even, tracing a more distant lineage, the pulley wheel in the locomotive; but also the rupture in direction, the mutation such that each machine is an absolute break in relation to the one it replaces, as, for example, the internal combustion engine in relation to the steam engine. Two powers which are really only one, since the machine in itself is the break-flow process, the break being always adjacent to the continuity of a flow which it separates from the others by assigning it a code, by causing it to convey particular elements.[5] Hence the fact that the machine is motherless does not speak for a cerebral father, but for a collective *full body*, the machinic agency on which the machine sets up its connections and produces its ruptures.

The machinic painters stressed the following: that they did not paint machines as substitutes for still lifes or nudes; the machine is not a represented object any more than its drawing is a representation. The aim is to introduce an element of a machine, so that it combines with something else on the full body of the canvas, be it with the painting itself, with the result that it is precisely the ensemble of the painting that functions as a desiring-machine. The induced machine is always other than the one that appears to be represented. It will be seen that the machine proceeds by means of an "uncoupling" of this nature, and ensures the deterritorialization that is characteristic of machines, the inductive, or rather the transductive quality of the machine, which defines recurrence, as opposed to representation-projection: *machinic recurrence versus Oedipal projection*. These opposing terms mark a struggle, or a disjunction, as can be seen, for example, in *Aeroplap(l)a*, or *Automoma*, and again in Victor Brauner's *Machine à connaître en forme Mère*.[6] In Picabia's work, the finished design connects up with the incongruous inscription, with the result that it is obliged to function with *this* code, with *this* program, by inducing a machine that does not resemble it. With Duchamp, the real machine element is directly introduced, either standing on its own merits or set-off by its shadow, or, in other instances, having its place in the ensemble determined by an aleatory mechanism that induces the still-present representations to change roles and statuses: *Tu m'* for example. The machine stands apart from all representation (although one can always represent it, copy it, in a manner however that is completely devoid of interest), and it stands apart because it is pure Abstraction; it is nonfigurative and nonprojective. Léger demonstrated convincingly that the machine did not represent anything, itself least of all, because it was in itself the production of organized intensive states: neither form nor extension, neither representation nor projection, but pure and recurrent intensities. It sometimes happens, as in Picabia, that the discovery of the abstract leads to the machinic elements, while at other times, as in the example of many a Futurist, the opposite road is traveled. Consider the old distinction drawn by the philosophers of the Enlightenment, the distinction between representative states and affective states that do not represent anything. The machine is the affective state, and it is false to say that modern machines possess a perceptive capacity or a memory; machines themselves possess only affective states.

When we contrast desiring-machines and Oedipus, we do not mean to say that the unconscious is mechanical (machines belong rather to metamechanics), or that Oedipus counts for nothing. Too many forces and too many people depend on Oedipus; there are too many interests at stake. To begin with, there would be no narcissism without Oedipus. Oedipus will prompt a great many moans and whimpers yet. It will inspire research projects that are more and more unreal. It will continue to nourish dreams and phantasies. Oedipus is a vector: 4, 3, 2, 1, 0 ... Four is the famous fourth symbolical term, 3 is the triangulation, 2 is the dual images, 1 is narcissism, and 0 is the death instinct. *Oedipus is the entropy of the desiring-machine*, its tendency to external abolition. It is the image or the representation slipped into the machine, the stereotype that stops the connections, exhausts the flows, puts death in desire, and substitutes a kind of plaster for the cracks; it is the *Interruptrice* (the psychoanalysts as the saboteurs of desire). For the distinction between the manifest content and the latent content, for the distinction between the repressing and the repressed, we must substitute the two poles of the unconscious: the schizo-desiring machine, and the paranoiac Oedipal apparatus, the connectors of desire, and its repressors. Yes, in fact, you will find as much of

Oedipus as you wish to find, as much as you call forth in order to silence the machines (necessarily so, since Oedipus is both the repressing and the repressed, which is to say the stereotype-image that brings desire to a standstill, and attends to it, representing it as being at a standstill). An image is something that can only be *seen* ... It is the compromise, but the compromise distorts both parties alike, namely, the nature of the reactionary repressor and the nature of the revolutionary desire. It is the compromise, but the compromise distorts both parties alike, namely, the nature of the reactionary repressor and the nature of the revolutionary desire. In the compromise, the two parties have gone over the same side, as opposed to desire which remains on the other side, beyond compromise.

In his two studies of Jules Verne, Moré came upon two themes, one after the other, which he presented simply as being distinct from each other: the Oedipal problem which Jules Verne lived both as father and as son, and the problem of the machine as the destruction of Oedipus and a substitute for women.[7] But the problem of the desiring-machine, in its essentially erotic nature, is not in the least that of knowing whether a machine will ever he capable of giving "the perfect illusion of woman." On the contrary, the problem is: in which machine to place woman, in which machine does a woman put herself in order to become the non-Oedipal object of desire, which is to say, nonhuman sex? In all the desiring-machines, sexuality does not consist of an imaginary woman-machine couple serving as a substitute for Oedipus, but of the machine-desire couple as the real production of a daughter born without a mother, a non-Oedipal woman (who would not be Oedipal neither for herself, nor for others). Yet there is no indication that people are growing tired of such entertaining narcissistic exercises as psychocriticism, which ascribes an Oedipal origin to the novel in general, bastards, foundlings. One must admit that the greatest authors lend themselves to this kind of misunderstanding, precisely because Oedipus is literature's counterfeit currency, or, what amounts to the same thing, its real exchange value. But, just when these writers appear to be up to their teeth in Oedipus, in the eternal mommy-wail, the eternal daddy-debate, in actual fact they are embarked upon a completely different venture, an orphan undertaking; they are assembling an infernal desiring-machine, putting desire in contact with a libidinal world of connections and breaks, flows and schizes that constitute the nonhuman element of sex, a world where each thing becomes a component of "the motor, desire," of a "lubric wheelwork," crossing, mixing, overturning structures and orders— mineral, vegetable, animal, juvenile, social—each time shattering the ridiculous figures of Oedipus, always pushing forward a process of deterritorialization. For not even childhood is Oedipal; as a matter of fact, it does not have the least possibility of being Oedipal. What is Oedipal is the abject childhood memory, the screen memory. And finally, an author most effectively reveals the inanity and the vacuity of Oedipus when he manages to inject into his work veritable recurrent blocks of childhood which again start up the desiring-machines, as opposed to old photos, to screen memories which flood the machine and turn the child into a regressive phantasy for little old people.

This can be seen clearly in the case of Kafka, a privileged example, the Oedipal terrain *par excellence*. The Oedipal pole that he (Kafka) waves and brandishes under the reader's nose masks a more subterranean undertaking: the nonhuman establishment of a totally new literary machine. Strictly speaking, it is a machine for literary practice and for de-Oedipalizing all too-human love. Kafka's machine plugs desire into the premonition of a perverse bureaucratic and technocratic machine, a machine that is already fascist, in which the names of the family lose their consistency in order to open onto the motley Austrian Empire of the machine-castle, onto the condition of Jews without identity, onto Russia, America,

China, continents situated well beyond the persons and the names of familialism. One can see a parallel undertaking in Proust: Kafka and Proust, the two great Oedipals, are make-believe Oedipals, and those who take Oedipus seriously will always be able to graft onto them their own mournful novels and commentaries. Just consider for a moment what they are losing: the comedy of the superhuman, the schizo laughter that shakes Proust or Kafka behind the Oedipal grimace—the becoming-spider, or the becoming-beetle.

In a recent text, Roger Dadoun develops the theory of two poles of dreams: the dream-program, the dream-machine or machinery-dream, the factory dream, in which the essential is desiring-production, machinic operation, the establishment of connections, the vanishing points or those of the deterritorialization of the libido being engulfed in the nonhuman molecular element, the circulation of flows, the injection of intensities—and, on the other hand, the Oedipal pole, the dream-theater, the dream-screen, which is no longer anything but an object of molar interpretation, and where the dream narrative has already prevailed over the dream itself, the visual and verbal images over the informal or material sequences.[8] Dadoun shows how Freud, with *The Interpretation of Dreams*, abandons a direction that was still possible during the period in which he wrote the "Project for a Scientific Psychology," and that henceforth psychoanalysis is committed to blind-alleys which it will set up as the very conditions of its own practice. One already finds in Gherasim Luca and in Trost, authors whose work goes strangely unrecognized, an anti-Oedipal conception of dreams which strikes us as being very fine. Trost reproaches Freud with having neglected the manifest content of dreams for the benefit of a unified theory of Oedipus, with having failed to recognize the dream as a machine for communication with the outside world, with having fused dreams to memories rather than to deliriums, with having constructed a theory of the compromise that robs dreams as well as symptoms of their inherent revolutionary significance. He exposes the action of the repressors or regressors in their role as representatives of "the reactionary social elements" that insinuate themselves into dreams by the help of associations originating in the preconscious and that of screen memories originating in waking life. Now these associations do not belong to dreams any more than do the memories; that is precisely why the dream is forced to treat them symbolically. Let there be no mistake, Oedipus exists, the associations are always Oedipal, but precisely because the mechanism on which they depend is the same as for Oedipus. Hence, in order to retrace the dream thought, which shares a common lot with sleepwalking insofar as they both undergo the action of distinct repressors, it is necessary to break up the associations. To this end, Trost suggest a kind of à la Burroughs cut-up, which consists in bringing a dream fragment into contact with *any* passage from a textbook of sexual pathology, an intervention that re-injects life into the dream and intensifies it, instead of interpreting it, that provides the machinic phylum of the dream with new connections. The risk is negligible, since by virtue of our polymorphous perversity, the passage *selected at random* will always combine with the dream fragment to form a machine. And no doubt the associations re-form, close up between the two components, but it will have been necessary to take advantage of the moment, however brief, of dissociation to cause desire to emerge, in its nonbiographical and nonmemorial nature, beyond as well as on this side of its Oedipal predeterminations. And this is indeed the direction indicated by Trost or Luca in several superb texts: bringing out an unconscious alive with revolution, straining towards a being, a non-Oedipal man and woman, the "freely mechanical being," "the projection of a human group still to be discovered," whose mystery resides in its function and not in its interpretation, the "wholly secular intensity of desire" (there has never been such a thorough denunciation of the authoritarian and pious nature of psychoanalysis).[9] In this sense, wouldn't the highest aim of the MLFI[10] be the machinic and revolutionary construction of the non-Oedipal woman, instead of the confused exaltation of mothering and castration?

Let us return to the necessity of breaking up associations: dissociation not merely as a characteristic of schizophrenia but as a principle of schizoanalysis. The greatest obstacle to psychoanalysis, the impossibility of establishing associations, is on the contrary, the very condition of schizoanalysis—that is to say, the sign that we have finally reached elements that enter into a functional ensemble of the unconscious as a desiring-machine. It is not surprising that the method called free association invariably brings us back to Oedipus; that such is its function. Far from testifying to a spontaneity, it presupposes an application, a mapping back that forces a preordained ensemble to associate with a final artificial or memorial ensemble, predetermined symbolically as being Oedipal. In reality, we still have not accomplished anything so long as we have not reached elements that are not associable, or so long as we have not grasped the elements in a form in which they are no longer associable. Serge Leclaire takes a decisive step when he sets the terms of a problem which, in his words, "everything impels us not to consider straight in the face ... What is involved, in brief, is the conception of a system whose elements are bound together precisely by the absence of any tie, and I mean by that, the absence of any natural, logical, or significant tie," "a set of pure singularities."[11] But, mindful of the need to remain within the narrow bounds of psychoanalysis, he takes the same step backwards: he presents the unbound ensemble as a fiction, its manifestations as epiphanies, which must be inscribed in a new restructured ensemble, if only through the unity of the phallus as the *signifier* of absence. Yet here indeed was the emergence of the desiring-machine, that which distinguishes it both from the psychic bonds of the Oedipal apparatus, and from the mechanical or structural bonds of the social and technical machines: a set of really distinct parts that operate in combination *as being really distinct* (bound together by the absence of any tie). Such approximations of desiring-machines are not furnished by surrealist objects, theatrical epiphanies, or Oedipal gadgets, which function only by reintroducing associations—in point of fact, Surrealism was a vast enterprise of Oedipalization of the movements that preceded it. But they will be found rather in certain Dadaist machines, in the drawings of Julius Goldberg, or, more recently, in the machines of Tinguely. How does one obtain a functional ensemble, while shattering all the associations? (What is meant by "bound by the absence of any tie"?).

In Tinguely, the art of real distinction is obtained by means of a kind of uncoupling used as a method of recurrence. A machine brings into play several simultaneous structures which it pervades. The first structure includes at least one element that is not operational in relation to it, but only in relation to a second structure. It is this interplay, which Tinguely presents as being essentially joyful, that ensures the process of deterritorialization of the machine, as well as the position of the mechanic as the most deterritorialized part of the machine. The grandmother who pedals inside the automobile under the wonderstruck gaze of the child—a non-Oedipal child whose eye is itself a part of the machine—does not cause the car to move forward, but, through her pedaling, activates a second structure, which is sawing wood. Other methods of recurrence can be put into play or added-on, as, for example, the envelopment of the parts within a multiplicity (thus the city-machine, a city where all the houses are in one, or Buster Keaton's house-machine, where all the rooms are in one). Or again, the recurrence can be realized in a series that places the machine in an essential relationship with scraps and residua, where, for example, the machine destroys its own object, as in Tinguely's Rotozazas, or the machine itself taps lost intensities or energies as in Duchamp's Transformer project, or it is itself made up of scraps as in Stankiewicz's Junk Art, or in the Merz and the house-machine of Schwitters, or, finally, where it sabotages or destroys itself, where "its construction and the beginning of its destruction are indistinguishable." In all these examples (to which should be added narcotics functioning as a desiring-machine, the junky machine) there appears a properly machinic death drive that stands in opposition to the Oedipal regressive death, to psychoanalytic euthanasia. And there is really not one of these desiring-machines that is not profoundly de-Oedipalizing.

Moreover, it is chance relations that ensure this, without, between elements which are really distinct as such, or the unconnective connection of their autonomous structures, following a vector that goes from mechanical disorder towards the less probable, and which we call the "mad vector." The importance here of Vendryes' theories becomes evident, for they make it possible to define desiring-machines by the presence of such chance relations within the machine itself, and by its production of Brownoid movements of the sort observed in the stroll or the sexual prowl.[12] And, in the case of Goldberg's drawings as well, it is through the realization of chance relations that the functionality of really distinct elements is ensured, with the same joy that is present in Tinguely, the schizo-laughter. What is involved is the substitution of an ensemble functioning as a desiring-machine positioned on a mad vector, for a simple memorial circuit or for a social circuit (in the first example, *You Sap, Mail that Letter*, the desiring-machine pervades and programs the three automated structures of sport, gardening, and the birdcage; in the second example, *Simple Reducing Machine*, the Volga boatman's exertion, the decompression of the stomach of the millionaire eating dinner, the fall of the boxer onto the ring, and the jump of the rabbit are programmed by the record insofar as it defines the less probable or the simultaneity of the points of departure and arrival).

All these machines are real machines. Hocquenghem is right in saying, "Where desire is active, there is no longer any place for the Imaginary," nor for the Symbolic. All these machines are already there; we are continually producing them, manufacturing them, setting them in motion, for they are desire, desire just as it is— although it takes artists to bring about their autonomous presentation. Desiring-machines are not in our heads, in our imagination, they are *inside the social and technical machines themselves.* Our relationship with machines is not a relationship of invention or of imitation; we are not the cerebral fathers nor the disciplined sons of the machine. It is a relationship of peopling: we populate the social technical machines with desiring-machines, and we have no alternative. We are obliged to say at the same time: social technical machines are only conglomerates of desiring-machines under molar conditions that are historically determined; desiring-machines are social and technical machines restored to their determinant molecular conditions. Schwitters' Merz is the last syllable of Komerz. It is futile to examine the usefulness or uselessness, the possibility or impossibility of these desiring-machines. Their impossibility and their uselessness become visible only in the autonomous artistic presentation, and there very rarely. Don't you see that they are possible because they are; they are there in every way, and we function with them. They are eminently useful, since they constitute the two directions of the relationship between the machine and man, the *communication* of the two. At the very moment you say, "this machine is impossible," you fail to see that you are making it possible, by being yourself one of its parts, the very part that you seemed to be missing in order for it to be already working, the dancer-danger. You argue about the possibility or the usefulness, but you are already inside the machine, you are a part of it, you have put a finger inside, or an eye, your anus, or your liver (the modern version of "You are in the same boat ...").

It almost appears as though the difference between social technical machines and desiring-machines were primarily a question of size, or one of adaptation, desiring-machines being small machines, or large machines suited to small groups. It is by no means a problem of gadgets. The current technological trend, which replaces the thermodynamic priority with a certain priority of information, is logically accompanied by a reduction in the size of machines. In another very joyful text, Ivan Illich shows the following: that heavy machines imply capitalist or despotic relations of production, involving the dependence, the exploitation, and the powerlessness of men reduced to the condition of consumers or servants. *The collective ownership of the means of production* does not alter anything in this state of affairs, and merely sustains a Stalinist despotic organization. Accordingly, Illich puts forward the alternative of *everyone's right to make use of the means of production,* in a "convivial society," which is to say, a desiring and non Oedipal society. This would mean the most extensive utilization of machines by the greatest possible number of people, the proliferation of small machines and the adaptation of the large machines to small units, the exclusive sale of machinic components which would have to be assembled by the users-producers themselves, and the destruction of the specialization of knowledge and of the professional monopoly. It is quite obvious that things as different as the monopoly or the specialization of most areas of medical knowledge, the complicated nature of the automobile engine, and the monstrous size of machines do not comply with any technological necessity, but solely with economic and political imperatives whose aim is to concentrate power or control in the hands of a ruling class. It is not a dream of a return to nature when one points out the extreme machinic uselessness of automobiles in cities, their archaic character in spite of the gadgets attached to them for show, and the potentially modern character of the bicycle, in our cities as well as in the Vietnam War. And it is not even on behalf of relatively simple and small machines that the desiring "convivial revolution" has to be made, but on behalf of machinic innovation itself, which capitalist or communist societies do everything in their economic and political power to repress.[13]

One of the greatest artists of desiring-machines, Buster Keaton was able to pose the problem of an adaptation of the mass machine to individual ends, or to those of a couple or small group, in *The Navigator*, where the two protagonists "have to deal with housekeeping equipment generally used by hundreds of people (the galley is a forest of levers, pulleys, and wires)."[14] It is true that the themes of reduction or adaptation of machines are not sufficient by themselves, and stand for something else. This is shown by the demand that everyone be able to make use of them and control them. For the true difference between social technical machines and desiring-machines obviously is not in the size, nor even in the ends they serve, but in the regime that decides on the size and the ends. *They are the same machines, but it is not the same regime.* This is not to say, by any means, that we should counter the present regime, which submits technology to the aims of an economy and a politics of oppression, with the notion of a regime in which technology presumably would be liberated and liberating. Technology presupposes social machines and desiring-machines, each within the other, and, by itself, has no power to decide which will be the engineering agency, desire or the oppression of desire. Every time technology claims to be acting on its own, it takes on a fascist hue, as in the techno-structure, because it implies not only economic and political investments, but libidinal investments as well, and they are turned entirely towards the oppression of desire. The distinction between the two regimes, as the regime of antidesire and that of desire, does not come down to the distinction between the collectivity and the individual, but to two types of mass organization, in which the individual and the collective do not enter into the same relationship. There exists the same difference between them as between the microphysical and the macrophysical—it being understood that the microphysical agency is not the machine-electron, but molecular machinizing desire, just as the macrophysical agency is not the molar technical object, but the antidesiring, antiproductive, molarizing social structure that currently conditions the use, the control and the possession of technical objects. In our present social order, the desiring-machine is tolerated only in its perverse forms, which is to say, on the fringes of the serious utilization of machines, and as a secondary benefit that cannot be avowed by the users, producers, or antiproducers (the sexual enjoyment experienced by the judge in judging, by the bureaucrat in stroking his files...). But the desiring-machine's regime is not a generalized perversion, it is rather the opposite, a general and productive schizophrenia that has finally become happy. What Tinguely says of one of his own works applies to desiring-machines: *a truly joyous machine, by joyous I mean free.*

3. The Machine and the full body: the investments of the Machine.

Nothing is more obscure, as soon as one considers the details, than Marx's propositions concerning productive forces and relations of production. The broad outline is clear enough: from tools to machines, the human means of production imply social relations of production, which however are external to these means and are merely their "index." But what is the meaning of "index"? Why does Marx project an abstract evolutive line meant to represent the isolated relationship of man and nature, where the machine is apprehended starting from the tool, and the tool in terms of the organism and its needs? It then necessarily follows that social relations appear external to the tool or to the machine, and impose on them from the outside another biological schema while breaking up the evolutive line according to heterogeneous social organizations[15] (it is among other factors, this interplay between productive forces and relations of production that explains the strange idea that the bourgeoisie was revolutionary at a given moment). It seems to us on the contrary that the machine has to be directly conceived in relation to a social body, and not in relation to a human biological organism. If such is the case, one cannot regard the machine as a new segment that succeeds that of the tool, along a line that would have its starting point in abstract man. For man and the tool *are already* components of a machine constituted by a full body acting as an engineering agency, and by men and tools that are engineered (*machinés*) insofar as they are distributed on this body. For example, there is a full body of the steppe which engineers man-horse-bow, a full body of the Greek city-state which engineers men and weapons, a full body of the factory which engineers men and machines ... Of the two definitions of a manufacture given by Ure, and cited by Marx, the first relates machines to the men who tend them, while the second relates the machines *and* the men, "mechanical and intellectual organs," to the manufacture as the full body that engineers them. It is in fact the second definition that is literal and concrete.

It is not through metaphors nor by extension that we consider public places and community facilities (*les lieux, les equipements collectifs*) the means of communication, and the social bodies as machines or machine components. On the contrary, it is by virtue of a restriction and a derivation that the machine will cease to designate anything but a technical reality but precisely under the conditions of a quite specific full body, the body of money-Capital, insofar as it gives the tool the form of fixed capital, which is to say, distributes the tools on the surface of an autonomous mechanical representative, and gives man the form of variable capital, which is to say, distributes men on an abstract representative of labor in general. An interlocking of full bodies all belonging to the same series: the full body of capital, that of the factory, that of mechanisms ... (Or indeed the full body of the Greek city-State, that of the phalange, that of the two-handed shield). The question we ought to ask is not how the technical machine follows after simple tools, but how the social machine, and which social machine, instead of being content to engineer men and machines, makes the emergence of technical machines both possible and necessary. (There were many technical machines before the advent of capitalism, but the machinic phylum did not pass through them, precisely because it was content to engineer men and tools. In the same way, there are tools in every social formation which are not engineered, because the phylum does not pass through them while the same tools are engineered in other social formations: hoplite weapons, for example).

The machine understood in this manner is defined as a desiring-machine: the ensemble composed of a full body that engineers, and men and tools engineered on it. Several consequences follow from this view of the machine, but we can only plot them here in a programmatic way.

Firstly, desiring-machines are indeed the same as technical and social machines, but they are their unconscious, as it were: they manifest and mobilize the investments of desire that "correspond" to the conscious or preconscious investments of interest, the politics, and the technology of a specific social field. To correspond does not at all mean to resemble; what is at stake is another distribution, another "map," that no longer concerns the interests established in a society, nor the apportionment of the possible and the impossible, of freedoms and constraints, all that constitutes a society's *reasons*. But, beneath these reasons, there are the unwanted forms of a desire that invests the flows as such, and the breaks in these flows, a desire that continually reproduces the aleatory factors, the less probable figures, and the encounters between independent series that are at the base of this society, a desire that elicits a love "for its own sake," a love of capital for its own sake, a love of bureaucracy for its own sake, a love of repression for its own sake, all sorts of strange things such as "What does a capitalist desire from the bottom of his heart?" and "How is it possible that men desire repression not only for others but for themselves?" and so on.

Secondly, the fact that desiring-machines are the internal limit, as it were, of the technical social machines is more easily understood if one bears in mind that the full body of a society, its engineering agency, is never given as such, but must always be inferred from terms and relations coming into play in that society. The full body of capital as a proliferating body, Money that produces more Money, is never given in itself. It implies a movement to the limit, where the terms are reduced to their simple forms taken in an absolute sense, and where the relations are "positively" replaced by an absence of ties. Consider the capitalist desiring-machine, for example, the encounter between capital and labor force, capital as deterritorialized wealth and labor capacity as the deterritorialized worker, two independent series or simple forms whose chance meeting is continually reproduced in capitalism. How can the absence of ties be positive? One meets again with Leclaire's question stating the paradox of desire: how can elements be bound together by the absence of any ties? In a certain sense, it can be said that Cartesianism, in Spinoza and Leibniz, has not ceased to reply to this question. It is the theory of real distinction, insofar as it implies a specific logic. It is because they are really distinct, and completely independent of each other, that ultimate elements or simple forms belong to the same being or to the same substance. It is in this sense, in fact, that a substantial full body does not function at all as an organism. And the desiring-machine is nothing other than a multiplicity of distinct elements or simple forms that are *bound together* on the full body of a society, precisely to the extent that they are "on" this body, or to the extent that they are really distinct. The desiring-machine as a movement to the limit: the inference of the full body, the eliciting of simple forms, the assigning of absences of ties. The method employed in Marx's *Capital* takes this direction, but its dialectical presuppositions prevent it from reaching desire as a part of the infrastructure.

Thirdly, the relations of production that remain outside the technical machine are, on the contrary, internal to the desiring-machine. Admittedly, they no longer exist as relations, but as parts of the machine, some being elements of production, and others elements of antiproduction.[16] J.J. Lebel cites the example of certain sequences of Genet's film that form a desiring-machine of the prison: two prisoners locked in adjoining cells, one of whom blows smoke into the other's mouth through a straw that passes through a little hole in the wall, while a guard masturbates as he watches. The guard is both an element of antiproduction and a voyeur component of the machine: desire is transmitted through all the parts. This means that desiring-machines are not pacified; they contain dominations and servitudes, death-carrying elements, sadistic parts and masochistic parts that are juxtaposed. Precisely in the desiring-machines, these parts assume, as do all the others, their strictly sexual dimensions. This is not to say, as psychoanalysis would have it, that sexuality has at its disposal an Oedipal code that would supplement the social formations, or even preside over their mental genesis and organization (money and anality, fascism and sadism, and so forth). There is no sexual symbolism, and sexuality does not designate another "economy," another "politics," but rather the libidinal unconscious of political economy as such. The libido, the energy of the desiring-machine, invests every social difference as being a sexual difference, including class differences, racial differences and so on, either in order to guard the wall of sexual differentiation in the unconscious, or, on the contrary, in order to blow this wall to pieces, to abolish it on behalf of nonhuman sex. In its very violence, the desiring-machine is a trial of the whole social field by desire, a test whose outcome can just as well be desire's triumph as its oppression. The test consists in the following: given a desiring-machine, how does it make a relation of production or a social difference into one of its component parts, and what is the position of this part? What about the millionaire's stomach in Goldberg's drawing, or the masturbating guard in Genet's film image? Isn't a captive factory boss a component of a factory desiring-machine, a way of responding to the test?

Fourthly, if sexuality as an energy of the unconscious is the investment of the social field by the desiring-machines, it becomes apparent that a social attitude vis-à-vis machines in general in no way expresses mere ideology, but the position of desire in the infrastructure itself, the mutations of desire in terms of the breaks and the flows that pervade this field. That is why the theme of the machine has a content that is so emphatically, so openly sexual. The epoch of the First World War was the meeting ground of the four great attitudes centering around the machine: the great molar exaltation of Italian Futurism, which counts on the machine to develop the national productive forces and to produce a new national man, without calling in question the relations of production; that of Russian Futurism and Constructivism, which conceive the machine in terms of new relations of production defined by collective appropriation (the tower-machine of Tatlin, or that of Moholy-Nagy, expressing the famous party organization as a democratic centralism, a spiral model, with a summit, a driving belt, and a base; the relations of production continue to be external to the machine, which functions as an "index"); the Dadaist molecular machinery, which, for its part, brings about a reversal in the form of a revolution of desire, because it submits the relations of production to the trial of the parts of the desiring-machine, and elicits from the latter joyous movements of deterritorialization that overcome all the territorialities of nation and party; and lastly, a humanist antimachinism, which wants to rescue imaginary or symbolic desire, to turn it back against the machine, standing ready to level it onto an Oedipal apparatus (Surrealism versus Dadaism, or Chaplin versus the Dadaist Buster Keaton). [17]

And precisely because it is not a matter of ideology, but of a machination that brings into play an entire group unconscious characterizing a historical epoch, the tie between these attitudes and the social and political field is complex, although it is not indeterminate. Italian Futurism clearly sets forth the conditions and the organizational forms of a fascist desiring-machine, with all the equivocations of a nationalist and war-hungry "left." Russian Futurists attempt to slip their anarchist elements into a party machine that crushes them. Politics is not the strong point of the Dadaists. Humanism effects a withdrawal of the investment of desiring-machines which nonetheless continue to operate inside it. But the problem of desire itself was posed in the confrontation of these attitudes, the problem of the position of desire, i.e., that of the relationship of respective immanence between desiring-machines and social technical machines, between those two extreme poles where desire invests paranoiac fascist formations, or, on the contrary, revolutionary schizoid flows. The paradox of desire is that it always requires such a long analysis, an entire analysis of the unconscious, in order to disentangle the poles and draw out the nature of the revolutionary group trials—for desiring-machines.

II
—

BEYOND ANALYSIS

5

GUERRILLA IN PSYCHIATRY:

FRANCO BASAGLIA

A war of liberation, waged for ten years to overthrow the traditional institution is presented to us in terms of militant struggle, in a literary fortnightly containing recorded accounts, book reviews, discussions, journal extracts, personal opinions, and articles. And it is done without the least bit of pedantry. There is straightaway a violent refusal of all scientific pseudoneutrality in this domain which is, for the authors, eminently political.

It all started in 1961. Under the impetus of Dr. Basaglia, the new direction of the hospital brought about "a sudden rupture of working solidarity" among the personnel and the breaking away of an "avant-garde" which refused to any longer fulfill the "mandate of the cure and of surveillance" entrusted to them by a repressive society. Step by step all services were to be opened: general meetings would be open to the institutionalized, communications, the organization of leisure, and sociotherapy would be intensified ...

At first "nobody would open their mouth"; but then there was a thaw, and intense interest spread to all the departments. The hospital held over fifty meetings a week, spectacular improvements were made, and patients were sent home after 10, 15, or 20 years in the hospital.

Basaglia and Minguzzi then decided to undertake a detailed investigation into similar experiments in institutional psychotherapy in France and therapeutic communities in England (i.e. at

Dingleton, under the direction of Maxwell Jones). They gradually developed their own conceptions, distancing themselves from other attempts that they considered to be too reformist, and questioning their own initial approaches.

Until then it had been the advanced group—the "avant-garde" —who "granted privileges" to patients. The dice were loaded. In 1965, Basaglia and his group decided to develop more thoroughly the "community culture" which, little by little, gained ground and modified the real relations of force between the personnel and the patients. Maxwell Jones's ideas were subjected to criticism. They decided that the techniques involved in *reaching a consensus* were, after all, only a new method of integrating the mentally ill into a society answering to the "ideal of the panorganization of neocapitalist society" (Lucio Schiter, p. 149). The famous "third psychiatric revolution" would be merely, as they put it, "a belated adaptation of modalities of social control of pathological behavior to the methods of production perfected over the last forty years by sociologists and technicians of mass communication" (p. 149).

Thus, they rejected every politics of improvement and the consolidation of hospitals, a politics which in France had led the most innovative trends in psychiatry to collaborate directly with the Minister of Health, and to elaborate, with the top-ranking civil servants, ministerial circulars for the reform of psychiatric hospitals, etc. In the long run, this experience was deceptive and bitter, and it drove certain of the best of French psychiatrists to despair. In addition, the recent psychiatric reform of teaching, finalized by Edgar Faure[1] for the departments, must have contributed to the spread of confusion among the ranks of the psychiatric opposition after May 1968. The society of institutional psychotherapy itself took cover during the May movement, certain psychiatrists estimating "that nothing happened in May," nothing in any case that could possibly concern institutional psychotherapy. Violently contradictory positions confronted one another during an international congress in Vienna in 1968, which Basaglia concluded by leaving and slamming the door behind him.

In Italy, where the state of the hospitals and the legislation is undoubtedly one of the most archaic in Europe, such illusions can hardly be dismissed—given the infamous stamp on the police record of psychiatric inmates, inmates denied their civil rights, and torture by strangulation: "a sheet, usually wet, is twisted tightly around the neck to prevent breathing: the loss of consciousness is immediate" (Basagila, p. 164). Basaglia harbors no illusions about the experiment of Gorizia: its future was doomed; at best, events would unfold as they did in Maxwell Jones's therapeutic communities at Dingleton, that is to say, in a "didactic and therapeutic engagement pursued on the staff level, but which retreats into the particular domain of institutional interests" (p. 100).

Unlike what generally happened elsewhere, the "psychiatric revolution" of Basaglia and his group was not "for laughs." From year to year, we witness an absolute escalation which has, moreover, lead to serious difficulties for its instigators. The *open door* [policy], ergotherapy, sociotherapy, sectorization—all these were implemented but did not cohere in a satisfying way. Was it the context of the Italian "creeping May" that entailed this permanent refusal of all self-satisfaction? Or was it the indifference of the Italian state and its inability to promote reform which discouraged every attempt at renewal? In any case, the "avant-garde" of Gorizia was no longer there: the "common goal" became "institutional change," the "negation of the institution," the Italian equivalent of the antipsychiatry of Laing and Cooper in England.[2]

The very honesty of this book leads us to question the desperate nature of this endeavor. Is it not secretly preoccupied by a desire to bring things to the verge of collapse? Isn't the dialectical process on the way to transforming itself in forward flight and, in a sense, betraying itself? For *antipsychiatry*, political intervention constitutes the prerequisite of all therapeutics. But doesn't the agreement around the "negation of the institution," which has meaning only if it is taken up by a real avant-garde and securely achored in social reality, risk serving as a springboard for a new form of social repression, this time at the level of global society and aiming at the very status of madness?

Basaglia states that with the medications that he administers "the doctor calms his own anxiety in the face of a patient with whom he does not know how to enter into contact nor find a common language" (p. 117). An ambiguous and perhaps demagogic expression: psychopharmacology is not, in itself, a reactionary science! It is the context of its use that must be called into question.

Nosography, too, is perhaps a little rashly thrown overboard. The ways of repression are sometimes subtle! Those who uphold normality at any price can become more effective than the police! With the best moral and political intentions in the world, one may come to refuse the mad the right to be mad; the claim that "society is to blame" can disguise a way of suppressing all deviance. Institutional negation would then become a denegation— *Verneinung* in the Freudian sense—of the singular fact of derangement. Before taking out an option on nosography, Freud devoted himself to really giving a voice to neurotics, freeing them from all the effects of suggestion. Giving up the idea of medical suggestion in order to fall into collective suggestion would only create an illusory benefit.

I think that Basaglia and his comrades might be led incisively beyond some of their current formulations and to "bend" their ears to mental alienation without systematically reducing it to social alienation. Matters are relatively straightforward and rightfully violent when it is a matter of repudiating repressive institutions. Things are much more difficult when they concern our understanding of madness. Then a few formulas from Sartrean or Maoist sources will not in this case suffice.

Political causality does not completely govern the causality of madness. It is perhaps, conversely, in an unconscious signifying assemblage that madness dwells, and which predetermines the structural field in which political options, drives, and revolutionary inhibitions are deployed, beside and beyond social and economic determinisms.

Fortunately, Basaglia's project has not fallen into a theoretical dogmatism. This book is invaluable in that it poses a thousand questions that the learned of contemporary psychiatry meticulously avoid.

6

LAING DIVIDED

The clear-cut alternatives between good and evil, the normal and the pathological, the healthy and the mad, are perhaps about to undergo a profound reshuffling, anticipating the awareness we may have of such a process. It became obvious that a number of judgments, which yesterday seemed to be self-evident, are now vacillating, that a number of roles no longer function according to the norms of common sense. Deviance has acquired authority. There is now a revolutionary front for homosexuals, an information group for common law prisoners, "Journals for Madness," etc.

The importance of Ronald Laing, one of the initiators of English antipsychiatry, is to be estimated in terms of this new context, as Danièle Sabourin says, within the framework of this "counterculture movement in which politics and the university come together."[1] Laing is first and foremost a deviant psychiatrist. For us he is first this disheveled and somewhat euphoric character whose irruption with Cooper at the conference on Alienated Childhood, organized in Paris in 1957 by Maud Mannoni and the journal *Recherches*, had the effect of a bombshell.

The whole psychiatric community is talking about Laing's antipsychiatry. But is Laing still speaking to the psychiatrists? He is already far away, very far away from their world and their concerns. He has himself taken the "trip" which he advocated for schizophrenics, he has abandoned his London activities and has gone to meditate, so they say, in a monastery in Ceylon. However, his books are quite present. Impossible to ignore them. They irritate, and shake up the specialized communities. Commentators started taking an interest, French translations followed one after the other: *The Politics of Experience* and *The Divided Self*, a theoretical work, *The Self and the Others*, a collection of eleven clinical monographs in collaboration with Estertson, and then this disconcerting, unclassifiable book, *Knots*, an unusual collection of logico-psychological poems. How can one interpret this public fascination? Since May '68 a public has appeared that has shown a particularly strong interest in everything concerning the problems of madness. More than twenty years after Artaud's death, and to borrow a term from Laing, the madman is about to become the hierophant of our society. The order of things and institutions have received such a jolt that one cannot refrain from questioning the future, with apprehension one searches for any form of opposition, any exemplary protest—the emotions stirred up around the Caro affair would have been unthinkable just five years ago!

In this light one can expect that Laing's work will be received by an even wider audience in the future. Is it not significant that a protest movement led by a group of urbanists, the CRAAAK,[2] used one of Laing's poems in childhood from *Knots* as their manifesto's epigraph? Laing, Cooper, Basaglia, Gentis, to name but a few, have done more in several months to change our view on madness than decades of patient and serious research, for instance those of the French Institutional Psychotherapy current which remained rigorously in the concrete territory of mental hygiene institutions.

To judge the root of the problems, it will still be necessary, however, to come back to this massive reality of the alienation of the psychiatric "populations," and to the inextricable problems the mental health workers have to deal with on a daily basis. In the last resort it is on this territory that the value of the antipsychiatric theories should be appreciated. Either antipsychiatry will be taken up by a mass practice which will profoundly modify the attitudes and power relations in daily practice, or it will remain what it still is, by force of circumstance: a literary phenomenon, and as such, it has already been "recuperated" to a large extent by the most reformist, even retrograde currents, that never retreat before verbal concessions.

We have to admit that up until now there have been no lasting experiments in antipsychiatry. All have been gallant last stands that were then liquidated by the orthodox institutions. Until now, not a single mass movement has pushed forward a true antipsychiatry (Cooper's experiment in Wing 21 in London was not followed up, no more than those of the House-hold, like Kingsley Hall, Basaglia had to leave Gorizia, etc.)

Antipsychiatry lays itself particularly open to the reformists' "recuperations" because on the doctrinal level it did not divest itself of a humanistic and personalistic ideology. Laing's antipsychiatry less than the others, but he is in a way the Left's voice in a line of thought which one must recognize as being, frankly, situated on the whole at a remove from the contributions of Marx and Freud regarding the understanding of mental and social alienation.

Laing is divided within himself: a revolutionary when he breaks with psychiatric practice, his written work escapes him and despite himself, it is used to ends that are foreign to his inspiration. It is perhaps in this light that one can explain his present research in Asia.

When Laing writes that the most important new phenomena is "the increasing discontent with which all theory or study of the individual in isolation from his context is received" (*The Self and Others*), it is the most traditional of family psychotherapy and sectorial psychiatry that are held accountable for this. When he holds society responsible for the genesis of psychosis, one only remembers that, for him, the cure should come from a "sincere confirmation between the parents." One feels relieved by such a return to fine sentiments, one feels delivered from this object, the cause of desire, brought to light by Lacan after Freud, an object radically heterogenous to the person, and whose identity and localization escapes intersubjective coordinates as well as the world of meanings.

In a note, Laing is worried that he might give the reader the impression that he pays no heed to "a person's actions upon itself" or that he minimizes "that which touches upon the sexuality awakened by family members, i.e. incest" (*Mental Equilibrium, Madness and the Family*). Hardly has he evoked the spectre of the sexual machine that he folds it back onto familialism and incest. His search for a "schizogeny" can never extricate itself from the personalistic "nexus." His project for an existentialist phenomenology of madness, in fact, amounts to following "the twists and turns of the person in relation to the various ways in which it invests itself more or less in the things that it does" (*The Self and the Others*). It is about nothing else than the "recognition of the person as an agent." It is the "false situations" that are pathogenic. What one must recover is the "true self," the "true confidence in the future" founded on Martin Buber's "true encounter."

One does not always have the feeling that Laing really masters the implications of what he has written. On certain points, he himself only commits himself with some reservation on themes that make up the common ground of antipsychiatry. For instance, he is far more cautious than Cooper[3] or Hochmann[4] when it comes to promoting the famous family psychotherapy which, at bottom, is nothing more than a disguised return to readaptation techniques, and suggestion techniques on a small group scale.

He is also reticent in his adherence to Bateson's neobehaviorist theory of the "double bind," which reduced the etiology of schizophrenia to a system of logical impasses and a personalistic alienation according to which "each time there is a double bind situation, there will always be a collapse, in any individual, of the capacity to distinguish between logical types" (*The Self and Others*).

It is not obvious, in fact, that a series of interpersonal collapses cannot alone produce a psychosis, or a neurosis, nor conversely could their resolution bring about a change! One is sometimes too quick in associating Laing's phenomenological exercises with Sartre's work. To tell the truth, Sartre never did get tied up in the mirror games which seem to fascinate Laing:

> She desires that he desire her
> He desires that she desire him
> To make her desire
> He pretends that he desires her ...
>   (*Knots*)

Sartre is a man situated in history and true commitment. He would certainly refuse the contemplative ideal which leads Laing to declare that we can do nothing more than "reflect the decomposition which surrounds us and which is in us."[5]

Is it possible today when dealing with madness to ignore the contributions of Freud and Lacan? Can one find refuge in a personalistic and mystic wisdom without becoming the unconscious prisoner of ideologies whose mission is to repress desire in all its forms?

Let us hope that Laing, who has distinguished himself in a remarkable way from the traditional role of the psychiatrist, will return to a concrete struggle against the oppression suffered by the mental patients, and that he will bring a more rigorous definition to the conditions of a revolutionary psychiatric practice, that is to say a nonutopian psychiatry which can be taken up in a massive way by the avant-garde of mental health workers and by the patients themselves.

7

MARY BARNES'S "TRIP"

In 1965, a community of about twenty people gather around R.D. Laing. They settle in the suburbs of London, at Kingsley Hall, an old building which for a long time was a stronghold of the British labor movement. For the next five years, the leaders of antipsychiatry and patients who, according to them, "make a career of schizophrenia," will explore collectively the world of madness. Not the madness of asylums, but the madness each of us carries within, a madness they intend to liberate in order to lift inhibitions and symptoms of every kind. At Kingsley Hall, they overlook, or rather, try hard to overlook, the distribution of roles among patients, psychiatrist, nurse, etc. No one is entitled to give or receive orders, to issue prescriptions ... Kingsley Hall then is a liberated piece of land, a base for the counterculture movement.

The antipsychiatrists want to go beyond the experiments in community psychiatry; according to them, these experiments still represent only reformist enterprises, which fail to really question the repressive institutions and traditional framework of psychiatry. Maxwell Jones and David Cooper,[1] two of the main instigators of these attempts, will actively participate in the life of Kingsley Hall. Antipsychiatry, then, can make use of its own recording surface, a kind of body without organs, with each corner of the house—the cellar, the terrace, the kitchen, the chapel ... Each part of the collective life functioning like the gears of a big collective machine, taking each individual away from his immediate self and from his petty problems, so that he either devotes himself to the service of others, or falls upon himself in the sometimes dizzying process of regression.

This liberated piece of land, Kingsley Hall, is besieged from all sides; the old world seeps in through all its cracks; the neighbors complain about its nocturnal life; the neighborhood children throw stones at the windows; on the slightest pretext, the cops are ready to ship the restless patients off to the *real* psychiatric hospital.[2]

However, the real threat against Kingsley Hall comes from within; the inhabitants freed themselves from recognizable constraints, but secretly the internalization of repression continues, and besides, they are left under the yoke of simplistic reductions to the hackneyed triangle of father, mother, and child, used to compress all cases not classified as "normal" behavior into the mold of Oedipal psychoanalysis.

Is it necessary to maintain a minimum of discipline at Kingsley Hall, or not? Internal struggles for power poison the atmosphere. Aaron Esterson, *leader* of the "hardcores" (Stalin under his arm, while Laing carries a book by Lenin) is finally eliminated, but nevertheless, it will always be difficult for the enterprise to find ways of self-regulation. In addition, the press, television, the "in" crowd are all involved; Kingsley Hall becomes the object of riotous publicity. Mary Barnes, one of the patients, becomes a kind of superstar of madness, at the cost of making herself the focal point of implacable jealousies.

From her experience at Kingsley Hall, Mary Barnes and her psychiatrist Joseph Berke wrote a book. It is a confession of disconcerting naïveté. It is at the same time both a model enterprise of the liberation of "mad desire" and a neobehaviorist dogmatism,[3] brilliant discoveries and an impenitent familialism akin to the most traditional Puritanism. The "mad" Mary Barnes elucidates in several chapters of confession what no other "antipsychiatrist" has ever revealed: the hidden side of the Anglo-Saxon antipsychiatry.[4]

Mary Barnes is a former nurse labeled schizophrenic. She might just as well have been classified among the hysterics. She takes Laing's advice on the "trip" literally. Her "regression into childhood" is achieved in the manner of a *kamikaze*. The "down" years several times lead her to the verge of death by starvation. Everyone around her panics; should she be hurried off to a hospital or not? This triggers off a "monumental crisis" in the community. Admittedly, during her "up" years, the problems of the group are no better: she will only relate to the few people whom she heavily endows with her familialism and mysticism, that is, first and foremost, Ronnie (Laing), whom she idolizes like a god, and Joe (Berke), her simultaneous father, mother, and spiritual lover.

She thus carved for herself a small Oedipal territory that will resound with all the paranoiac tendencies of the institution. Her pleasure crystalizes into the painful realization, which tortures her relentlessly, of the *evil* she generates around her. She opposes Laing's project; and yet, this project is her most dear possession! The more guilty she feels, the more she punishes herself, the worse her condition gets, unleashing reactions of panic all around her. She reconstitutes the infernal circle of familialism by involving more than twenty people, which makes matters worse!

She acts like a baby; she has to be bottle-fed. She walks around naked, covered with shit, pissing in all the beds, breaking everything, or letting herself starve to death. She tyrannizes Joe Berke, forbids him to leave, persecutes his wife, to the point that, one day, unable to stand it any longer, he hits her. Irrepressible becomes the temptation to resort to the well-known methods of the psychiatric hospital! Joe Berke asks himself how it could be that "a group of people devoted to demystifying the social transactions of disturbed families should revert to behaving like one of them"?

Fortunately, Mary Barnes is an extreme case. Not everyone behaves as she does at Kingsley Hall. Yet, isn't she presenting the real problems? Is it certain that understanding, love, and all the other Christian virtues, together with a method of mystical regression, suffice to exorcize the demons of the Oedipal madness?

Laing is unquestionably among those most engaged in the attempt to destroy psychiatry. He passed the walls of the asylum, but it seems he remained the prisoner of other walls, those he carries with himself; he has not yet succeeded in ridding himself of the worst constraint, the most dangerous of the *double binds*,[5] namely "psychoanalysm"—to borrow Robert Castel's apt expression—with its signifying, interpretative delusion, its echoed representations, and its derisive abyss.

Laing believed it possible to elude neurotic alienation by focusing the analysis on the family, on its internal "knots." For him, everything begins with the family. He wouldn't mind, though, getting out of it. He would like to melt with the cosmos, to shatter the routine of everyday existence. But the style of his explanation cannot free the subject from the familialist hold which he wanted only as a starting point and which catches up with him at every corner. He tries to resolve the difficulty by taking refuge in an Oriental type of meditation which, however, cannot ward off indefinitely the intrusion of a capitalist subjectivity equipped with quite subtle means. You don't compromise with Oedipus; as long as you don't attack head-on this essential mechanism of capitalist repression, you won't be able to effect major changes in the economy of desire and consequently in the status of madness.

Throughout the book, there is a constant flow of either shit, piss, milk, or paint. However, it is significant to note that there is practically never mention of a flow of money. We do not exactly know what goes on from this angle. Who is in charge of money, who decides to buy what, who gets paid? The group seems to live out of thin air; Peter, Mary's brother, undoubtedly much more involved than she in the schizo process, cannot stand the bohemian style of Kingsley Hall. There is too much noise, too much chaos, and moreover, what he wants most is to keep up with his job.

But his sister harasses him; he must stay with her at Kingsley Hall. Relentless proselytism of regression: you will see, you will have your trip, you will be able to paint, you will go to the end of your madness … But Peter's madness is somewhat more disturbing. He is not very anxious to throw himself into this kind of venture! Perhaps here we can grasp the difference between a real schizo trip and the petty bourgeois style of familialist regression. A schizo is not very much interested in "human warmth." His concern lies elsewhere, on the side of the most deterritorialized flux; the flow of the "miraculating" cosmic signs, and also the flow of monetary signs. The schizo does not overlook the reality of money (even if his use of it is out of the ordinary), any more than he overlooks any other reality. A schizo does not act like a child. For him, money is a point of reference like any other, and he needs to make use of as many systems of reference as possible, precisely to enable him to keep his distance. Exchange for him is a way to avoid mix-ups. In short, Peter cannot be bothered with all these stories about community, which only invade and threaten his singular relation to desire.

Mary's familialist neurosis is something altogether different— she does not stop establishing small familial grounds; it is a kind of vampirism of "human warmth." Mary hangs on to the image of the other; for example, she asked Anna Freud to be her analyst—but for her, this meant that she would settle at her place, with her brother, and that they would become her children. This is what she tried to do again with Ronnie and Joe.

Familialism consists of magically denying social reality, and avoiding all connections with the actual flux. The only remaining possibilities are the dream and the infernal closed-door of the conjugal-familial system, or better still, during the great moments of crisis, a small decrepit territory in which to isolate oneself. It was in this manner that Mary Barnes operated at Kingsley Hall; as a missionary of Laing's therapy, a militant of madness, as a professional.

We learn more through this confession than we would by reading a dozen theoretical writings on antipsychiatry. We can finally glimpse the repercussions of "psychoanalysm" in the methods of Laing and his friends.

From the Freud of *Studies on Hysteria* to the structuralist analysts who are the current rage, the whole psychoanalytic method consists of reducing any situation by means of three criteria:

1) *Interpretation*: a thing will always *have meaning* but only obliquely through a game of signifying clues;

2) *Familialism*: these signifying clues are essentially reducible to familial representations. To reach them, one proceeds by means of regression; the subject will be induced to "recapture" his childhood. It will be in fact a kind of "powerless" representation of childhood, a recollected, mythical, and sheltered childhood, negative of the present intensities and without any connection to the positive aspects of childhood;

3) *Transfer*: in line with interpretative reduction and familialist regression, desire is restored onto a wilted space, a small, miserable world of identifications (namely the analyst's couch, the look, the assumed attention). The rule of the game is that everything that comes up is to be reduced in terms of interpretation and daddy-mommy images; one need only proceed to the ultimate reduction of the signifying batter itself, which must henceforth function with a single term: the silence of the analyst, against which all sorts of questions are to lean. Psychoanalytical transfer, a churn used to cream the reality of desire, makes the subject sink in a dizziness of abolition, a narcissistic passion, which, though less dangerous than Russian roulette, doesn't lead him on any less (if it works) to an

irreversible fixation of cheap subtleties which will end by expropriating him from all other social investment.

We have known for a long time that these three criteria work badly with the insane. Their interpretations, their images are too removed from dominant social coordinates. Instead of giving up this method at Kingsley Hall, they try to improve these criteria to reinforce their effects. Thus, the silent interpretation of dual analysis is replaced with a collective, and loud, interpretation, a kind of collective interpretative delusion. It is true that the method becomes operational; no longer is it simply a minor game between the words of the patient and the silence of the analyst, but rather it involves objects, gestures, and the interaction of forces. Joe Berke, initiated in the big game of Mary Barnes's regression, grunts, acts like a crocodile, bites and pinches her, rolls her in bed ... things still not very common among typical psychoanalysts.

We are almost there! On the verge of penetrating another practice, another semiotic. The ropes will be broken with the sacred principles of significance and interpretation. Not so, each time the psychoanalyst recovers by reinstating the familialist coordinates. He is then caught at his own game; when Joe Berke needs to leave Kingsley Hall, Mary tries everything to stop him. Not only has the analysis become endless, but the session also! Only by losing his temper can Berke free himself from his "patient" for a few hours, to participate in a meeting on the Vietnam war.

The interpretative contamination has become boundless. Paradoxically, Mary is the first one who breaks the cycle through her painting. In a few months she has become a famous painter.[6] Even this is subject to interpretation; if Mary feels guilty taking drawing courses, it is because painting was her mother's hobby and she could be upset if she found out her daughter was a better painter. Paternally speaking, things are no better: "Now, with all these paintings, you have the penis, the power, and your father is threatened."

Mary tries to ingest all this psychoanalytical rubbish with touching diligence. Thus in the communal atmosphere of Kingsley Hall, Mary refuses to work with just anyone. She turns down others because she wants to make sure the person working with her is a firm disciple of Ronnie. "When I got the idea of the breast, a safe breast, Joe's breast, a breast I could suck, without being stolen from me, there was no holding me back ... Joe Clattari putting his finger in my mouth was saying, 'Look I can come into you but I'm not controlling you, possessing, stealing you.'"

Even the psychoanalyst ends up being overwhelmed by the interpretative machine he helped start. He admits: "She interpreted everything that was done for her (or for anyone else for that matter) as therapy. If someone brought her a glass of water when she was thirsty, this was therapy. If the coal was not delivered when ordered, that was therapy. And so on, to the most absurd conclusions." This doesn't prevent Joe Berke from continuing to fight with his own interpretations, aimed only at making his relation with Mary part of the Oedipal triangle: "By 1966, however, I had a pretty good idea of what and who I was for her when we were together. 'Mommy' took the lead when she was Mary the baby. 'Daddy' and 'brother Peter' vied for second place. In order to protect my own sense of reality and help Mary break through her web of illusion, I always took the trouble to point out when I thought Mary was using me as someone else." But it will be impossible for him to disentangle himself from this spider web. Mary trapped the whole house inside it.

Let us deal next with the technique of regression into child-hood and with transfer; developed in a communal atmosphere, their "derealization" effects are accentuated. In the traditional ana-lytical face-to-face situation, the dual relation, the artificial and limited character of the scenario form a kind of barricade against imaginary outbursts. At Kingsley Hall, it is with a real death that

Mary Barnes is confronted at the end of each trip, and the whole of the institution is overcome by a kind of sadness and anxiety just as real. Aaron Esterson ends up having to resort to the old methods of authority and suggestion: Mary was brought close to death by her starvation; she is forcefully forbidden to continue fasting.

It is with the same brutality that a few years before a Catholic psychoanalyst forbade her to masturbate, telling her, as she recalls, that it was a worse sin than sleeping with a man without being married. It worked then also. In fact, isn't this return to authority and suggestion the inevitable correlative to the technique of regression in all directions? A sudden relapse close to death, a daddy-cop creeps out of the shadows. The imaginary faculties, especially those of the psychoanalyst, do not form a defense against social repression; they secretly bring it on instead.

One of the richest lessons of this book is perhaps that it shows us to what extent it is foolish to hope to find raw desire, pure and hard, by heading off to look for knots, hidden in the unconscious, and secret keys of interpretation. Nothing can unravel, by the sheer magic of transfer, the real micropolitical conflicts that emprison the subject. No mystery, no inner world. There is nothing to discover in the unconscious. The unconscious needs to be created. If the Oedipus of transfer does not resolve the familial Oedipus, it is because it is deeply attached to the familialized individual.

Whether alone on the couch or in the group, in an institutional regression the "normal-neurotic" (you and I) or the neurotic of the psychiatrist (the "insane") continues to ask again and again for Oedipus. Imbued with the reducing drug of interpretation through their training and practice, the psychoanalysts could only reinforce the policy which amounts to crushing desire, transfer is a way of detouring the investments of desire. Far from slowing down the race toward death, it seems instead to accelerate it, cumulating, as a cyclotron, "individuated" Oedipal energies in what Joe Berke calls "the vicious spiral of punishment-anger-guilt-punishment." It can only lead to castration, self-denial, and sublimation: a shoddy asceticism. The objects of the collective culpability follow one after the other, and accentuate the punitive and self-destructive impulses by doubling them with a real repression made of anger, jealousy, and fear.

Guilt becomes a specific form of the libido—a capitalist Eros—when it exists in conjunction with the deterritorialized flows of capitalism. It then finds a new way, an unedited solution, outside the framework of family, asylum, or psychoanalysis. I shouldn't have, what I did was bad, and the more I feel it's bad, the more I want to do it, because then I can exist within the realm of the intensity of guilt. Except that this realm, instead of being made "corporeal," attached to the body of the subject, to his ego, to his family, will take possession of the institution; actually, the real boss of Kingsley Hall was Mary Barnes. She knew it well. Everything centered around her. All she ever did was play Oedipus, while the others were indeed well caught in a collective Oedipus.

Once Joe Berke finds her covered with shit and shaking with cold, and his nerves crack. He then becomes aware of her extraordinary capacity for "conjuring up everyone's favorite nightmare and embodying it for them." Thus, transfer at Kingsley Hall is no longer "contained" by the analyst. It goes in all directions and threatens even the psychoanalyst. Everyone becomes a psychoanalyst! Yet they were so close to having none, to letting the desiring intensities, the "partial objects," follow their own lines of force without being haunted by the systems of interpretation or duly codified by the social frame of "dominant reality."

What is the reason for this desperate attempt on the part of Joe Berke to glue together the scattered multiplicity by which Mary "experiments" with the dissolution of her ego and seeks to explode her neurosis? Why this return to familial poles, to the unity of the person, which prevents Mary from opening up to the outside world, after all potentially quite rich? "The initial process of her coming together was akin to my trying to put together a jigsaw puzzle without having all the pieces. Of those pieces at hand, many had had their tabs cut off and their slots stuffed, so it was almost impossible to tell what went where. This puzzle, of course, was Mary's emotional life. The pieces were her thoughts, her actions, her associations, her dreams, etc."

What proof do we have that the solution for Mary Barnes lies within infantile regression? What proof do we have that the origin of her problems lies in the disturbances, the blocked intrafamilial communication system of her childhood? Why not consider instead what went on around the family? We note, in fact, that all the doors leading outside were forcefully closed upon her when she tried to open them; this is surely how she came upon an even more repressive familialism around the family than the one she knew in childhood. And what if the poor father and mother Barnes were only the pitiful and peripheral connections to the repressive tempest raging outside? Mary was not *fixated* in childhood: she just did not find the exit! Her desire to leave was too strong and too demanding to adapt itself to compromises of the outside world.

The first crisis strikes in school. "School was dangerous." She sat in her chair, paralyzed, terrorized; she fought with the teacher. "Most things at school worried me." She pretended to read, sing, draw ... What she always wanted, however, was to be a writer, a journalist, a painter, a doctor! All this, she will be told, meant that she wanted to become a man. "I was ashamed of wanting to be a doctor. I know that this shame was bound up ... (and here goes the *interpretationite*) with the enormous guilt I had in connection with my desire to be a boy. Anything masculine in myself must be hidden, buried in secret, hardly admitted."

Priests and cops of all types tried to make her feel guilty, about anything and mainly about masturbation. When she resigns herself to being a nurse and enlists into the army, she finds herself in another dead end. Once, she wanted to go to Russia because she heard that over there "women with babies and no husbands were quite acceptable." When she decides to enter a convent, her religious faith is questioned: "What brought you into the Church?"

Priests are probably right; her wish for saintliness smells fishy! It finally all leads to the asylum. Even there, she is ready to do something, give herself to others. She once brings flowers to a nurse to be told: "Get out! You should not be here!" It is impossible to recount all the social traumas and tortures she has gone through. As a nurse, her right to go into higher education is challenged. At the beginning, Mary Barnes was not interested in the family, but in society! But everything brought her back to the family. And (this is hard to say), this holds true even for her stay at Kinglsey Hall! Since familialist interpretation was the favorite game of the place, and since she adored everyone there, she also got into it. And with what a gusto!

She is, at bottom, the real analyst of Kingsley Hall. She played to the full all the neurotic mainsprings of the enterprise, the underlying paranoia of the fathers and mothers of Kingsley Hall. Has Mary-the missionary at least helped the antipsychiatrists clarify the reactionary implications of their psychoanalytical assumptions?

8

THE BEST CAPITALIST DRUG

Arno Munster: *For a long time Freudo-Marxists and left-wing Freudians have struggled for the recognition of psychoanalysis by the labor movement, for the integration of psychoanalysis into political combat, for a synthesis of dialectical materialism and psychoanalysis. After the failure of this attempt, shouldn't you fear that your critique might be taken up at least in part by the Right which has long fought Freudianism because of its materialism, because it destroys society's hypocrisy in matters of sexuality?*

Félix Guattari: There are two parts to your question. First, when the communist movement deigns at last to pay attention to the problems of the unconscious, of sexuality, when a great reconciliation is at hand, are we going to spoil the whole deal? Second, the recovery by the Right. On the first point, it's precisely my belief that all the consequences must be drawn from the fact that the communist movement, the socialist movement, the leftist movements, etc., have never unreservedly accepted to consider the desiring economy in its relation to the work of revolutionaries. Let it suffice to mention the famous conversation between Lenin and Clara Zetkin.

A certain degree of tolerance undoubtedly exists today between the labor movement and psychoanalysis. There are two ways of looking at it: on the one hand, there are the resistances manifested by the revolutionary movement, the labor movement, and on the other there is the psychoanalytical movement proper. It is quite obvious that the labor movement and the revolutionary movement participate in the repression of desire; therefore they are not very willing to face questions which could eventually break their internal bureaucratic equilibrium. In this sense your question is justified. It should, however, be added immediately that the psychoanalytic movement has contributed a good deal to these resistances; indeed, it has consistently promoted them. The psychoanalytical movement has organized itself on the basis of a complete split between social formations and unconscious ones; it has set up a radical separation between what happens in political and social struggles and what takes place in "private life" with the couple, the child, etc. Psychoanalysts have discarded social issues and politicians have considered that desiring economy did not concern them. The two groups finally appear to be acting in complicity. Such a reconciliation between Marxism and Freudianism is inseparable from their respective entry into the University. The preliminary step was the emasculation of Marxism. It was thus necessary, on the one hand, that Freudianism shift once and for all from its origins to an ideology of the Oedipus, of the signifier, and that Marxism, on the other hand, reduce itself to an exercise in textual practice so that the welding of the two could be worked out. As for the text, nothing is left of it but a powerless residue cut off from any revolutionary opening.

The warders of the labor movement now agree to deal with the family and with desire just as long as the issue is confined to sterilized institutional objects: the "quality of life" and other nonsense. But as soon as other objects, dynamite carriers, come into the picture—homosexuality, criminality, abortion—they call in the cops! They are willing to take into consideration the problems of the couple, of women, housing, tenants, but they are not really inclined to tackle seriously with libido-revolutionary problems. Psychoanalysts, on the other hand, do not mind investigating social formations, but on the express condition that no one will question the status of the family, of the school, etc.

If a psychoanalyst wanted to stop being an accomplice, if he wanted to bring about this rupture you mentioned, what should he do? Your book gives an answer—perhaps not a completely satisfying one—to this question: one must "de-Oedipianize" psychoanalysis, replace it by another institutional practice conceived as an attempt to break down the familialism of traditional psychoanalysis and create a completely different psychoanalytical practice. But is it sufficient, in the context of the system, to avoid giving a hand to authority and repression? Is this "de-Oedipianization" of psychoanalysis possible, is it possible without a total revolution of psychoanalysis and of the institutional framework of psychiatry, which, as one of the authors of The Kursbuch Number 28 concerning "the misery of the psyche" very correctly points out, continues to fight mental illness by repressing the patient? How does Anti-Oedipus operate in this perspective and what can "schizoanalysis" do here?

The problem once again is to avoid considering the institutions of psychiatry and psychoanalysis as confined arenas. We remain in some sort of "social objectity" as if there were a particular battle to fight with the workers in the factories, another in hospitals with the sick, yet another in the University with the students, etc. ... We must question this "containing-contained" approach of institutions which are supposed to be filled with people. Sociologists and technocrats see things that way. The problem of the University—we certainly found out in May '68—is not the students and the professors; it is the problem of the entire society inasmuch as it involves the relationship between the transmission of knowledge, the training of executives, the desire of the masses, the requirements of industry, and, finally, everything which could intermingle in the setting of the University. What was the magnificent answer of the governmental reformists? To refocus the problem on the object itself, to confine it to the University's structure and organization. The same holds for psychiatry and the associations for psychoanalysis; what we should try to elucidate today is not how to alter the role of the psychiatrist, of the psychoanalyst, the attitude of groups of patients, but, more fundamentally, how society functions in order to bring about such a situation. Marxism raises the very same question which is not to know how the situation in the concentration camps could have been improved, but what was the process that led to them. We assert that a society which overcodes production through the law of capitalist profit tends to create an inseparable split between desiring- production and social production. Desire is thrown upon private life while sociality recedes into profit-making labor.

The real question is whether a production of desire, a dream, a passion, a concrete Utopia, will finally acquire the same existential dignity in social life as the manufacturing of cars or fads. It is naïve to think that production can be reduced to the simple opposition of the variable investment of work forces and the constant investment of technical means. Underlying the whole problem is the division which will determine what component of desire will be accepted and what will be rejected. The capitalist is interested only in the different machines of production that he can connect to his machine of exploitation: your arms, if you are a janitor; your brains, if you are an engineer; your looks, if a cover girl. Not only doesn't he give a damn about the rest, but he won't hear a word about it. To speak in the name of the rest would upset—could only upset—the normal process of his production. At the heart of industrial machines, there are desiring-machines which are split, separated, and tapped by the dominant system. The point at issue is whether this division which is considered to be legitimate and human—this castrating slash by machines which is supposed to give access to who knows what sacrosanct sublimation—can or cannot be overcome.

Will the revolutionaries ever come to grips with this separation, this castration which people constantly run up against, this recuperation by the family, by the school, etc?

As for the second part of your question—the recovery by the Right—I agree completely! It is even surprising that this book elicited, let us say, so many responses. We didn't anticipate any. I believe that the explanation can be found, to a certain extent, in a blend of several elements: a revolutionary current which was fed up with being overcoded by all these psychoanalytical concepts and perhaps a long-standing hatred of the reactionary Right which was happy, finally, to find people who could support an attack that it had never known how to lead. But, in the end, such a misunderstanding is not fundamental. Anything can always be recovered: the most daring artistic production, the most untimely philosophy, as long as it does not depart from the framework of writing, books, the University …

But by attacking psychoanalysis' fixation upon Oedipus and upon the superego, you also attack part of the theoretical heritage of Freud. Your theory of schizophrenia is at variance with Freudian theory.

Freud didn't understand much about schizophrenia. Many inner struggles in the psychoanalytic movement would be understood if Freud's fundamental hostility toward psychosis were finally acknowledged. Psychosis and revolution have always been taboo. Normality was identified with the acceptance of family life. From its origin Freudianism was built upon a vision of the family man. Freud despised delirium: for example that of President Schreber. He also held women in contempt. His representation of sexuality and society is entirely "phallocentric" as the Women's Liberation Movement would say. In *Analysis Terminable and Interminable* (1937), the problem of castration appeared as the stumbling block which analysis hit upon; the man refuses the necessary castration because he does not want to be "like a woman," while the woman does not accept the lack of a penis, etc. In no way does Freud elucidate the element of political struggle which underlies this kind of "resistance." Women refuse castration as much as men (if, indeed, the latter succeed in doing so). The key term is the superego. The question is whether the superego is a formation derived from the social milieu and transmitted through the family in such a way that the individual comes to desire repression and to assume his own curbing as the ultimate link in a long chain which begins with the father, or if the superego is to be accepted as a necessary split at the core of the psychic topography which alone would allow the subject to reach a satisfactory equilibrium and guarantee the ego a good adaptation to reality. In this perspective, the authority of the father and the images of social hierarchy would only be accessories to this necessary, sacrosanct castration. It all boils down to these alternatives: either desire comes to desire repression and actively supports its aims, thus preserving itself as desire, or desire revolts against repression and loses itself as desire. Quite a clever mechanism!

About ten years ago I introduced the notion of *transversality* to express the capacity of an institution to remodel the ways of access it offers the superego so that certain symptoms and inhibitions are removed. Modification of the local coefficient of transversality implies the existence of an erotic focal point, a group eros, and a takeover—even if partial—of local politics by a group-subject. A social formation can modify the erotic "causality" which sets off the activity of the superego. This modification of the ways it accommodates the superego leads to a radical transformation of the whole of the topography. Under these conditions, repression and inhibition take on a completely different meaning. Psychoanalysis is simply reactionary when it covers up for what happens at school, in the family, in the army, etc. No existential dehiscence, no splitting of the ego, no lack, no castration can justify the intervention of a repressive third party. To no avail are we told that we don't have to deal anymore with the real father, that what's really at stake is a structural logic without which the "subject" could not establish himself as desire within the signifying chain, that we must at all costs renounce the undifferentiated Imaginary pleasures in order to accede to the "Symbolic" order—the Symbolic is mere twaddle (you have it or you don't, and that's that). All this sordid paraphernalia is there only to safeguard the comfort of the couch. Let society have it its own way, we'll take care of desire, we will assign it the small, secret domain of the couch. And it works! Psychoanalysis works only too well. That's what makes it so dangerous! It's the best of all capitalist drugs. Denouncing it is not enough; something has to be found to replace it.

Psychoanalytical struggle has to be shifted into the social domain. Instead of attacking the institutional framework of traditional psychoanalysis, we should fight it in the context of politics, which would one day allow us to destroy the conditions out of which the "social Oedipus" originates, dismantle family life, etc.

I agree completely.

Yes, but the point is not completely elucidated in the book ...

The second part of *Capitalism and Schizophrenia*[1] will have to deal with the concrete conditions of schizoanalytical struggle—in other words, a political struggle on all fronts of desiring-production. We should avoid centering the struggle on a single field. The problem of psychoanalysis is the problem of the revolutionary movement, the problem of the revolutionary movement is the problem of madness, the problem of madness is the problem of artistic creation. Transversality is, at heart, nothing but this nomadism ... The unconscious is in the first place a social set-up, the collective distribution of virtual utterances. Statements such as "this is yours and that is mine" will only be differentiated in a second phase. The unconscious recognizes the private property of statements no more than it recognizes the private property of desire. Desire is always extraterritorial—deterritorialized-deterritorializing; it passes over and under all barriers. Although psychoanalysis readjusts its concepts and passes them through a linguistical, logical, and anthropological sieve, it cannot leave its home base, which is that of familialism and capitalism. It serves capitalism as a substitute religion. Its function is to update repression, to give it a personal touch so it sells better—as has been done for the Ford Pinto or Plymouth Duster. Sin and confession don't work the way they used to. Desire has to be given leeway. Gadgets aren't enough. Something imperishable, waterproof, and imputrescible is needed: a subjective prostitution, an interminable ritual. Once hooked on this new drug, there is no longer any reason to fear that the subject will truly invest its energy into social struggle. Reality must remain at the door of the consulting room. The objective is not really to defend the values of capitalism but only to pretend not to be aware of them. Revolutionary struggle must act upon such a representation of social production and of labor in general. This shift of emphasis you mentioned must be operated in all places where familial repression is exerted on desire, women, children, drug addicts, alcoholics, homosexuals, etc. This "micro class struggle" can not be undertaken in the sole territory of psychoanalysis. Whatever conceptual references we adopt, we should never lose sight of the true stakes, the real institutional objects of this class struggle. The complicity between psychoanalysis and left-wing trends is based upon ideas, never upon practice. When militants in groupuscules or in revolutionary parties are asked what their real attitude is in regard to children, homosexuals, etc., what their bureaucrats get off on, or what depresses or maddens their comrades … no answer. When things get out of hand, the psychoanalyst or the psychiatrist is called for.

You said: "micro class struggle." Can we truly separate it from the "macro struggle"?

No more than we can separate atomic chemistry from molecular chemistry.

This confirms an article you wrote immediately after the events of May '68, in which you asserted that as many "subject-groups" should be created as possible, and that the struggle should also be led against "seriality"[2] which was responsible, according to Sartre, for the inertia inherent in groups, parties, unions, etc. In short, political action had to be started off again. Here the psychoanalyst and militant are inter-mingled. Where, in an identical strategy, is the place of the patient, the place of the psychoanalyst, in this radical psychoanalysis you call "schizoanalysis"?

The place of contemporary psychoanalysis in the revolutionary struggle—I don't see it! Which does not mean that all analytical exercises, including "dual" analysis, must be condemned. But there are two facets to the question: on the one hand, shifting the focus of analysis to "subject-groups" involved in political reality or in an activity of creative self-analysis, and, on the other hand, a constant fight against the insidious reinjection of repressive social patterns. A group analysis of the Slavson or Ezriel type can be as thoroughly harmful as a "dual" analysis if the real function of parental poles is not elucidated; what element of the father and mother intervenes in a neurotic relation? Does the father serve as an integrating symbolic pole or is he, despite himself, only the homing head of the social hydra? Take, for example, the case of Kafka.[3] Photographs are a constant theme of his work. There are several ways of looking at it. We might reduce the theme by interpreting it: photos could refer to a crystallization of the imaginary, the theme of the double, narcissicism, whatever. Many a theory would be elaborated here ... But wouldn't it be much more interesting to try to find out how photos really function in the work, when they appear, what networks they modify, etc. In one section of *The Trial*, a series of identical pictures appear: it is one of the "hottest" moments of the work, at a juncture where Joseph K. is almost freed from the hold of the Oedipal process. Instead of saying, "Hey, things are strangely resolved in identity, there is a duplication, etc.," schizoanalysis will find paths of differentiation which originate there. There is no such thing as a father in general. There is only a father who works at the bank, who works in a factory, who is unemployed, who is an alcoholic: the father is only the element of a particular social machine. According to traditional psychoanalysts, it's always the same father and always the same mother—always the same triangle. But who can deny that the Oedipal situation differs greatly, depending on whether the father is an Algerian revolutionary or a well-to-do executive? It isn't the same death which awaits your father in an African shanty town as in a German industrial town; it isn't the same Oedipus complex or the same homosexuality. It may seem stupid to have to make such obvious statements, and yet such swindles must be denounced tirelessly; there is no universal structure of the human mind!

Is the schizoanalyst, then, someone who wants to synthesize the analysis of social economy and of libidinal economy in this society?

Synthesis is a big word! Instead of reducing things to no more than a logical skeleton, we must enrich them, follow sequences, the real tracks, the social implications. Difference originates in repetition. Repetition is not the law, the finality of something; on the contrary, it marks the threshold to "deterritorialization," the indication of a desiring mutation. Blocked representation, catatonia as a response to aggression, group photos, etc., don't play the same role in the work of Kafka before and after his meeting with Felice Bauer. The family picture crystallizes Kafka's anti-Oedipal hatred from the time of *The Trial*. Hate and fascination. Kafka being a top level executive—not at all a shabby bureaucrat—is also confronted with his own Fascist desire to master the other in the framework of bureaucratic hierarchy, for instance. A tele-mastery. The other, fixed in the photo, is crystallized in some sort of submission ritual. The attempt to possess Felice from a distance through the interplay of love letters is inserted in a much larger practice of remote possession based on the power of titles and functions. We will thus come closer and closer to the social ties "holding" Felice and Kafka; both of them are bureaucrats fascinated by the power of bureaucracy. Kafka's denunciation is only a denial. The analysis of a "perversion" of the letter, of a bureaucratic perversion, leads him to analyze the decaying bureaucracy of Austria-Hungary and the cultural turmoil out of which Nazi Eros will rise. Analysis will move in this direction. But if one is content to point out Kafka's impossible identification with his shopkeeper of a father, one completely overlooks the social dynamic of desiring-energy. Kafka is not, in spite of what has been said, a writer of the nineteenth century. He is a writer of the twenty-first century who describes a desiring process in embryo, the scope of which we have scarcely begun to grasp.

Your book is, above all, a plea for the liberation of desire, a revolt against the overcoding of individuals by the fluxes of capitalism. But you go farther still, you call for an identification of the analyst, the patient and the militant. Exactly what does this mean?

To start with, we never said: "identification of the analyst and the schizophrenic." We say that the analyst, like the militant, the writer or whoever it may be, is more or less involved in a "schizo-process" to be distinguished from the locked-up schizophrenic whose own "schizo-process" runs aimlessly or is blocked up. We don't say that revolutionaries ought to identify with free-wheeling madmen, but that they should model their action on the "schizo process." The schizophrenic is a person who, for whatever reason, has been touched off by a desiring flow which threatens the social order. There's an immediate intervention to ward off such a menace. The issue is libidinal energy in its process of "deterritorialization" and not at all the interruption of this process. Like the militant, the analyst must drift with the process instead of serving the "Oedipianizing" social repression by stating, for instance that "All you do is the result of an abnormal homosexual desire." (So they claim to interpret President Schreber's delusion.) Or "It's so because, in your case, the death instinct and Eros are not properly interrelated." Schizoanalysis, on the other hand, meets with the revolutionary struggle to the extent that it strives to free the flows, to remove the bolts—the axiomatics of capitalism, the overcoding of the superego, the primitive territorialities artificially reconstructed, etc. The work of the analyst, the revolutionary, and the artist meet to the extent that they must constantly tear down systems which reify desire, which submit the subject to the familial and social hierarchy (I am a man, I am a woman, I am a son, I am a brother, etc.). No sooner does someone say, "I am this or that" than desire is strangled.

One last question on this new analytical practice. Your activities as a psychoanalyst are closely linked to the experience of the La Borde clinic at Cour Cheverny where institutional psychoanalysis is practiced.[4] *Do you think this institution (the clinic) takes on special importance for your project of liberation, or is it to be considered a compromise solution with all the characteristics of contemporary reformism in psychoanalysis? Don't the determinations of the general sociological framework condemn it to a failure at the outset?*

Yes and no. It effectively partakes in reformism, being surrounded by Social Security, the way patients perceive their illness, the whole medical ideology and social hierarchy, money, etc. ... So, in this sense it is but a small-scale experiment which is easily repressed and even recuperated. It is, however, sufficiently alien to the rest of society to offer a number of people new conceptual instruments. If I had had to work as a psychoanalyst in private practice or as a professor it would have been much more difficult for me to challenge psychoanalytic dogmas. Our teamwork, although it is prey to all the mechanisms you were referring to, has nevertheless allowed us to pursue somehow or other a positive collective experiment with the French Communist Party, the radical "groupuscules," the Movement of March 22.[5] If we had worked in a traditional hospital, this would have been impossible. It is important to preserve a few pals, a network which allows us to escape from this abominable solitude which capitalist society brings us to.

So, yes and no. No, it's not a vanguardist undertaking; it is nevertheless by progressively modifying the tutelages which weigh on desire, that we will succeed in setting up revolutionary machines of a new type. As much as I am against the illusion of a step by step transformation of society—"small reforms which make up great transformations"—I believe that microscopic attempts at creating communities, setting up analytic groups among militants, organizing a day-care center in a university, are crucial. It is out of such small attempts that one fine day we will bring about a great big rip like May '68. At the outset, the Movement of March 22 was almost a joke! I believe in a permanent reformism of the revolutionary organization. It's better to have ten consecutive failures or insignificant results than a besotted passivity before the mechanisms of retrieval.

9

EVERYBODY WANTS TO BE A FASCIST

I have chosen to discuss fascism for several reasons: because it is a real political problem, and not a purely theoretical consideration, and because I think it is a key theme to use in approaching the question of desire in the social realm. Besides, isn't it a good idea to discuss it freely while we still can?

A micropolitics of desire is not a proposal for the establishment of a bridge between psychoanalysis and Marxism, looking at them as completely formalized theories. This seems to me to be neither desirable nor possible. I do not think that a system of concepts can function with validity outside of its original environment, outside of the collective arrangements of enunciation which produced it. For example, much of the talk about pleasure is very interesting, but in contrast with desire, it is absolutely impossible to transfer these two notions, drawn from a certain type of practice and a certain vision of psychoanalysis, to the social field; in no way do they help us grasp the functioning of the libido in, for example, a fascist situation. Therefore, it must be understood that when I speak of desire I am not borrowing this notion from orthodox psychoanalysis or from Lacanian theory. I do not pretend to lay the foundation of a scientific concept; I will simply try to erect the scaffolding of a provisional theoretical construct in which the operation of desire within the social realm will be discussed. The starting point is simple: it is not possible to bind together in the same sentence the term "pleasure" with the term "revolution." You cannot say that a "pleasure of revolution" could exist. But nowadays no one is surprised to hear someone speak of a "desire for revolution" or a "revolutionary desire." It seems to me that this is tied to the fact that the meaning generally given to pleasure is inseparable from a certain mode of individuation of subjectivity, and psychoanalytic pleasure is even less independent from this kind of inward folding individuation which, quite to the contrary, managed to find some kind of fulfillment within the confines of the couch. With libido and desire, however, things are altogether different.

Desire is not intrinsically linked to an individuation of the libido. A machine of desire encounters forms of individuation, that is, of alienation. Neither desire nor its repression is an ideal formation; there is no desire-in-itself, no repression-in-itself. The abstract objective of a "successful castration" partakes of the worst reactionary mystifications. Desire and repression function in a real society, and are marked by the imprint of each of its historical stages. It is therefore not a matter of general categories which could be transposed from one situation to another. The distinction which I propose between micropolitics and macropolitics of desire would have to function as something which would lead to the liquidation of the pretended universality of psychoanalytic models, a notion which ostensibly secures the psychoanalyst against political and social contingencies. It is said that psychoanalysis is concerned with something which takes place on a small scale, barely the scale of the family and the person, whereas politics is concerned only with large social groupings. I would like to demonstrate that, on the contrary, there is a politics which addresses itself to the individual's desire, as well as to the desire which manifests itself in the broadest social field. And it has two forms: either a macropolitics aiming at both individual and social problems, or a micropolitics aiming at the same domains (the individual, the family, party problems, state problems, etc.). The despotism which exists in conjugal or family relationships arises from the same kind of libidinal disposition that exists in the broadest social field. Inversely, it is by no means absurd to approach a number of large scale social problems (for example, the problems of bureaucratism and fascism), in the light of a micro-politics of desire. The problem therefore is not to put up bridges between already fully constituted and fully delimited domains, but to put in place new theoretical and practical machines, capable of sweeping away the old stratifications, and of establishing the conditions for a new exercise of desire. In that case, it is no longer a simple question of describing preexisting social objects, but one of engaging in a political struggle against all machines of the dominant power, whether it be the power of the bourgeois State, the power of any kind of bureaucracy, the power of academia, familial power, phallo-cratic power in male/female relationships, or even the repressive power of the superego over the individual.

Three methods of approach to these questions can be schematized: first, a sociological approach, which we will call analytic-formalist; secondly, a neo-Marxist, synthetic-dualist approach; and thirdly, an analytic-political approach. The first and second approaches preserve the distinction between large and small social groupings, while the third approach attempts to go beyond this distinction.

Sociological analytic formalist thought attempts to disengage common traits and to separate out species, either by a method of perceptible analogies—in that case, it will try to settle small relative differences (for example, it will distinguish the three types of fascism: Italian, German, and Spanish); or, by a method of *structural homologies*—in that case, it will try to determine absolute differences (such as the differences between fascism, Stalinism and the Western democracies). On the one hand, the differences are minimized, in order to disengage a common feature, and on the other, the differences are magnified, in order to separate levels and construct species.

Synthetic dualist neo-Marxist thought claims to go beyond such a system by always refusing to sever representation from a militant social practice, but generally this practice gets caught up in another kind of gap, this time between the reality of the masses' desires, and the instances that are supposed to represent these desires. Sociological thought's system of description proceeded by reducing social objects into things, and by failing to recognize the desire and creativity of the masses; the militant Marxist system of thought surmounts this failure, but constitutes itself as the collective system of representation of the masses' desires. This system recognizes the existence of a revolutionary desire, but it imposes mediations on it: that of the theoretical representation of Marxism, and that of the practical representation of the party which is supposed to be its expression. A whole mechanism of transmission belts is thus put into place between the theory, the direction of the party, and the militants, so that the innumerable differences which run through the desire of the masses find themselves "massified," restored to standardized formulations whose necessity is deemed to be justified in the name of the cohesion of the working class and party unity. We have switched from the impotence of a system of mental representation to the impotence of a system of social representativity. In fact, it is no accident if this neo-Marxist method of thought and action is swamped in bureaucratic practices; this owing to the fact that it has never really disengaged its pseudodialectic from an obdurate dualism between representation and reality, between the caste who holds the passwords and the masses, who are heard alphabetizing and catechizing like good children. Neo-Marxist thought contaminates by its reductive dualism, its conception of the class struggle, its schematic opposition between the city and the country, its international alliances, its politics of "the peace camp and the war camp," etc. The two terms of each of these oppositions always revolve around a third object which, though a third, still does not constitute a "dialectical synthesis"; this third object is, essentially, the State, the power of the State, and the party which is a candidate for the taking of that power. Any partial struggle must be brought back to these transcendent third objects; everything must be given its *meaning* by them, even when real history reveals them for what they are—namely, lures, lures just like the phallic object of the triangular Oedipal relationship. In addition, it could be said that this dualism and its transcendent object constitute the nucleus of the militant Oedipus, which must be confronted by a *political analysis*.

In fact, this analysis refuses to maintain the disjunction between large social groupings and individual problems, family problems, academic problems, professional problems, etc. This analysis will no longer concern itself with mechanically chipping the problematic of concrete situations down to a simple alternative of classes or camps. It will no longer pretend to find all the answers in the action of a unique revolutionary party standing as a central depository of theoretical and practical truth. Therefore, a micropolitics of desire would no longer present itself as *representing* the masses and as *interpreting* their struggles. Which does not mean that it would condemn, *a priori*, all party action, all idea of party line, of program or even of centralism, but it would endeavor to locate and relativize this party action in terms of an analytic micropolitics which, at every turn, would stand in opposition to the Manichean dualism that presently contaminates the revolutionary movements. It would no longer seek support from a transcendent object in order to provide itself with security. It would no longer center itself on a unique object— the power of the State, which could only be conquered by a representative party acting in lieu of and instead of the masses—but rather, it would center on a multiplicity of objectives, within the immediate reach of the most diverse social groupings. Starting from the plurality of partial struggles (but the term is already equivocal: they are not part of an already constituted whole), far-reaching collective struggles could be launched. There would no longer be mass, centrally ordered movements which would set more or less serialized individuals in motion on a local scale. Rather, it would be the connection of a multiplicity of molecular desires which would catalyze challenges on a large scale. This is what happened at the beginning of the movement of May '68: the local and singular manifestation of the desire of small groups began to resound with a multiplicity of repressed desires which had been isolated and crushed by the dominant forms of expression and of representation. In such a situation there is no longer an ideal *unity* which *represents* and *mediates multiple* interests, but rather, there is a *univocal multiplicity* of desires whose process secretes its own systems of tracking and regulation. This multiplicity of desiring-machines is not made of standardized and regulated systems which can be disciplined and hierarchized in relation to a unique objective. It is stratified according to different social groupings, to classes formed by age groups, sexes, geographic and professional localizations, ethnic origins, erotic practices, etc. Thus, it does not realize a totalizing unity. It is the univocity of the masses' desire, and not their regrouping according to standardized objectives, which lays the foundation for the unity of their struggle. The unification of struggles is antagonistic to the multiplicity of desires only when it is totalizing, that is, when it is treated by the totalitarian machine of a representative party.

Seen from this perspective, theoretical expression no longer comes between social object and praxis. The social object can speak without representative instances. For political struggle to coincide with an analysis of desire, you have to be in a position to listen in on whoever is speaking from a position of desire, and above all, "off the track." At home, a child "off the track" is put down, and this continues in school, in the barracks, in the factory, in the trade union, and in the party cell. You must always stay "on the right track" and "in line." But by virtue of its very nature, desire always has the tendency to "stray from the subject," "to get off the track," and to drift from its proper course. A collective arrangement of enunciation will say something about desire without referring it to a subjective individuation, without centering it around a pre-established subject and previously codified meanings. Henceforth, the analysis is not something which takes place after the terms and relationships of force are established, or after the *socius* is crystallized into various closed instances which remain opaque to one another: it participates in this very crystallization. The analysis becomes immediately political. "When saying is doing." The division of labor between the specialists of saying and the specialists of doing ceases.

Collective arrangements of enunciation produce their own means of expression—it could be a special language, a slang or a return to an old language. For them, working on semiotic flows, or on material and social flows is one and the same thing. Subject and object are no longer face-to-face, with a means of expression in a third position; there is no longer a tripartite division between the realm of reality, the realm of representation or representativity, and the realm of subjectivity. You have a collective set-up which is, at once, subject, object, and expression. The individual is no longer the universal guarantor of the dominant meanings. Here, everything can participate in enunciation: individuals, as well as zones of the body, semiotic trajectories, or machines that are plugged in on all horizons. The collective disposition of enunciation thus unites semiotic flows, material flows, and social flows, well short of its possible recuperation within a theoretical corpus. How is such a transition possible? Are we talking about a return to anarchist utopias? Isn't it an illusion to want to give the masses permission to speak in a highly differentiated industrial society? How could a social object—a subject group—substitute itself for the system of representation and for ideologies? Gradually, as I go on with this statement, a paradox thrusts itself on me: how is it conceivable to speak of these kinds of collective dispositions of enunciation while seated on a chair facing a group that is soberly arranged in a room? In reality, everything I say tends to establish that a true political analysis cannot arise from an individuated enunciation, especially when it is the act of a lecturer, who is unacquainted with the problems of his audience! An individual statement has no bearing except to the extent that it can enter into conjunction with collective set-ups which already function effectively: for example, which are already engaged in real social struggles. If this doesn't happen, then who are you speaking to? To a universal interlocutor? To someone who already knows the codes, the meanings, and all their possible combinations? The individuated enunciation is the prisoner of the dominant meanings. Only a subject-group can manipulate semiotic flows, shatter meanings, open the language to other desires and forge other realities!

Let's come back to this question of fascism and to its relation to Stalinism and Western style "democracies." We are not interested in establishing reductive comparisons, but, on the contrary, in complexifying the models. Any halt in the course of this analytic path will come only once one has reached a position where one has a minimum of real grasp on the ongoing process. There are all kinds of fascisms, all kinds of Stalinisms and all kinds of bourgeois democracies. These three groupings break up as soon as one begins to consider, at the heart of each grouping, the relative status of, for example, the industrial machine, the banking machine, the military machine, the politico-police machine, the techno-structures of the State, the Church, etc. The analysis will have to consider each of these subgroupings while, at the same time, not losing sight of the fact that, in each case, it is only concerned with provisional stages of molecular reduction. Contemporary totalitarian systems have invented a number of prototypes for a police party; the Nazi police party would merit being studied in comparison with the Stalinist police party; in fact, perhaps they are closer to each other than the corresponding structures of the State. It would be interesting to pick out the different kinds of machines of desire that go into their composition. But we would then discover that it is not enough to consider things from so far off. The analysis would have to progress constantly in the direction of a molecularization of its object to be able to grasp, from up close, the role that it plays in the heart of the large groupings within which it functions. There is not one Nazi party; not only has the Nazi party evolved, but during each period it has had a different function, according to the various domains wherein it has carried out its action. Himmler's SS machine was not the same as the SA machine or as that of the mass organizations conceived by the Strasser brothers. Certain points of view of quasi-religious inspiration are found at the very heart of the SS machine—remember that Himmler wished the SS to be trained using methods similar to those of the Jesuits—coexisting with openly sadistic practices, like those of a Heydrich ... We are not talking about a gratuitous investigation, but about a refusal of those sim-plifications which prevent us from perceiving the *genealogy* and the *permanence* of certain fascist machineries. The Inquisition had already put together a type of fascist machinery which kept devel-oping and perfecting itself up to our own time. Thus, we see that the analysis of the molecular components of fascism can deal with quite a variety of areas. It is the same fascism under different forms which continues to operate in the family, in school, or in a trade union. A struggle against the modern forms of totalitarianism can be organized only if we are prepared to recognize the continuity of this machine.

There are all kinds of ways in which to approach these questions concerning desire in the social field. We can simply ignore them, or else reduce them to simplified political alternatives. We can also try to grasp their mutations, their displacements, and the new possibilities which they afford to revolutionary action. Stalinism and fascism are generally placed in opposition, since they seemingly answer to radically different definitions, while the different forms of fascism have been placed under the same rubric. And yet, the differences are, perhaps, much greater between the fascisms than between certain aspects of Stalinism and certain aspects of Nazism. It is in no way contradictory to want to preserve these differences, and, at the same time, wish to disengage the continuity of a totalitarian machine which pursues its course through all structures: fascist, Stalinist, democratic-bourgeois, etc. Without going all the way back to the Late Empire of Diocletian and Constantine, its filiation can be traced from the repression against the Communards of 1871, right up to its present forms. In this way, different totalitarian systems produced different formulas for a collective seizing of desire, depending on the transformation of productive forces and the relationships of production. We must endeavor to disengage its machinic composition, much as we would a chemical composition, but a social chemistry of desire which runs not only through History, but also through the whole social space. The historical transversality of the machines of desire on which totalitarian systems depend is, in fact, inseparable from their social transversality. Therefore, the analysis of fascism is not simply a historian's specialty. I repeat: what fascism set in motion yesterday continues to proliferate in other forms, within the complex of contemporary social space. A whole totalitarian chemistry manipulates the structures of state, political and union structures, institutional and family structures, and even individual structures, inasmuch as one can speak of a sort of fascism of the superego in situations of guilt and neurosis

But what is this bizarre totalitarian machine that traverses time and space? Some prop in a science-fiction story? I can already hear the sarcastic remarks of the right-minded psychoanalysts, Marxists, and epistemologists. "What a confusion of levels! Everything's been thrown into the same bag ..." May I point out that it was only by conducting an analysis at the molecular and atomic levels that the chemists later succeeded in realizing syntheses of complex elements! But they will still say: that's nothing but mechanistic talk! Granted; up to this point we're only making a comparison. And besides, what's the use of polemicizing: the only people who will put up with listening to me any longer are those who feel the interest and urgency of the micropolitical antifascist struggle that I'm talking about. The evolution of the social division of labor has necessitated the creation of ever more gigantic productive groupings. But this gigantism of production has involved an increasing molecular-ization of those human elements activated in the machinic combinations of industry, of the economy, of education, of infor-mation, etc. It is never a person who works—the same can be said for desire—but a combination of organs and machines. An individual does not communicate with his fellow humans: a transhuman chain of organs is formed and enters into conjunction with semiotic chains and an intersection of material flows. Today the productive forces provoke the explosion of traditional human territorialities, because they are capable of liberating the atomic energy of desire. This phenomenon being irreversible, and its revolutionary scope impossible to calculate, the totalitarian-bureaucratic capitalist and socialist systems are forced to constantly perfect and miniaturize their repressive machines. Therefore, it seems to me that the con-stant search for this machinic composition of totalitarian powers is the indispensable corollary of a micropolitical struggle for the liberation of desire. The minute you stop facing it head-on, you can abruptly oscillate from a position of revolutionary openness to a position of totalitarian foreclosure: then you find yourself a prisoner of generalities and totalizing programs, and representative instances regain their power. Molecular analysis is the will to a molecular power, to a theory and practice which refuse to dispossess the masses of their potential for desire. Contrary to a possible objection, we are not trying to look at the smallest side of history, nor do we claim, like Pascal, that if Cleopatra's nose had been bigger, the course of history would have changed. We simply don't want to miss the impact of this totalitarian machine which never stops modifying and adapting itself to the relationships of force and societal transformations. Certainly the role of Hitler as an individual was negligible, but it remains fundamental inasmuch as it helped crystallize a new form of this totalitarian machine. Hitler can be seen in dreams, in deliriums, in films, in the contorted behavior of policemen, and even on the leather jackets of some gangs who, without knowing anything about Nazism, reproduce the icons of Hitlerism.

Let's return to a question which involves, in other forms, the present political situation. After the debacle of 1918 and the crisis of 1929, why is it that German capitalism didn't resort to a simple military dictatorship for support? Why Hitler rather than General von Schleicher? Daniel Guérin says that large capital hesitated to "deprive itself of this incomparable, irreplaceable means of penetrating into all the cells of society, the organization of the fascist masses." Indeed, a military dictatorship does not compartmentalize the masses in the same way as a party that is organized like a police force. A military dictatorship does not draw on libidinal energy in the same way as a fascist dictatorship, even if some of their results may seem identical, and even if they happen to resort to the same kinds of repressive methods, the same tortures, etc. The conjunction, in the person of Hitler, of at least four libidinal series, crystallized the mutation of a new desiring machinism in the masses:

1) A certain plebeian style that put him in a position to have a handle on people who were more or less marked by the socio-democratic and Bolshevik machines.

2) A certain veteran-of-war style, symbolized by his Iron Cross from the war of 1914, which made it possible for him to at least

neutralize the military staff elements, for want of being able to win their complete confidence.

3) A shopkeeper's opportunism, a spinal flexibility, a slackness, which enabled him to negotiate with the magnates of industry and finance, all the while letting them think that they could easily control and manipulate him.

4) Finally, and this is perhaps the essential point, a racist delirium, a mad, paranoiac energy which put him in tune with the collective death instinct released from the charnel houses of the First World War. To be sure, all this is still too schematic. But the point that I wanted to insist upon, and that I could only allude to, is the fact that we cannot consider as indifferent those local and singular conditions which allowed this mechanical crystallization on the person of Hitler. I insist that historico-psychoanalytic generalities are not enough: today within political and trade union movements, within groupuscules, in family life, academic life, etc., we are witnessing other fascisizing microcrystallizations, which take over from the phylum of the totalitarian machine. By pretending that the individual has a negligible role in history, they would like to make us believe that we can do nothing but stand with hands tied in the face of the hysterical gesticulations or paranoiac manipulations of local tyrants and bureaucrats of every kind. A micropolitics of desire means that henceforth we will refuse to allow any fascist formula to slip by, on whatever scale it may manifest itself, including within the scale of the family or even within the scale of our own personal economy. Through all kinds of means—in particular, movies and television—we are led to believe that Nazism was just a bad moment we had to go through, a sort of historical error, but also a beautiful page in history for the good heroes. And besides, was it not touching to see the intertwined flags of capitalism and socialism? We are further led to believe that there were real antagonistic contradictions between

the fascist Axis and the Allies. This is a way of concealing the nature of the selection process which was to lead to the elimination of a fascist formula which, after a while, the bourgeoisie finally decided was dangerous. Radek defined Nazism as something external to the bourgeoisie, somewhat like iron bands used by the bourgeoisie, in an attempt to consolidate "capitalism's leaky tank." But wasn't this image a bit too reassuring? Fascism only remained external to a certain type of bourgeoisie, which rejected it only because of its instability and because it stirred much too powerful forces of desire within the masses. The remedy, welcomed in the paroxystic phase of the crisis, later seemed far too dangerous. But international capitalism could only consider its elimination to the extent that other means were available by which to control class struggle, not to mention totalitarian formulas for subduing the desire of the masses: as soon as Stalinism had "negotiated" this replacement formula, an alliance with it became possible. The Nazi regime never really mastered its internal contradictions; the Fuhrer's practically insoluble mission consisted of an attempt to establish a sort of compromise between different machines of power which fully intended to maintain their autonomy: the military machine, the politico-police factions, the economic machine, etc.[1] At the same time, he had to keep in mind that the revolutionary effervescence of the masses threatened to sway them towards a Bolshevik style revolution. In fact, the alliance of the Western democracies and totalitarian Stalinism was not formed to "save democracy." It was formed only because of the catastrophic turn which the fascist experiments had taken, and, above all, in response to the deadly form of libidinal metabolism which developed in the masses as a result of these experiments. During this whole period, the planet was seized by a crisis that seemed like the end of the world. Of course, we shouldn't forget that the leftist organizations in Italy and Germany had been liquidated at the very beginning.

But why did these organizations collapse like houses of cards? They never offered the masses a real alternative, at any rate, none that could tap their energy of desire, or even divert this energy from the fascist religion (on this subject I find Reich's analysis final). It is often asserted that, at their outset, the fascist regimes supplied a minimum of economic solutions to the most urgent problems—an artificial boost to the economy, a reabsorption of unemployment, a large-scale public works program, control of capital. These measures are then contrasted, for example, with the powerlessness of the socio-democratic governments of the Weimar Republic. Explanations like, "The socialists and communists had a bad program, bad leaders, a bad organization, bad alliances," are considered sufficient. Their deficiencies and betrayals are endlessly enumerated. But nothing in these explanations accounts for the fact that the new totalitarian desiring machine was able to crystallize in the masses to such an extent that it was felt, by international capitalism itself, to be even more dangerous than the regime that came out of the October revolution. What almost everyone refuses to acknowledge is that the fascist machine, in its Italian and German forms, became a threat to capitalism and Stalinism because the masses invested a fantastic collective death instinct in it. By reterritorializing their desire onto a leader, a people, and a race, the masses abolished, by means of a phantasm of catastrophe, a reality which they detested and which the revolutionaries were either unwilling or unable to encroach upon. For the masses, virility, blood, vital space, and death took the place of a socialism that had too much respect for the dominant meanings. And yet, fascism was brought back to these same dominant meanings by a sort of intrinsic bad faith, by a false provocation to the absurd and by a whole theater of collective hysteria and debility. Fascism simply took a much longer detour than, for example, Stalinism. All fascist meanings stem out of a composite representation of love and death, of Eros and Thanatos now made into one. Hitler and the Nazis were fighting for death, right up to and including the death of Germany; the German masses agreed to follow along and meet their own destruction. How else are we to understand the way they were able to keep the war going for several years after it had been manifestly lost? Beside such a phenomenon, the Stalinist machine seemed much more sensible, especially when viewed from the outside. It is no wonder that English and American capitalism felt few qualms about an alliance with it. After the liquidation of the Third International, Stalinist totalitarianism could appear to the capitalist strategy as a replacement system, having certain advantages over the different forms of fascism and classical dictatorship. Who could be better equipped than the Stalinist police and their agents to control any excessively turbulent movements of the working class, the colonial masses, or any oppressed national minorities? The last World War will thus have been the opportunity to select the most efficient totalitarian machines, those best adapted to the period.

Unlike fascism, capitalist totalitarian machines manage to divide, particularize, and molecularize the workers, meanwhile tapping their potentiality for desire. These machines infiltrate the ranks of the workers, their families, their couples, their childhood; they install themselves at the very heart of the workers' subjectivity and vision of the world. Capitalism fears large-scale movements of crowds. Its goal is to have automatic systems of regulation at its command. This regulatory role is given to the State and to the mechanisms of contractualization between the "social partners." And when a conflict breaks out of the preestablished frameworks, capitalism seeks to confine it to economic or local wars. From this standpoint, it must be acknowledged that the Western totalitarian machine has now completely surpassed its Stalinist counterpart. And yet, Stalinism had the advantage, over

Fascism, of greater stability; the party was not put on the same level as the military machine, the police machine, and the economic machine. In effect, Stalinism overcoded all the machines of power, meanwhile keeping the masses under an implacable control. Furthermore, it succeeded in keeping the avant-garde of the international proletariat strung along on a tight leash. The failure of Stalinism, which is no doubt one of the most striking developments in the modern period, evidently stems from the fact that it could not adapt itself to the evolution of the productive forces and in particular to what I have called the molecularization of the work force. Inside the USSR, this failure was translated into a series of political and economic crises and into a series of successive slips which restored, to the detriment of the party, a relative autonomy to the technocratic machines of the State and of production, to the army, to the regions, etc. Outside of the USSR, this was translated into the chaotic relationships with the popular democracies—rupture with China, foundation of a *de facto* polycentrism within the communist parties. Everywhere, national and regional questions, particularisms once again took on decisive weight. Among other things, this allowed the capitalist countries to recuperate and partially integrate their local communist parties. From this standpoint, Stalin's legacy was completely lost. Of course, Stalinism continues to outlive itself in a certain number of parties and unions, but, in fact, it now operates on the old social-democratic model, and revolutionary struggles, struggles of desire, like May '68 or Lip, tend more and more to escape its influence. Under these conditions, the capitalist system is forced to search internally for new formulas of totalitarianism. And so long as these are not found, capitalism will have to face struggles on unforeseeable fronts (managerial strikes, struggles of immigrants and racial minorities, subversion in the schools, in the prisons, in the asylums, struggles for sexual liberty, etc.) This new situation, which involves heterogeneous social groupings whose action is not channeled into purely economic objectives, is met by proliferation and exacerbation of repressive responses. Alongside the fascism of the concentration camps, which continue to exist in numerous countries,[2] new forms of molecular fascism are developing: a slow burning fascism in familialism, in school, in racism, in every kind of ghetto, which advantageously makes up for the crematory ovens. Everywhere the totalitarian machine is in search of proper structures, which is to say, structures capable of adapting desire to the profit economy. We must abandon, once and for all, the quick and easy formula: "Fascism will not make it again." Fascism has already "made it," and it continues to "make it." It passes through the tightest mesh; it is in constant evolution, to the extent that it shares in a micropolitical economy of desire itself inseparable from the evolution of the productive forces. Fascism seems to come from the outside, but it finds its energy right at the heart of everyone's desire. We must stop, once and for all, being misled by the sinister buffooneries of those socio-democrats who are so astonished that their army, allegedly the most democratic in the world, launches, without notice, the worst of fascist repressions. A military machine as such crystallizes a fascist desire, no matter what the political regime may be. Trotsky's army, Mao's army, and Castro's army have been no exceptions: which in no way detracts from their respective merits. Fascism, like desire, is scattered everywhere, in separate bits and pieces, within the whole social realm; it crystallizes in one place or another, depending on the relationships of force. It can be said of fascism that it is all-powerful and, at the same time, ridiculously weak. And whether it is the former or the latter depends on the capacity of collective arrangements, subject-groups, to connect the social libido, on every level, with the whole range of revolutionary machines of desire.

Discussion

Félix Guattari: I think that it was Bassi who proposed—if I have understood it correctly—a program inspired by David Cooper which consists of making love everywhere, as an alternative to getting mired in discourse. Of course, I'm in agreement with this! But perhaps it is necessary to clarify that "making love" is not restricted to interpersonal relations. There are all kinds of ways to make love: one can make it with flowers, with science, with art, with machines, with social groups ... Once the personological framework of Oedipal sexuality is shattered, a nonhuman transsexuality is established in the social realm, that is to say, through a multiplicity of material and semiotic fluxes. It's the entire individual libidinal economy closed back onto itself that is put into question. From this point of view, I am not at all certain that Laing and Cooper have made a very significant breakthrough. It seems to me that they very quickly lock the libido back up into a system of intrafamilial communications. I think that they are overly influenced by American communications theorists. Let us say, to proceed quickly, that it is not information but transformation that is at stake here.

I would like to say to Emmanuele Amadio that there are all sorts of equivalents of psychoanalysis that are used to arrive at the same result: the neutralization of desire. One proceeds by reterritorializing it on familialism, on a technique of the body, on group therapy, on mystical practices, etc. Until a new order is achieved, psychoanalysis will remain the mastermind, the implicit frame of reference for these efforts. And this is happening even in the United States, where psychoanalysis has not gone off on a structuralist tangent, and where it tends to pale in significance next to body techniques and mysticism. In the Soviet Union and the Eastern European countries there is a budding interest in psychoanalysis, but they are trying to adapt it to local conditions. In all likelihood, the goal will be to promote a normalization, an adaptation of individuals to the bureaucratic system. Thus, the technique of Oedipalization, the chasing of desire back into familialism, is not an activity which is confined to the analyst's consulting room. It is of increasing interest to pedagogues, priests, and political commissioners of all stripes. In the end, wasn't the preparation of the Moscow trials already a kind of psychoanalysis? Perhaps physical torture didn't play the most important role. It was in the name of the party, thought of as one large family, that the absolute submission of the accused was obtained.

I am quite in agreement with Ricci and Bonetti: it's true that there is something absolutely artificial in speaking within the framework of a meeting such as this and above all in speaking about collective organizations of enunciation.

I would like to respond to my translator, and to Pietrantonio. It is not a question of conjuring away the relationship of the subject to language, but, on the contrary, of clearing the field of a host of illusions concerning the structures of enunciation. The irreducible opacity of the relation of desire to language is not miraculously revealed by the silent listening of the psychoanalyst. On the contrary, I think that it is by breaking off, one way or another, with the techniques of semiotic interpretation that one can pave the way for a political analysis, eliminating the primacy psychoanalysis has granted to the significations that rule over desire. A micropolitics of desire would refute the imperialism of signifying semiologies that cut desire off from the real. In refusing to consider the principles of signification and interpretation as immanent, this micropolitics would refuse to accept the organization of dominant realities as an act of fate. It is not a question, for example, of magically denying signification by rendering language absurd and falling back into the techniques of word play, which psychoanalysts baptized "signifying interpretations," but of placing different semiotic systems in conjunction with each other, beginning with asignifying semiotics, that is to say those semiotic practices which use signs in order to transform the real and which constitute, precisely, the privileged site for the investment of desire in the social arena. One has to search for the semiotic opacity of desire on the side of asignifying fluxes, for example in the fluxual economy of economic signs, in music, in art and in "incomprehensible" revolutionary transformations. From that point onward, it is no longer surprising to discover the irreducible character of desire in language: desire is inseparable from the existence of semiotic chains of all kinds, and at the same time, it has nothing to do with the redundancies of significant semiologies, with dominant mental representations and repressive interpretations—except when it invests them as such in a fascist-Oedipal micropolitics.

I think that I have already begun to respond to Calligaris, who, it seems to me, was also speaking in the name of Finzi. I repeat here that Deleuze and I do not intend to elaborate a scientific theory which would guarantee the existence of different social praxes. To advance theory, it is certainly desirable to reread Marx, but also to reread Hitler, and above all to follow everything that emerges concerning struggles and current conflicts; indeed, one should not lose sight of the fact that this is the terrain above all where the major theoretical ruptures have occurred, as in May '68 in France, or today in Chile and in the Middle East. Collective organizations of enunciation, such as those mentioned here, depart less from coherent theoretical constructions than from provisional semiotic scaffolds, elaborated on the basis of contingent situations. Whenever they are cut off from practice, these scaffolds are always at risk of being recuperated by the machines of power. Actually, in science, theory doesn't work in any other way.

I would like to conclude by commenting on an aspect of my translator's question which I did not answer: the risk of returning to an evolutionist way of thinking. Indeed, there is a point there which I haven't really been able to address in my exposition, even though it nevertheless was the essence of what I wanted to say. What insures the transition of the great classical fascist entities to the molecularization of fascism we are witnessing today? What drives the deterritorialization of human relations, what makes them lose their foundation in territorial and familial groupings, the body, age classifications, etc? What is this deterritorialization which engenders, in turn, the mounting of microfascism? This involves not only a simple question of ideological orientation or of strategy on the part of capitalism, but a fundamental material process: it's because industrial societies function on the basis of semiotic machines which increasingly decode all realities, all of the former territorialities; and it's because technical machines and economic systems are increasingly deterritorialized that they are capable of liberating increasingly greater fluxes of desire; or, more exactly, it's because their mode of production is forced to carry out this liberation, that the forms of repression are equally incited to become molecularized. A simple massive repression is no longer enough. Capitalism is obliged to construct and impose models of desire; and its survival depends on its success in bringing about the internalization of these models by the masses it exploits. It is preferable that everyone be attributed with: a childhood, a sexual positioning, a relationship to knowledge, a representation of love, of honesty, of death, etc. Capitalist relations of production are not simply established on the scale of great social groupings; from the cradle onward, they shape a certain type of producer-consumer individual. The molecularization of the processes of repression, and by extension, this prospect of a micropolitics of desire, are not therefore linked to an ideal evolution of history or to ideological mystifications, but to a transformation of material processes, to a deterritorialization of all forms of production, whether it involves social production or a desiring-production.

10

LA BORDE: A CLINIC UNLIKE ANY OTHER

Since 1955 I have worked at the clinic of La Borde; I was invited to collaborate on this experiment by my friend Jean Oury, who is its founder and principal director. The Château de la Borde is situated ten miles south of Blois [one hour south of Paris] in the Cour-Cheverny district. During these early years, it was truly fascinating to participate in the formation of the institutions and facilities of what would become the first experiment in "Institutional Psychotherapy" in the context of a private establishment. Our material resources were even smaller than they are today, but our freedom of action was greater. There were no psychiatric hospitals in the department of Loir and Cher at this time, the one in Blois having been closed during the war. Also, the authorities looked favorably upon the establishment of this clinic "like no other" that almost completely fulfilled the needs of the department.

It was then that I learned about psychosis and the impact that institutional work could have on it. These two aspects are profoundly interconnected, because psychotic traits are essentially disfigured in the context of traditional prison systems. Psychosis can show its true face only in a collective life developed around it within appropriate institutions, a face that is certainly not one of strangeness or violence, as one all too often believes, but one of a different relation to the world.

With the exception of a few pilot programs like those of Saint Alban in Lozère, or Fleury-les-Aubrais in the Loiret, French psychiatry in the 1950s had the grisly look one still finds today, for example, in Greece on the island of Leros or in the hospital of Daphni near Athens. Psychotics, objects of a system of quasi-zoological guardianship, necessarily take on an almost bestial allure, turning in circles all day long, knocking their heads against the walls, shouting, fighting, crouching in filth and excrement. These patients, whose understanding and relations with others are disturbed, slowly lose their human characteristics, becoming deaf and blind to all social communication. Their guardians, who at that time had no training at all, were forced to retreat behind a sort of armor of inhumanity if they wanted to avoid depression and despair themselves.

So I frequented Jean Oury since the early 1950s. He had been trained in the profession by François Tosquelles at Saint Alban, where a truly internal revolution had occurred during the war through the struggle for collective survival, the opening up to the outside world, the introduction of group methods, workshops, psychotherapies. Before meeting Jean Oury, I, too, thought madness embodied a sort of inversion of the world—strange, disquieting, and fascinating. In the communal style of life at La Borde in those years, the patients appeared to me in a completely different aspect: familiar, friendly, human. A sense of true emulation existed among personnel at the meetings that were held each evening at six o'clock to keep everyone informed about what had been said and done in the course of the day. For instance: such and such a catatonic had just spoken for the first time, or another had come of his own free will to work in the kitchen.

Jean Oury then asked me to join his team—and, consequently, to interrupt my studies in philosophy—because he needed my help, so he believed, in developing an intrahospital committee: the

Patients' Club, to be specific. My presumed competence in this domain was due to the fact that since the age of sixteen I had always been a "militant" in organizations like the "Youth Hostels" and a whole range of activities for the extreme left. In a few months' time, I had contributed to the establishment of multiple collective proceedings: general assemblies, joint commissions between patients and personnel, and "workshops" of all kinds—newspaper, drawing, sewing, chickens raising, gardening, etc.

But to do this, it was not enough to mobilize the sick, one also had to count on a maximum of personnel members getting involved. This presented no difficulty at all with the original team of organizers, who had been co-opted, as I myself had been, on the basis of a common goal and a certain anterior "activism." But it was not the same with the staff members who were local and had left a job or farm in order to work at the clinic as a cook, gardener, maid, or maintenance man. How then were these newcomers to be initiated to our psychiatric methods? How did one avoid creating a rift between the presumably "noble" tasks of the medical staff and the thankless, material tasks of the service personnel? (Depending on their position, the latter nonetheless regarded manual labor alone to be effective, while the "supervisors" merely babbled at useless meetings.)

At this stage of development, the institutional process demanded that an internal mini-revolution be undertaken: it required all service personnel work to be integrated with medical work, and that, reciprocally, medical staff be drafted for material tasks such as cleaning, cooking, dishwashing, maintenance, etc. Paradoxically, the second aspect of this mini-revolution posed fewer problems than the first. The medical staff, without too much fuss, agreed to take turns with the material chores, which enriched their encounters and dialogue with the patients. By contrast, it was much more difficult to get people who had been hired as laundresses, maids, or bookkeepers to collaborate in the care of patients and collective activities. Some were afraid of giving injections, others couldn't bear working at night or organizing meetings. And yet, in a few months time, the clinic's institutional landscape would change radically. An old washerwoman proved very capable at running the print workshop and editorial committee of the newspaper; another excelled in sporting activities, a former metallurgist showed great talent leading mime shows ...

The organization of the staff got more complex as tasks became more differentiated. Henceforth, one could no longer be content with a simple work schedule and holidays. A very elaborate "grid," or table, with dual-entries for the amount of time and the type of task, was used to account for those, in particular, who worked on a rota basis and to ensure that nursing, supervisory, and ordinary custodial activities were made compatible. In order to manage such a schedule, it became necessary to put a group of supervisors in place with an overall view of the needs of the institution and, in some respects, to assume the function of a chief of personnel, which had never existed before at La Borde.

A description as condensed as this may lead one to believe there was a linear development, while in practice the most unforeseen difficulties never stopped coming up because of certain resistances, blunders, practical obstacles of all kinds. Again and again, each problem had to be taken-up and reargued without ever losing sight of the basic orientation that consisted of gradually desegregating the doctor-patient relationship as much as that between medical staff and service personnel. This constant activity of calling things into question seems pointless and confusing in the eyes of an organizer-counsel, and yet it is through this activity alone that individual and collective assumptions of responsibility can be instituted, the only remedy to bureaucratic routine and passivity generated by traditional hierarchical systems.

A word that was fashionable then was "seriality," which defined, according to Jean-Paul Sartre, the repetitive and empty character of a mode of existence arising from the way a practico-inert group functioned. What we aimed for through our multiple activities, and above all through the assumption of responsibility with regard to oneself and to others, was to be disengaged from seriality and to make individuals and groups reappropriate the meaning of their existence in an ethical and no longer technocratic perspective. It was a matter of bringing forward the sort of activities that favor an assumption of collective responsibility and yet are founded on a resingularization of the relation to work and, more generally, personal existence. The institutional machine that we positioned didn't simply remodel the existing subjectivities, but endeavored, instead, to produce a new type of subjectivity. The supervisors created by the "rotations," guided by the "schedule," and actively participating in the "information meetings," gradually became, with training, very different people from what they had been upon arrival at the clinic. Not only did they familiarize themselves with the world of madness (as the Labordian system revealed it to be), not only did they learn new techniques, but their whole way of seeing and living was modified. More specifically, they shed that protective armor with which so many nurses, educators and social workers guard themselves against an alterity that unsettles them.

It was the same with the psychotic patients: some of them revealed expressive capacities totally unforeseen—for example, of a pictorial nature—which pursuing their lives in an ordinary setting would never have permitted them to become remotely aware of. The office employees preferred to assume the material tasks, farmers devoted themselves to managing the patient club, and both got more out of it than mere entertainment: they discovered a whole new relationship to the world.

And this is the essential thing, this change of relation with the world that, for the psychotic, corresponds to a readjustment of the components of personality. The world and the "other" no longer speak to him with the same voice or with that troubling insistence that replaces a reassuring neutrality. But let's not be mistaken: this alterity, or world, with which psychosis has a dialogue is not exclusively of an imaginary, delirious, or fantasy order. It also manifests itself in quotidian, social, and material reality. On the imaginary side, psychotherapies can intervene by way of "projective equivalents" in order to restore the body, mend wounds to the self, and forge new existential territories. On the real sides, it is the intersubjective field and the pragmatic context that can be expected to bring about new responses. For example, Gisela Pankow, in her attempts at dynamic restructuration of the psychotic body, frequently uses the medium of modeling plaster in order to allow plastic expression where spoken language fails. At La Borde, our modeling plaster is the institutional matter engendered throughout the tangle of workshops and meetings, as well as daily life in the dining rooms and bedrooms, in sports, games, and cultural life ... The range of expressive possibilities is not given in advance like the colors in a painting, but for the most part is reserved for innovation and improvisation of new activities.

Collective life, conceived according to rigid schemas, according to a ritualization of the quotidian, a regular and terminal hierarchization of responsibility—in short, "serialized" collective life—can become a desperate plight for patients as well as medical staff. It is surprising to realize that with the same microsociological "notes" one can compose a completely different institutional score. At La Borde, one can count about forty different activities for a population consisting of just a hundred patients and seventy staff members. There is an almost baroque treatment at the institution, always in search of new themes and variations in order to confer its seal of singularity—i.e., of finitude and authenticity—to the slightest gestures, the shortest encounters that take place in such a context.

One can only dream of what life could become in urban areas, in schools, hospitals, prisons, etc., if instead of conceiving them in a mode of empty repetition, one tried to redirect their purpose in the sense of permanent, internal re-creation. It was in thinking of such a virtual enlargement of the institutional practice of subjectivity-production that I developed the concept of "institutional analysis" in the early 1960s. It was not simply a matter, then, of calling psychiatry into question, but also of pedagogy—at least that kind of "institutional pedagogy" practiced and theorized by the group of instructors united around Fernand Oury, the older brother of Jean Oury—and also the conditions of study in which the problem, I dare say, began to seethe at the very heart of the Students' National Insurance (*Mutuelle Nationale des Etudiants*), where I had become a "technical counselor," and in the National Union of Students (*UNEF*), which had become a catalyst for the events of 1968. As I see it, all social segments should undergo, step by step, a veritable molecular revolution, i.e., a permanent reinvention. In no way did I suggest extending the experiment of La Borde to the whole of society, no single model being materially transposable in this way. Yet it seemed to me that subjectivity, at any stage of the *socius* worth considering, did not occur by itself, but was produced by certain conditions, and that these conditions could be modified through multiple procedures in a way that would channel it in a more creative direction.

Already in archaic societies, myths and initiation rites work to mould the subjective positions of each individual within age group, sex, function, race. In developed industrial societies, one finds the equivalent of these systems-of-entry in subjective arrangements, but under standardized forms producing nothing more than a serialized subjectivity. The "fabrication" of a subject now passes through a long and complicated process involving the family, school, "machinic" systems (like TV, various media, sports, etc.). I must insist on the fact that it is not only the cognitive content of subjectivity that undergoes modelization, but also every other facet, whether affective, perceptive, volitional, mnemonic ...

By working day to day with its hundred or so patients, La Borde gradually found itself involved in wider, global issues of health, pedagogy, prison conditions, femininity, architecture, urbanism. About twenty sector-based research groups were organized around the thematic of "institutional analysis," which implied that the analysis of formations of the unconscious did not only concern the two protagonists of classical psychoanalysis, but could encompass other, more ample social segments. Toward the mid-1960s, these groups were confederated in an organism called the FGERI (*Fédération des Groupes d'Etude et de Recherche Institutionnelle*). This organism was soon superseded by an institutional research center, CERFI (*Centre d'Etude, Recherche, et Formation Institutionnelle*), which published a magazine called *Recherches*. Fifty special issues of this magazine were published. The most famous of these was, no doubt, the one entitled "Three Billion Perverts," edited by Guy Hocquenghem and René Schérer, which dealt with "deviant" forms of sexuality. This issue led to legal proceedings for "offending established values," a trial at which I was convicted as director of the magazine.[1]

Another memorable issue of *Recherches*, around 1966, was devoted to the program planning of psychiatric facilities. The crust of French psychiatry had united around two program planners appointed by the Ministry of Health and around a group of young architects of the FGERI, both proponents of the Institutional Psychotherapy trend as well as the *Secteur* trend, preoccupied above all with extra-hospital facilities such as nursing homes, day hospitals, workshops, and dispensaries. We recommended, then, a stop to any new construction of psychiatric hospitals—institutional dinosaurs destined to disappear anyway—and the planning of facilities with fewer than a hundred beds, directly located in urban areas corresponding to the new *Secteur* divisions. Time has shown we were right. But we were not heard. In fact, Georges Pompidou, President of the Republic at the time, who favored development, had offered construction companies an immense market that consisted in equipping each regional department with new psychiatric hospitals, conceived according to the old model, i.e., the prison type—cut off from the social fabric and hyperconcentrated. This was a decision that, after several years, proved to be completely shortsighted, the new facilities corresponding in no way to real needs. It was also in this special edition on "Architecture and Psychiatry" that I made the acquaintance of an Italian group that would have great importance to me: Franco Basaglia, Giovanni Jervis, and Franco Minguzzi.

Two issues of the magazine were devoted to the "Days of Alienated Childhood" organized by Maud Manonni with the participation of Jacques Lacan. It was then that I met Ronald Laing and David Cooper who, also, would become friends and a source of inspiration, although I never espoused their brand of "antipsychiatry." If one puts aside certain demagogic exaggerations that occurred (along the lines of: "madness does not exist," or "all psychiatrists are cops"), the antipsychiatry movement can be credited with shaking up opinion about the fate reserved in society for the mentally ill, which the different reformist tendencies of European psychiatry had never succeeded in doing. Unfortunately, the revelation for the public at large, with respect to madness as portrayed in films like Kenneth Loach's *Family Life* or the work of Mary Barnes, was not accompanied by a single concrete proposition for reforming the situation. Communal experiments like that of "Kingsley Hall" in London remained the exception, yet did not seem broadly applicable in any general way that could transform English psychiatry as a whole. Another criticism I would make against Laing and Cooper's school of thought was their acceptance of a pretty reductionist conception of mental illness, psychosis appearing to them as the consequence of intrafamilial conflicts. It was at this time that the famous "double bind" was popularized, which was supposed to generate the most serious behavioral problems as a consequence of the reception, by the "designated patient," of a contradictory message by members of his family ("I ask you to do something, but I secretly want you to do the opposite"). It was clearly a very simplistic interpretation of the etiology of psychoses which had, among other negative effects, the one of laying the blame on psychotics' families who had already experienced enough difficulties as it was.

For its part, the Italian school *Psichatria Democratica*, which had formed around its charismatic leader, Franco Basaglia, never bothered with such theoretical considerations about the genesis of schizophrenia or curative techniques. It focused most of its activity on the global social field, allying itself to the parties and unions of the left with the goal, pure and simple, of closing psychiatric hospitals in Italy. It finally succeeded in doing this ten years ago with Law 180, whose adoption, unfortunately, roughly coincided with Basaglia's own death. The psychiatric hospitals were closed, in general, under the worst conditions, i.e., without setting up any real alternative. Patients were abandoned, as was the case in the USA with the "Kennedy Act," which closed the big American psychiatric hospitals for purely economic reasons, forcing tens of thousands of the mentally ill into the streets. In Italy, associations of the families of the mentally ill were organized to demand the reopening of the old asylums. The solution, which consisted of placing psychiatric services in the middle of general hospitals, proved illusory, these services being isolated and marginalized like the "poor cousins" of other hospital functions. It must be said, however, that a great distance had been covered between the initial discussions surrounding this project and the enactment of Law 180. The whole idea of the suppression of psychiatric hospitals appeared in the context of the social activism of the 1960s, favorable as it was to all sorts of innovations. But in 1980, this contestatory and creative wave was washing out, giving way to a new form of social conservatism. Whatever the case, Italian reformers of psychiatry had put their finger on the essential problem: only the sensitization and mobilization of the entire social context could create conditions favorable to real transformation. Certain experiments like that of Triest offered living proof. In his film *Fous à délier* (Madmen Unbound) Marco Bellochio showed seriously ill people welcomed in the context of industrial enterprise by union militants who declared that their presence had modified, in a more humane way, the entire climate of the workplace. The idealist character of these experiments makes one smile these days, considering the development of increasingly computerized and robotized industries, yet the global aims of the Italians remain sound. To resituate psychiatry in an urban context does not mean to artificially insert facilities and clinical teams there, but to reinvent it, while at the same time developing other social practices with the direct participation of the populations concerned.

In 1975, on the initiative of a group of friends, Mony Elkaïm (a world-renowned Moroccan psychiatrist specializing in family therapy) convoked a meeting in Brussels during which an International Network of Alternatives to Psychiatry was launched. We proposed to combine and, if possible, to surpass the diverse initiatives inspired by Laing, Cooper, Basaglia, etc. We wanted, above all, to disengage ourselves from the almost exclusively mass-mediatized character of anti-psychiatry in order to launch a movement that effectively engaged mental health workers and patients. Under the aegis of this network, important meetings took place in Paris, Triest, San Francisco, as well as in Mexico and Spain. This network continues to exist today. It is principally led by the successors of Franco Basaglia in Triest who have regrouped around Franco Rotelli. Because of certain developments, by which I mean a certain intellectual evolution, it has renounced many of its initial positions, at least in their more utopian aspects. The Triest teams are concentrating on converting existing psychiatric facilities by opening them up not only to the urban scene (as French proponents of the politics of *Secteur* had recommended in a somewhat more formal fashion), but by opening them up to the social in general. There is an important nuance here. One can create light psychiatric facilities in the midst of the urban fabric without necessarily working in the social field. One has simply miniaturized the old, segregative structures and, despite oneself, internalized them. The practice being developed today in Triest is different.

Without denying the specificity of the problems posed by the mentally ill, the institutions created, like the cooperatives, concern other categories of the population that are also in need of assistance. In this way, issues relating to drug-addiction, ex-convicts, troubled youths, etc., are no longer artificially separated. The work done through the cooperatives is not a simple ergotherapy; it is integrated into the wider social field, which does not prevent particular approaches being adapted for different kinds of handicaps. Here, then, one is moving in the direction of a general desegregation.

Unfortunately, in France and many other countries, official orientation is toward reinforcing segregation: the chronically ill are placed in establishments for the "long-term," which means, in fact, leaving them to crouch in isolation and inactivity; acute cases get special services as do alcoholics, drug users, Alzheimer's patients, etc. Our experience at La Borde has shown us, on the contrary, that a mixture of different nosographic categories and regular encounters between different age groups could constitute nonnegligible therapeutic vectors. Segregative attitudes form a whole: those one encounters among mental illnesses; those that isolate the mentally ill from the "normal" world; those one finds with respect to "problem children"; those that relegate the old to a sort of geriatric ghetto—all participate in the same continuum where one finds racism, xenophobia, and the rejection of cultural and existential differences.

The creation of communal "lifespaces" (*lieux de vie*), independent of official structures, had assumed a certain importance in the south of France. The few "lifespaces"—opened to disturbed children and ex-psychiatric patients alike—that still manage to survive do so with great difficulty, the ministerial guardians having never given up on the idea of establishing certain norms for them despite the fact that their true value consists in the inventiveness they show outside of established frameworks. And yet, more than ever now, the lack of these alternative structures is being felt. They alone can prevent, in some cases, the costly, pathogenic hospitalizations that take place in official structures.

One always comes back to this terrible burden of the state, which weighs heavily on the structures of care and assistance. Vital and creative institutions are long in the making; they involve the formation of dynamic teams who know each other well, with a common background, so many factors that cannot be dictated to by way of administrative circulars. For it should be understood that even now it is the French Minister of Health and Welfare who decides the appointments of psychiatrists in the psychiatric wards and who reviews them about once every two years. An absurd situation: not one psychiatric hospital is under the full directorship of the psychiatrists. All the power is concentrated in the hands of administrators who control entirely the services in the person of directors of general health. This condemns in advance all innovation, be it ever so slight. An experiment like that of François Tosquelles, during the last World War and after the Liberation, at Saint Albans Hospital in Lozère, would be impossible today. Among the younger generations of psychiatrists, psychologists and nurses, surely the same proportion of people exists today as before, willing to break out of the mediocrity in which French psychiatry is steeped. But these younger generations have their hands tied by a statute that reduces them to mere functionaries. It's an entire conception of public service that should be reconsidered. The state technocracy is accompanied by a kind of corporate spirit among the medical staff. Fortunately, there are some exceptions, as revealed by a few dozen thriving experiments within certain *Secteurs* and certain psychiatric services inspired by institutional psychotherapy. But these experiments are extremely minor and very precarious at the mercy of an untoward shuffling of posts for their principal directors. When the iron curtain was falling over Eastern Europe, an opportunity was lost to sweep our own front door by liquidating all the bureaucratic archaisms that prolong the more absurd and harmful psychiatric institutions. Only a veritable "de-Statization" of French psychiatry can allow the development of a climate of emulation between various innovative programs. I do not recommend here the privatization of psychiatry—private clinics too often simply isolate their patients in rooms without developing a therapeutic social life around them. But to me, it seems that the management of existing facilities, both intra- and extrahospital, be given to those associations and foundations in which all concerned parties are brought together: medical staff, patients (by the intermediary of the therapeutic clubs), family associations, local collectivities, public authorities, Social Security, unions, etc. A maximum number of participants should be involved in the reform of psychiatry to prevent it from folding back on itself. Controls and a priori regulations should be checked and a mechanism for dialogue set up, as well as, naturally, an a posteriori evaluative mechanism. It seems that this is the only way to get French psychiatry out of the present morass. Let those who want to innovate and be open-minded be able to do so. Let those who prefer to stand still stay as they are (no one can make them change by force!). Yet, a social competition will develop, opinion will exert pressure in one way or another. Anything is better than the present mediocrity with its pseudodebates around abusive internments, etc. It is psychiatry in its entirety that is abusive. One point one can never insist on enough is that medical and technical personnel as well as psychiatrists and psychologists are equally victims of present circumstances in which both patients and staff are literally dying of boredom.

It is also appropriate to expose the behavioralist ideologies at the core of French psychiatry, which relies on the most mechanistic conditioning programs, without taking social life or the singularities and psychic virtualities of the mentally ill into account. It is intolerable that one should turn away from the very essence and existence of humanity, its sense of freedom and responsibility.

Certain dangers also exist with the influence of systemic theories with reference to family therapy. They basically are concerned with intrafamily interaction (the concept of which is perfectly fuzzy) and consist very often of some sort of psychodrama by which the sessions are ritualized and coded according to pseudo-mathematical theories which have no other purpose except to confer a scientific veneer over their operators. Here, I completely set apart the antireductionist school run by Mony Elkaïm who, on the contrary, is essentially preoccupied with the resingularization of treatment, i.e., with engaging the therapist in what is most personal, in what permits an irreplaceable seal of authenticity and truth to be conferred on the relation formed between the therapist and the family.

For one thing, the psychoanalytic tendency, which has declined markedly in France, is, up to a certain point, equally responsible for the divestment of young psychiatrists with regard to institutional life. In particular, psychoanalysis of the Lacanian stamp with its esoteric, pretentious character, cut off from all apprehension of the terrain of psychopathology, entertains the idea that only an individual treatment allows access to the "symbolic order" by transcendent routes of interpretation and transference. The truth is completely different and access to neurosis, psychosis, and perversion requires other routes than this type of dual relation. I think that in a few years the "Lacanian pretension" will appear to be exactly what it is: simply ridiculous. The psyche, in essence, is the resultant of multiple and heterogeneous components. It engages, assuredly, the register of language, but also nonverbal means of communication, relations of architectural space, ethological behaviors, economic status, social relations at all levels, and, still more fundamentally, ethical and aesthetic aspirations. Psychiatry is confronted with all these components, including biological dimensions, to which more and more access is being given through psychopharmacology, which makes greater and greater progress every year. I don't mean the use of the "chemical camisole" of the neuroleptics in several psychiatric hospitals, to neutralize the patients. Medications, like any other therapeutic vector, must be "negotiated" with the patients; they require a delicate appreciation of their effects; the dosage, the times taken have to become the object of a sustained dialogue between the patient and the doctor who prescribes them.

Psychoanalysis continues to be marked by an original defect which consists in having been born under the aegis of a scientific (or at least scientistic) paradigm. Freud and his successors always wanted to present themselves as scientists who were discovering the universal structures of the psyche. The truth is that they invented the unconscious and its complexes as great visionaries in other epochs invented new religions, new ways of experiencing the world and social relations. It in no way devalorizes the invention of psychoanalysis in thus placing it under the aegis of an aesthetic paradigm. Treatment is not a work of art, yet it must proceed from the same sort of creativity. Interpretation does not furnish standard keys for resolving general problems founded upon what Lacan called the "mathemes of the unconscious," but it does announce or mark an irreversible bifurcation of the production of subjectivity. In short, it is on the order of "performance," in the sense assumed by this term in the field of contemporary poetry.

The knowledge of the psychoanalyst remains unchallenged up to now. It is a theology in which psychoanalysis has been soaking itself since its infancy. Here again the aesthetic paradigm can be a real help to us. Knowledge is what it is; one can hardly avoid it for the purpose of acquiring a minimum of *tonus*, of consistency, when faced with a patient or faced with an institution. But it is basically made in order to be channeled off into other things. The concepts of art, like those of analysis, come out of this tool box of modelization—the same box (which I introduced over twenty years ago) having been taken up, to my great joy, by Michel Foucault, in order to struggle against the always reemergent dogmatisms. A concept is only worth the life one invests it with. Its function is less for the purpose of guiding representation and action than of catalyzing the universe of reference that frames a pragmatic field. My intention today was not to explain my own concepts of metamodelization, which attempts to construct a processual unconscious that is turned towards the future rather than fixated upon the stases of the past, starting with the four functions: flows, machinic phyla, existential territories, and the universe of reference. In no way do they propose a more scientific description of the psyche, but they are conceived such that the formations of subjectivity be essentially open to an ethico-aesthetic pragmatic. Four imperatives are echoed here:

1) that of the *irreversibility* of the event-encounter, which gives its stamp of authenticity, of *jamais vu* to the analytic process;

2) that of *singularization*, which implies a permanent availability to the occurrence of any rupture of meaning that takes place in opening a new constellation of the universe of reference.

3) that of *heterogenesis*, which leads to the search for the specificity of the ontological terrain from which diverse partial components of subjectivation present themselves;

4) that of *necessitation*, which presupposes the obligation of an affect, percept, or concept to be actualized in an existential territory marked by finitude and the impossibility of being "translated" into whatever hermeneutic.

One sees that these schizoanalytic imperatives would be equally applicable in the fields of pedagogy, ecology, art, etc. It is the ethico-political root of the analysis—here conceived, I repeat, as the production of subjectivation at any given level.

The activity of theoretical modelization has an existential function. As such, it cannot be the privilege of theoreticians. One day, the right to theory and metamodelization will be inscribed on the pediments of every institution having anything to do with subjectivity.

It is obvious, then, that I do not propose the clinic of La Borde, for example, as an ideal model. Yet I do believe this experiment, despite its various shortcomings, can still be credited with raising certain important issues and indicating the axiological directions by which psychiatry might redefine its specificity, which I would like to sum up in conclusion:

1) Individual subjectivity, whether that of the patient or the medical staff, cannot be separated from the collective arrangements

of subjectivity-production; these arrangements involve microsocial dimensions, but also material and unconscious dimensions.

2) The mental health institution could become, if permanently rearranged for this purpose, a very elaborate instrument for the enrichment of individual and collective subjectivity and for the reconfiguration of existential territories concerning—all at once—the body, the self, living space, relations with others ...

3) To properly maintain their position within the therapeutic process, the material dimensions of the institution imply that the said "service" personnel be involved in every institutional facet according to appropriate modalities.

4) Information and training constitute important aspects of a therapeutic institution, but they do not replace the ethico-aesthetic aspects of human life considered in its finitude. No institutional arrangement, any more than an individual treatment, can function authentically unless in the register of truth, i.e., the unicity and irreversibility of the sense of life. This authenticity is not the object of instruction, but could, however, work itself out through individual and collective analytic practices.

5) Thus, the ideal situation would be one in which no two institutions were alike and no individual institution ever cease evolving in the course of time.

11

BEYOND THE PSYCHOANALYTICAL

UNCONSCIOUS

Individual and collective behavior are governed by multiple factors. Some are of a rational order, or appear to be, like those that can be treated in terms of power relations or economics. Others, however, appear to depend principally on nonrational motivations whose ends are difficult to decipher and which can sometimes even lead individuals or groups to act in ways that are contrary to their obvious interests.

There are numerous ways to approach this "other side" of human rationality. One can deny the problem, or fall back on the usual logic regarding normalcy and proper social adaptation. Considered that way, the world of desires and passions leads to nothing in the end, except to the "jamming" of objective cognition to "noise" in the sense that communication theory uses the term.[1] From this point of view, the only course of action is to correct these defects and facilitate a return to prevailing norms. However, one can also consider that these behaviors belong to a different logic, which deserves to be examined as such. Rather than abandon them to their apparent irrationality they can be treated as a kind of basic material, as an ore, whose life-essential elements, and particularly those relating to humanity's desires and creative potentialities can be extracted.

According to Freud, this is what the original task of psycho-analysis was supposed to be. But to what extent has it achieved this objective? Has it really become a new "chemistry" of the unconscious psyche, or has it remained a sort of "alchemy" whose mysterious powers have waned with time, and whose simplifications and "reductionism" (whether in its orthodox currents or structuralist offshoots) are less and less tolerable?

After years of training and practice, I have come to the conclusion that if psychoanalysis does not radically reform its methods and its theoretical references it will lose all credibility, which I would find regrettable on several counts. In fact, it would hardly matter to me if psychoanalytic societies, schools, or even the profession itself were to disappear, so long as the analysis of the unconscious reaffirms its legitimacy and renews its theoretical and practical modalities.

The very first thing which must be thought anew is the conception of the unconscious itself. Today the unconscious is supposed to be part of everone's essential baggage. No one doubts its existence. It is spoken about in the same way as memory or will, without anyone wondering about what it really is. The unconscious is supposed to be something at the back of the head, a kind of black box where mixed feelings and weird afterthoughts accumulate; something that should be handled with care.

Certainly professional psychoanalysts are not content with such a vague consideration. Explorers or guardians of a domain they consider to be their own, covetous of their prerogatives, they consider that access to the world of the unconscious can only be made after long and costly preparation, with a sort of strictly controlled asceticism. In order to succeed, didactic analysis, like ordinary analysis, demands much time and the use of a very particular apparatus (e.g., transference between analyst and analysand, controlling anamneses, exploring identifications and fantasies, lifting resistances through interpretation, etc.).

No one seems to wonder why this unconscious, supposedly loged at the core of every person, and referred to in connection with a great variety of domains like neuroses, psychoses, daily life, art, social life, etc., is the exclusive concern of specialists. So many things that seemed to belong unquestionably to everyone, like water, air, energy, and art, are now about to become the property of new industrial and commercial branches. So why not fantasies and desire as well?

I am interested in a totally different kind of unconscious. It is not the unconscious of specialists, but a region everyone can have access to with neither distress nor particular preparation: it is open to social and economic interactions and directly engaged with major historical currents. It is not centered exclusively around the family quarrels of the tragic heroes of ancient Greece. This unconscious, which I call "schizoanalytic," as opposed to the psychoanalytic subconscious, is inspired more by the "model" of psychosis than that of neurosis on which psychoanalysis was built. I call it "machinic" because it is not necessarily centered around human subjectivity, but involves the most diverse material fluxes and social systems. One after the other, the old territories of Ego, family, profession, religion, ethnicity, etc., have been undone and deterritorialized. The realm of desire can no longer be taken for granted. This is because the modern unconscious is constantly manipulated by the media, by collective apparatuses and their cohorts of technicians. It is no longer enough to simply define it in terms of an intrapsychic entity, as Freud did when he was conceiving his different topics. Would it suffice to say that the machinic unconscious is more impersonal or archetypical than the traditional unconscious? Certainly not, since its "mission" is precisely to circumscribe individual singularities more closely, in order to tie them down more strictly to social relations and historical realities of the "machinic age." Simply put, the questions raised by the unconscious no longer fall squarely within the realm of psychology. They involve the most fundamental choices for both society and desire, "existential choices" in a world which is criss-crossed by a myriad of machinic systems that expropriate the processes of singularization and fold them back over standardized—real as much as imagined—territorialities.

This model of the unconscious is not opposed point-by-point to the old psychoanalytic model. It takes up some of its elements, or, at least, reshuffles them as variants or exemplars. Actually, an unconscious pattern really does exist within an intrapsychic "familialized" space where certain mental materials elaborated during early stages of psychic life are tied together. No one can deny that such a place where hidden and forbidden desires, a sort of secret kingdom, a state within the state exists, which seeks to impose its law over the whole psychism and its behaviors. But this formula, a private individualized and Oedipal unconscious, assumes premier importance in developed societies where most of their power depends upon systems of guilt and internalizations of norms. Still, I repeat, a new kind of analysis must discover and promote what could only be a variant to the notion of the unconscious, realigned according to other possiblities.

The Freudian model of the unconscious, one recalls, obeyed a double movement: 1) repulsing "representative drives" that the unconscious and the preconscious could not tolerate (utterances, images, and forbidden fantasies); 2) attracting those which originate in always already repressed psychic formations (originary repression). Thus forbidden contents had first to travel through the conscious and the unconscious before falling into something like an "unconscious-discharge" governed by a particular syntax called the "primary processes" (for example the condensations and displacements at the heart of dreams). This double movement did not allow for creative processes that would be specific to the unconscious. (Freud: "The dream Work is never creative.") Everything there was played out in advance, every possible path marked out: the psychoanalytic unconscious was programmed like destiny.

Instead of relying on such a binary mechanism—a system of repression proper and a system of originary repression—the schizo-analytic unconscious implies a proliferation made up not only of typical "part objects"—the breast, the feces, the penis; or mathemes like Lacan's "a-object"—but also a multitude of singular entities, fluxes, territories, and incorporeal universes, making up *functional arrangements* that are never reducible to universals.

To recapitulate some characteristics of the machinic unconscious:

1) It *is not* the exclusive seat of representative contents (representations of things or representations of words, etc.). Rather it *is* the site of *interaction between semiotic components and extremely diverse systems of intensity*, like linguistic semiotics, "iconic" semiotics, ethological semiotics, economic semiotics, etc. As a consequence, it no longer answers to the famous axiom formulated by Lacan, of being "structured like a language."

2) Its different components *do not depend upon a universal syntax*. The configuration of its contents and its systems of intensity (as these may be manifested in dreams, fantasies, and symptoms) depend upon *processes of singularization* which necessarily resist reductive analytic descriptions, like castration or Oedipus complexes (or intrafamilial systematizations). Collective arrangements that relate to specific cultural or social contexts account for such machinic instances.

3) *Unconscious interindividual relationships do not depend on universal structures* (like those that the disciples of Lacan try to base on a sort of "game theory" of intersubjectivity). Both imaginary and symbolic interpersonal relations obviously occupy a nodal point at the heart of unconscious arrangements, but they don't account for them all. Other, no less essential dispositions, come from systems of abstract entities and concrete machines that operate outside human identifications. The machinic unconscious is like a department store—you can find whatever you want there. This

explains both its subservience to consumer society, its rich creativity and openness to innovation.

4) The unconscious can fall back on a nostalgic imaginary, *open up to the here and now*, or take chances on the future. Archaic fixations on narcissism, the death instinct, and the fear of castration can be avoided. They are not, as Freud assumed, the rock bottom of the whole edifice.

5) The machinic unconscious is not the same all over the world: *it evolves with history*. Obviously, the economy of desire of Malinowsky's Trobrianders is different from the inhabitants of Brooklyn, and the fantasies of Precolumbian Teotihuacans have little to do with those of contemporary Mexicans.

6) The structures of unconscious analytic enunciations do not necessarily require the services of the corporation of analysts. *Analysis can be pursued individually or collectively.* The notions of transference, interpretation and neutrality, based on a "typical cure," should also be revised. They are only admissible in very particular cases, within a very limited range of circumstances.

No matter what upheavals of history or technological and cultural transformations may be in store, isn't it inevitable that structural elements will always be found within unconscious transformations? Don't the oppositions self/other, man/woman, parent/child, etc., criss-cross in such a way as to constitute a kind of universal mathematic grid of the unconscious? But why should the existence of such a grid preclude the possibility of a diversity of unconsciousnesses? Even the people who are most open to a "schizoanalytic revision" sometimes come back to these kinds of questions. I should therefore emphasize several of the reasons that lead me to reject "universals" of expression as much as universals of content as bases for the unconscious.

One of Freud's major discoveries was to bring to light the fact that there is no negation in the unconscious, at least not the kind of negation that is found in the logic of consciousness. It is a mental world where rigid oppositions don't have to apply, where self and other, man and woman, parent and child can—and actually do—exist simultaneously in the same person. What matters then, is not the existence of reified, polarized entities, but rather processes that Gilles Deleuze and I have called "becomings." Becoming-women, becoming-plants, becoming-music, becoming-animals, becoming-invisible, becoming-abstract ... The "primary processes" of the Freudian unconscious (whose reductionist interpretations, based on normalized noetic structures patterned on dominant coordinates and signification we cannot condone) only gives us access to a universe of transformations of an incorporeal nature: when everything appears to he stratified and definitively crystalized, it introduces virtualities of meaning and praxis that are extrinsic to the opposition reality/representation.

For example, if it happens that a patient tells his analyst about a problem concerning his boss or the President of the Republic, one can be sure that only mechanisms of paternal identification will be called forth. Behind the woman post-office official, or the female television announcer, will loom the maternal imago, or a universal structural matheme. More generally, behind all the forms that come to life around us, the different analytical schools only locate sexual symbols and references to symbolic castration. But in the long run, such a one-track reading obviously loses its appeal.

If the symbolic father is often lurking behind the boss—which is why one speaks of "paternalism" in various kinds of enterprises—there also often is, in a most concrete fashion, a boss or hierarchic superior behind the real father. In the unconscious, paternal functions are inseparable from the socio-professional and cultural involvements which sustain them. Behind the mother, whether real or symbolic, a certain type of feminine condition exists, in a socially defined imaginary context. Must I point out that children do not grow up cut off from the world, even within the family womb? The family is permeable to environmental forces and exterior influences. Collective infrastructures, like the media and advertising, never cease to interfere with the most intimate levels of subjective life. The unconscious is not something that exists by itself to be gotten hold of through intimate discourse. In fact, it is only a rhizome of machinic interactions, a link to power systems and power relations that surround us. As such, unconscious processes cannot be analyzed in terms of specific content or structural syntax, but rather in terms of enunciation, of *collective enunciative arrangements*, which, by definition, correspond neither to biological individuals nor to structural paradigms. Unconscious subjectivity engendered by these arrangements is not "ready made." It locates its processes of singularization, its subjective ensemble, within orders which differ greatly from each other (signs, incorporeal universes, energy, the "mechanosphere," etc.), according to open configurations, in the way that we speak today of opening up creative possibilities in the visual arts, in materials, substances, forms ...

The customary psychoanalytical family-based reductions of the unconscious are not "errors." They correspond to a particular kind of collective enunciative arrangement. In relation to unconscious formation, they proceed from the particular micropolitics of capitalistic societal organization. An overly diversified, overly creative machinic unconscious would exceed the limits of "good behavior" within the relations of production founded upon social exploitation and segregation. This is why our societies grant a special position to those who specialize in recentering the unconscious onto the individuated subject, onto partially reified objects, where methods of *containment* prevent its expansion beyond dominant realities and significations. The impact of the scientific aspirations of techniques like psychoanalysis and family therapy should be considered as a gigantic industry for the normalization, adaption and organized division of the *socius*.

The workings of the social division of labor, the assignment of individuals to particular productive tasks, no longer depend solely on means of direct coercion, or capitalistic systems of semiotization (like monetary remuneration based on profit, etc.). They depend just as fundamentally on techniques modeling the unconscious through social infrastructures, the mass media, and different psychological and behavioral devices. The deterritorialization of the libido by productive forces that support World Integrated Capitalism (WIC) effectively develops a kind of collective anguish, as a counterpoint to the scope of science and technology, resurrecting factors like religious ideologies, myths, archaisms, etc. It is more than probable to expect that despite the amplitude of subjective operations reterritorializing the *socius* and the imaginary by diverse forces of WIC (like capitalist regimes, socialist bureaucracies, Third World dictatorships, etc.), the machinic integration of humanity will continue. What we don't know yet are its eventual modalities. Will it continue to move at counter- currents to the creative lines of desire and the most fundamental human ends? Just consider the immense physical and moral misery that reigns over the greater part of this planet. On the other hand, will the economy of desire be able to harmonize itself to technical and scientific progress? Only a profound transformation of social relationships at every level, an immense movement by machines of desire to "get their hands on" technical machines, a "molecular revolution" correlative to analytical practices and new micropolitics, will enable such a readjustment. Even the outcome of the class struggle of the oppressed—the fact that they constantly risk being sucked into relations of domination—appears to be linked to such a perspective.

An analytic and micropolitical approach towards collective formations of desire should constantly renew its methods, diversify and enrich itself through contact with every domain of creation, so that it can become "everybody's business." In short, it must do everything that the psychoanalytic profession of today does not do.

III

MINOR POLITICS

12

TO HAVE DONE WITH THE MASSACRE

OF THE BODY*

No matter how much it proclaims its pseudotolerance, the capitalist system in all its forms (family, school, factories, army, codes, discourse ...) continues to subjugate all desires, sexuality, and affects to the dictatorship of its totalitarian organization, founded on exploitation, property, male power, profit, productivity ...

Tirelessly it continues its dirty work of castrating, suppressing, torturing, and dividing up our bodies in order to inscribe its laws on our flesh, in order to rivet to our subconscious its mechanisms for reproducing this system of enslavement.

With its throttling, its stasis, its lesions, its neuroses, the capitalist state imposes its norms, establishes its models, imprints its features, assigns its roles, propagates its programs ... Using every available access route into our organisms, it insinuates into the depths of our insides its roots of death. It usurps our organs, disrupts our vital functions, mutilates our pleasures, subjugates all lived experience to the control of its condemning judgments. It makes of each individual a cripple, cut off from his or her body, a stranger to his or her own desires.

To reinforce its social terror, which it forces individuals to experience as their own guilt, the capitalist army of occupation

---

* Published anonymously in the special issue of *Retherches*, "Three Billion Perverts," March 1973.

strives, through an ever more refined system of aggression, provocation, and blackmail, to repress, to exclude, and to neutralize all those practices of desire which do not reproduce the established form of domination.

In this way the system perpetuates a centuries-old regime of spoiled pleasures, sacrifice, resignation, institutionalized masochism, and death. It is a castrating regime, which produces a guilty, neurotic, scrabbling, submissive drudge of a human being.

This antiquated world, which stinks everywhere of dead flesh, horrifies us and convinces us of the necessity of carrying the revolutionary struggle against capitalist oppression into that territory where the oppression is most deeply rooted: the living body.

It is the body and all the desires it produces that we wish to liberate from "foreign" domination. It is "on that ground" that we wish to "work" for the liberation of society. There is no boundary between the two elements. 'I' oppress myself inasmuch as that 'I' is the product of a system of oppression that extends to all aspects of living.

The "revolutionary consciousness" is a mystification if it is not situated within a "revolutionary body," that is to say, within a body that produces its own liberation.

Women in revolt against male power—a power that has been forced on their bodies for centuries—homosexuals in revolt against a terroristic "normality," young people in revolt against the pathological authority of adults: these are the people who, collectively, have begun to make the body a means of subversion, and have begun to see subversion as a means for meeting the "immediate" needs of the body.

These are the people who have begun to question the mode of production of desires, the relationship between pleasure and power, the relationship between the body and the individual. These are the people who question the function of such relationships in all spheres of capitalist society, including within militant groups.

These are the people, of both sexes, who have finally broken that perennial barrier between "politics" and reality as it is actually lived—a barrier that has served the interests of both the leaders of bourgeois society and those who have claimed to represent and speak for the masses.

These are the people, of both sexes, who have opened the way for a great uprising of life against the forces of death—even as these latter continue to infiltrate our organisms in order to subjugate, with greater and greater subtlety, our energies, our desires, and our reality to the demands of the established order.

A new cutting edge, a new line of more radical and more definitive attack has been opened up, and because of it there will necessarily be new alignments among revolutionary forces.

We can no longer sit idly by as others steal our mouths, our anuses, our genitals, our nerves, our guts, our arteries, in order to fashion parts and works in an ignoble mechanism of production which links capital, exploitation, and the family.

We can no longer allow others to turn our mucous membranes, our skin, all our sensitive areas into occupied territory—territory controlled and regimented by others, to which we are forbidden access.

We can no longer permit our nervous system to serve as a communications network for the system of capitalist exploitation, for the patriarchal state; nor can we permit our brains to be used as instruments of torture programmed by the powers that surround us.

We can no longer allow others to repress our fucking, control our shit, our saliva, our energies, all in conformity with the prescriptions of the law and its carefully-defined little transgressions. We want to see frigid, imprisoned, mortified bodies explode to bits, even if capitalism continues to demand that they be kept in check at the expense of our living bodies.

This desire for a fundamental liberation, if it is to be a truly revolutionary action, requires that we move beyond the limits of our "person," that we overturn the notion of the "individual," that we transcend our sedentary selves, our "normal social identities," in order to travel the boundaryless territory of the body, in order to live in the flux of desires that lies beyond sexuality, beyond the territory and the repertories of normality.

So it is that some of us have felt the vital need to act as a group in liberating ourselves from those forces that have crushed and controlled desire in each one of us.

Everything that we have experienced on the level of personal, intimate life we have tried to approach, explore, and live collectively. We want to break down the concrete wall, erected by the dominant social organization, that separates being from appearance, the spoken from the unspoken, the private from the social.

Together, we have begun to explore all the workings of our attractions, repulsions, our resistances, our orgasms, the universe of our representations, our fetishes, our obsessions, our phobias. The "unconfessable secret" has become for us a matter for reflection, public discussion, and political action—where politics is taken as the social manifestation of the irrepressible aspirations of the "living being."

We have decided to break the intolerable seal of secrecy which the power structure has placed on the reality of sensual, sexual, and affective practices; thus we will break the power structure's ability to produce and reproduce forms of oppression.

As we have explored collectively our individual histories, we have seen to what extent all of our desiring life has been dominated by the fundamental laws of the bourgeois capitalist state and the Judeo-Christian tradition; all of our desires are subjected to capitalism's rules concerning efficiency, surplus value, and reproduction. In comparing our various "experiences," no matter how free they may have appeared, we recognized that we are always and forever obliged to conform to the officially sanctioned sexual stereotypes, which regulate all forms of lived experience and extend their control over marriage beds, houses of prostitution, public bathrooms, dance floors, factories, confessionals, sex shops, prisons, high schools, buses, etc.

Let us discuss this officially sanctioned sexuality, which has been defined as the one and only possible sexuality. We do not wish to manage it, as one manages the conditions of one's imprisonment. Rather, we wish to destroy it, eliminate it, because it is nothing more that a mechanism for castrating and recastrating; it is a mechanism for reproducing everywhere, in every individual, over and over again, the bases for a system of enslavement. "Sexuality" is a monstrosity, whether in its restrictive forms, or in its so-called "permissive" forms. It is clear that "liberalizing" attitudes and "eroticizing" the social reality through advertising is something organized and controlled by the managers of "advanced" capitalism for the sake of a more efficacious reproduction of the officially sanctioned libido. Far from reducing sexual misery, these transactions only increase frustrations and feelings of "failure," hence permitting the transformation of desire into a compulsive consumer need, while also guaranteeing "the production of demand," which of course is the very motor of capitalist expression. There is no real difference between the "immaculate conception" and the seductive female of advertising, between dutifully-fulfilled marital obligations and the promiscuity of bourgeois women on the go. The same censorship is at work in all cases. The same will to put to death the body-that-desires perpetuates itself. Only a change of strategy has occurred.

What we want, what we desire, is to burst through the screen of sexuality and its representations in order to know the reality of our bodies, of our bodies-that-desire.

We want to free this living body, make it whole again, unblock it, clear it, so that it may experience the liberation of all its energies, desires, intensities, which at present are crushed by a social system that prescribes and conditions.

We want to recover the full use of all our vital functions, complete with their particular potentials for pleasure

We want to recover such elementary faculties as the pleasure of breathing, which has literally been strangled by the forces that oppress and pollute. We want to recover the pleasure of eating and digesting, which has been disrupted by the rhythms imposed by Productivity and by the bad food that is produced and Prepared according to criteria of marketability.

And let us not forget the pleasure of shitting and the pleasures of the anus, systematically destroyed by the coercive conditioning of the sphincter—a conditioning used by capitalist authority to inscribe even onto the flesh its fundamental principles (relationships of exploitation, neurotic accumulation, the mystique of property and of cleanliness, etc.). Or the pleasure of masturbating happily and without shame, with no anguished feelings about failure and compensation, but simply for the pleasure of masturbating. Or the pleasures of shaking oneself, of humming, of speaking, of walking, of moving, of expressing oneself, of feeling delirious, of singing, of playing with one's body in every possible way. We want to recover the pleasures of producing pleasure and of creating— pleasures which have been ruthlessly quashed by educational systems charged with manufacturing obedient worker-consumers.

We want to open our bodies to the bodies of other people, to other people in general. We want to let vibrations pass among us, let energies circulate, allow desires to merge, so that we can all give free reign to our fantasies, to our ecstasies, so that at last we can live without guilt, so that we can practice without guilt all pleasures, whether individual or shared by two or more people. All of this pleasure we desperately need if we are not to experience our daily reality as a kind of slow agony which capitalist, bureaucratic civilization imposes as a model of existence on its subjects. And we want to excise from our being the malignant tumor of guilt, which is the age-old root of all oppression.

Obviously we are aware of the formidable obstacles that we will have to overcome if our aspirations are not to remain simply the dream of a tiny set of marginalized people. We are quite aware that the liberation of the body and the freeing of sensual, sexual, affective, and ecstatic feelings are indissolubly linked to the liberation of women and the abolition of every kind of sexual categorization. Revolutionizing desire means destroying male power and rejecting all its modes of behavior and its ideas about couples; revolutionizing desire means destroying all forms of oppression and all models of normality.

We want to put an end once and for all to the roles and identities instituted by the Phallus.

We want to put an end once and for all to any rigid assigning of sexual identity. We do not want to think of ourselves anymore as men and women, homosexuals and heterosexuals, possessors and possessed, older and younger, masters and slaves, but rather as human beings who transcend such sexual categorization, who are autonomous, in flux, and multifaceted. We want to see ourselves as beings with varying identities, who can express their desires, their pleasures, their ecstasies, their tenderness without relying on or invoking any system of surplus value, or any system of power at all, but only in the spirit of play.

We have begun with the body, the revolutionary body, as a place where "subversive" energies are produced—and a place where in truth all kinds of cruelties and oppressions have been perpetuated. By connecting "political" practice to the reality of this body and its functioning, by working collectively to find means to liberate this body, we have already begun to create a new social reality in which the maximum of ecstasy is combined with the maximum of consciousness. This is the only way that we will be able to directly combat the hold that the Capitalist State exercises over us. This is the only step that will truly make us STRONG against a system of domination that continues to strengthen its power, that aims to weaken and to undermine each individual in order to force him or her to bow to the system, that seeks, in effect, to reduce us all to the level of dogs.

13

THREE BILLION PERVERTS ON THE STAND

1. Prefatory Note

The object of this file—homosexualities, today, in France—cannot be approached without questioning again the standard methods of research in the social sciences where, under a pretext of objectivity, all care is taken to maximize the distance between the researcher and the object of study. To arrive at the radical decentering of scientific enunciation that is required for the analysis of such a phenomenon, it is not sufficient to *"give voice"* to the subjects concerned—which at times amounts to a formal, even Jesuitical, intervention. Rather, it is necessary to create the conditions for a total, indeed a paroxysmic, exercise of that enunciation. Science should have nothing to do with just measures and compromises for the sake of good taste! It is not readily apparent how to break through the barriers of established knowledge, in fact of dominant power. At least three sorts of censure must be thwarted:

1) that of the pseudo-objectivity of *social surveys*, in the manner, for example, of the Kinsey Report, transposed onto the *"sexual behaviour of the French"*—which contain a priori all possible responses, and in such a way as not to reveal to the public anything that does not accord with what the observer and the director of the study wish to hear;

2) that of *psychoanalytic prejudices* which preorganize a psychological, topical, and economic *"comprehension"*—in fact a recuperation—of homosexuality, such that, with the persistence of the most traditional sexology, will continue to be held within a clinical framework of perversion, which implicitly justifies all the forms of repression it has suffered. Here, then, there will be no question of "fixation" at the pregenital, pre-Oedipal, presymbolic, or pre-anything stages, which would define the homosexual as lacking something—at the very least normality and morality. Far from depending on an *"identification with the same-sex parent,"* homosexual maneuvering effects a break with all possible adequation to a prominent parental pole. Far from resolving itself by fixation on the Same, it is an opening into Difference. For the homosexual, refusal of castration does not indicate a shrinking from his or her social responsibilities, but rather, at least potentially, indicates an attempt to expunge all normalizing, identificatory processes—processes which are, fundamentally, no more than the remnants of the most archaic rituals of submission;

3) that, finally, of *traditional militant homosexuality*. Likewise, in this domain, the period of the "Case of Uncle Tom" has passed. Here, the defense of the legitimate and unassailable claims of oppressed minorities will no longer be at issue; and no question, either, of a quasi-ethnographic exploration of a mysterious *"third sex"*... Homosexuals speak for us all—speak in the name of the silent majority—by putting into question all forms, whatever they may be, of desiring-production. Nothing in the order of artistic creation or of revolution can be accomplished in ignorance of their questioning. The era of homosexual geniuses, who set about separating and diverting their creativity from their homosexuality, forcing themselves to conceal that their creative spirit originated in that very break with the established order, has now passed.

Incidentally, for the deaf: the gay, no more than the shizo, is not *of himself* a revolutionary—the revolutionary of modern times! We are simply saying that, among others, he *could* be, *could* become, a site for an important libidinal disruption in society—a point of emergence for revolutionary, desiring-energy from which classical militantism remains cut off. We do not lose sight, insofar as it also exists, of an infinitely unfortunate commitment to asylums, or an indefinitely shameful and miserable Oedipal homosexuality. And yet, even with these cases of extreme repression, one should stay in touch.

May '68 taught us to read the writing on the walls, and, since then, we have begun to decipher the graffiti in prisons, asylums, and now in urinals. There is a *"new scientific spirit"* to recapture!

2. A Letter to the Court

In recent years, the position of homosexuals in society has greatly evolved. In this area, as in many others, one observes a discrepancy between reality and psychiatric theory, medical-legal and juridical practice. Homosexuality is less and less felt to be a shameful malady, a monstrous deviance, a crime. This evolution has become increasingly pronounced since May '68, when the forces of social struggle took on previously neglected causes, such as life in prisons and in asylums, the condition of women, the question of abortion, of quality of life, etc. There has been, moreover, a homosexual political movement which, considering homosexuals to be a marginal minority, has defended their human dignity and demanded their rights. Some of these movements, in the United States for example, have joined forces with other protest groups: movements against the Vietnam War, civil rights movements for Blacks, Porto Ricans, feminist movements, and so on.

In France, this evolution has been different. The revolutionary movement, the FHAR [*Front homosexuel d'action revolutionnaire*], was launched with a political agenda right from the start. There was no conjunction of marginal homosexual movements with political movements: the problems of homosexuality were immediately posed as political questions. This spontaneist Maoist movement, formed around the journal *Tout!*—the product of May '68—refused not only to accept that homosexuality was an illness or a perversion, but advanced the view that it concerned all normal sexual life. Similarly, the women's liberation movement, the MLF (*Mouvement de liberation des femmes*), argued that feminine homosexuality was not only a form of struggle against male chauvinism, but also a radical questioning of all dominant forms of sexuality.

Homosexuality would be, thus, not only an element in the life of each and everyone, but involved in any number of social phenomena, such as hierarchy, bureaucracy, etc. The question has thus been shifted: homosexual men and women refuse the status of an oppressed minority, and intend to lead a political offensive against the enslavement of all forms of sexuality to a system of reproduction, and to the values of bureaucratic capitalist and socialist societies. This is, in fact, more about transsexuality than homosexuality: at issue is the definition of what sexuality would be in a society freed from capitalist exploitation and the alienation it engenders on all levels of social organization. From this perspective, the struggle for the liberty of homosexuality becomes an integral part of the struggle for social liberation.

The ideas arising from this line of thought were explored in the issue of *Recherches* for which I have been charged—as the director of the publication—for "affronting public decency." In fact, the problems raised by this issue of *Recherches* are fundamentally, and only, political. The charge of pornography is merely a pretext, all too easily invoked in this particular domain; the main thing is suppression for the sake of "an example."

Recherches, in addition to a number of current publications, endeavors to break with the practice common to radio, television, and most print media of selecting information according to reigning prejudices, of making themselves the judges of decency and indecency, of transposing the voice of those concerned by a particular problem into a language deemed acceptable; in short, of substituting themselves. On the situation in prisons, for example, one would solicit commentary from a judge, a policeman, a former prisoner (one of exceptional character—one, for example, who had committed a crime of passion), but never from an average prisoner. The same applies for mental illness. At a push, one might bring forward an insane genius, but never would one seek out actual witnesses to the miserable life of a psychiatric hospital.

We wanted, therefore, to give direct voice to homosexuals. And the result? We are reproached for our impropriety. But of what nature is this impropriety, if it is not political? In fact, what is said in this issue of *Recherches*, and in the manner in which it is said, is clearly less than what can be found not only in publications for sex-shops—our goal was hardly to compete!—but also in scientific publications. The originality of the issue—that which shocks, and for which we are charged—lies in that, for perhaps the first time, homosexuals and nonhomosexuals speak of these problems for themselves and in an entirely free manner.

3. 17th Magistrate's Court

(Notes for the trial)

1) I will not repeat the terms of my letter to the court; it seems, as Mr. Kiejman has advised me, that this would have a negative effect,

— I am summoned as the director of the journal *Recherches* for its special issue on homosexuality: "Three Billion Perverts: An Encyclopedia of Homosexualities,"

2) what does the fact that I am held responsible for this issue signify?

• *Recherches* is the expression of a group
• this issue, in particular, was collectively produced
• all of its participants asked to be charged

3) what does the fact of holding someone responsible for something signify?

- I am responsible, I represent *Recherches*
- you represent the law
- members of Parliament represent the people
- the President of the Republic: France
- universities: knowledge
- gays: perversion

4) *Recherches* wishes to have done with this sort of representation, with all the bad theatre to which officials and institutions
resort.

What we want is to give voice to those who never manage to
be heard.

5) At CERFI (*Centre d'études, de recherches et de formations insti-
tutionnelles*), we are often questioned on the issues surrounding these
problems. It is, undoubtedly, for those who are interested to seek
answers themselves! Sometimes, however, we cannot restrain ourselves
from expressing our own ideas.

6) Recently, the Minister of Justice asked us if we would agree
to study what the "spatial disposition of a Law Court" could be.

There is at least one comment that I could make at the moment:
that is that judges should be in the room, and that speakers, whoever
they may be, should *face the public*.

7) Can one speak seriously in a Court?

- when I was a young militant, I would have refused to participate in this "masquerade,"
- I would have said to you: "So, now, to express myself freely
in a journal, one must pay. Fine. Write up the bill and we won't
waste any more time." And I would have thrown you a fistful of
bills or change for the bailiffs to pick up.

Then you would have sentenced me with contempt of court
and everyone would have been satisfied!

• now I think a bit differently. I know that things go on everywhere, even in the magistrature, even in the police, even in the prefecture,

• finally, then, this trial interests me: I would like to know if everything was played out in advance, if everything was already inscribed in the "pharmacopoeia" of laws ... In this case, then, I grant you, in advance, that this issue of *Recherches* is indefensible. (Even though, I am sure, Mr. Merleau-Ponty, Mr. Kiejman, and Mr. Domenach would know how to prove otherwise!)

8) What purposes do texts serve: whether it be a text of law or a text of *Recherches*? Are they not inseparable from the social relations that underlie them, and from what linguists call the context, the implicit? Isn't the important thing to look at life itself, at the evolution of what one could call the "jurisprudence of everyday life"? One would see that homosexuality has evolved in recent years—at the very least, its "customary law"—and it is of that which we must speak.

9) But before continuing, I would like to ask you two things, Your Honour, for the enrichment of our proceedings:

1. have all the witnesses, up to the present, enter together,

2. give free voice to everyone in the room who asks to speak.

This affair has two sides:

1) a ridiculous side,

2) a serious side.

The ridiculous side: In April of 1973, I was in Canada participating in an extremely interesting conference. Unfortunately, I could not delay my return to France because of consultations that I could not reschedule. Arriving home in Paris, suitcases in hand, I found several people with whom I had appointments sitting in the stairway, in front of my padlocked door.

It took me a moment to realize that the padlock, roughly screwed on the door (which cost me 150 francs to repair), had been put there by the police after searching the premises. The two statutory witnesses to this search had been, in my absence, my upstairs neighbours and ... the locksmith! All of my papers and my clothes had been gone through, and the bathroom turned upside down. During this time, ten police officers had undertaken a similar search of the clinic of La Borde where I work. *Dozens* of search warrants had been issued ... to what end? It defies belief! To find copies of the seized issue of *Recherches*, while that same issue was on sale in bookstores, and had been for weeks!

When I protested these proceedings to the examining judge, I must say that he remained largely perplexed. I thought then that there had been a mistake and that the case would be adjourned *sine die.*

The serious side: What exactly caused such a commotion? The content or the form?

a) *The content of the issue*
The content is certainly exceptionally rich, particularly insofar as it involved:

1) the position of the homosexual in society,

2) the way in which different immigrant groups from North Africa live their homosexuality,

3) the sexual misery of young people,

4) the racist fantasies which are sometimes invoked in relations of sexual dependence, etc.

5) masturbation: some extremely interesting accounts of this relatively unknown subject were brought together. But it would require at least three hours for the witnesses summoned today to deal with these different subjects.

b) *The form of the issue*

It is the form that was the target of repression, undoubtedly because the issue doesn't fit into any pre-established category:

1) it's not an "art" book,

2) nor is it a porno magazine,

3) nor an erotic novel for the elite,

4) and nor is it a text that austerely presents itself as a scientific communication.

We dispensed here with the notions of an author and a work. When the examining judge asked me, for example, who had written this or that article, supposing I would even answer, I was not able to do so. More often than not, the articles were, in effect, made up of reports, discussions, and montages of text, which makes it impossible to determine individual responsibility! Even the layout was done collectively, and certain sentences were taken directly from graffiti! How can the law determine who is responsible! Rather than asking questions regarding the substance, one has opted for the ease of holding responsible: the legal director!

5) Is it irresponsible to allow people to speak, without precautions, without supporting documentation, and without a pseudo-scientific screen? (Even though scientific research, at a second level, works with documents as up to date.)

How otherwise to conceive of a study, whether it be in psychiatry, pedagogy, or in areas that concern justice?

Is it really dangerous to let people speak of things as they feel them, and with their language, their passions, their excesses?

Must we institute a police for dreams and fantasies? For what good do we suppress the public expression of popular spontaneity on the walls—or in the subways, as in New York ... How can we not understand that to forbid expression, on this level, is to favor a transition to actions that will present undoubtedly larger inconveniences to the social organization?

We think that the expression of desire is synonymous with disorder and irrationality.

But the neurotic order that forces desire to conform to dominant models perhaps constitutes the real disorder, the real irrationality.

It is repression that makes sexuality shameful and sometimes aggressive.

Desire that can open itself up to the world ceases to be destructive and can even become creative.

This trial is political. It makes a cause of a new approach to daily life, to desire, and the new forms of expression that have erupted since 1968.

Will we finally allow people to express themselves without having recourse to "representatives"? Will we allow them to produce their own journals, their own literature, theatre, cinema, etc?

Violence engenders violence.

If we repress the new forms of expression of social desire, we will head for absolute revolt, desperate reactions, even, indeed, for forms of collective suicide (as was, in certain respects, Hitlerian fascism).

Thus, it's for the judges to choose as well. Do they situate themselves, a priori, on the side of the dominant order?

Or are they capable of giving a hearing to another order that seeks to build another world?

14

I HAVE EVEN MET HAPPY DRAG QUEENS

The Mirabelles are experimenting with a new type of militant theatre, a theatre separate from an explanatory language, and long
tirades of good intentions, for example, on gay liberation. They
resort to drag, song, mime, dance, etc., not as different ways of illus-
trating a theme, to "change the ideas" of the spectators, but in order
to trouble them, to stir up uncertain desire-zones that they always
more or less refuse to explore. The question is no longer to know
whether one will play feminine against masculine or the reverse, but
to make bodies, all bodies, break away from the representations and
restraints of the "social body," and from stereotyped situations, attitudes and behaviors, of the "breastplate" of which Wilhelm Reich
spoke. Sexual alienation, one of capitalism's foundations, implies that
the social body is polarized in masculinity, whereas the feminine
body is transformed into an object of lust, a piece of merchandise to
which one cannot have access except though guilt and by submitting
to all the system's mechanisms (marriage, family, work, etc.). Desire,
on the other hand, has to manage as best it can. In fact it deserts
man's body in order to emigrate to the side of the woman, or more
precisely, to the becoming woman side. What is essential here is not
the object in question, but the transformational movement. It's this
movement, this passage, that the Mirabelles help us explore: a man
who loves his own body, a man who loves a woman's body or another
man's is himself always secretly characterized by a "becoming-woman."

This is, of course, much different than an identification to the woman, even less to the mother, as psychoanalysts would have us believe. Instead, it is a question of a different becoming, a state in order to become something other than that which the repressive social body has forced us to be. Just as workers, despite the exploitation of their work power, succeed in establishing a certain kind of relationship to the world's reality, women, despite the sexual exploitation which they undergo, succeed in establishing a true relationship to desire. *And they live this relationship primarily on the level of their bodies.* And if at the economic level the bourgeoisie is nothing without the proletariat, men aren't much where bodies are concerned, if they do not achieve such a becoming-woman. From whence comes their dependence on the woman's body or the woman image which haunts their dreams and their own bodies, or which they project onto their homosexual partner's body. From whence comes the counterdependence to which they try to reduce women or the predatory sexual behaviors which they adopt in regard to them. Economic and sexual exploitation cannot be dissociated. Bureaucracies and the bourgeoisie maintain their power by basing themselves on sexual segregation, age, classes, races, the codification of attitudes and class stratification. Imitation of these same segregations and stratifications by militants (for example, refusal to look closely at the concrete alienation of women and children, at possessive and dominating attitudes, at respect for the bourgeois separation of private life and public activity, etc.) constitutes one of the foundations of the present bureaucratization of the revolutionary workers' movement. Listening for the real desires of the people implies that one is capable of listening to one's own desire and to that of one's most immediate entourage. That doesn't at all mean that we should put class struggles way down on the ladder beneath desire struggles. On the contrary, each juncture between them will bring an unexpected energy to the former.

That is the "front" on which, with much modesty and tenacity, the Mirabelles work. But they especially don't want us to take them seriously; they are struggling for something more important than what is "serious." (Their motto: "Drag and monetary crisis. Drag green bean ...") What interests them is to help pull homosexuality out of its ghetto, even if it is a militant ghetto; what interests them is that shows like theirs touch not only homosexual circles, but also the mass of people who just don't feel good about themselves.

15

BECOMING-WOMAN

In the global social field, homosexualities function somewhat as movements, chapels with their own ceremonial, their initiation rites, their myths of love as Renée Nelli puts it.[1] Despite the intervention of groupings of a more or less corporatist nature like Arcadia, homosexuality continues to be tied to the values and interactional systems of the dominant sexuality. Its dependence in regard to the heterosexual norm is manifested in a politics of the secret, a hiddenness nourished by repression as well as by a feeling of shame still lively in "respectable" milieus (particularly among businessmen, writers, show-biz people, etc.) in which psychoanalysis is presently the reigning master. It enforces a second degree norm, no longer moral, but scientific. Homosexuality is no longer a moral matter, but a matter of perversion. Psychoanalysis makes an illness of it, a developmental retardation, a fixation at the pregenital stage, etc.

On another, smaller and more avant-garde level is found militant homosexuality, of the FHAR type. Homosexuality confronts heterosexual power on its own terrain. Now heterosexuality must account for itself; the problem is displaced, phallocratic power tends to be put into question; in principle, a conjunction between the actions of feminists and homosexuals then becomes possible.

However, we should perhaps distinguish a third level, a more molecular one in which categories, groupings, and "special instances" would not be differentiated in the same way, in which clear cut oppositions between types would be repudiated, in which, on the contrary, one would look for similarities among homosexuals, transvestites, drug addicts, sadomasochists, prostitutes, among women, men, children, teenagers, among psychotics, artists, revolutionaries, let's say among all forms of sexual minorities once it is understood that in this realm there could only be minorities. For example, it could be said, both at the same time: 1) that all forms of sexuality, all forms of sexual activity are fundamentally on this side of the personological oppositions homo-hetero; 2) that nonetheless, they are closer to homosexuality and to what could he called a feminine becoming.

On the level of the social body, libido is caught in two systems of opposition: class and sex. It is expected to be male, phallocratic, it is expected to dichotomize all values—the oppositions strong/weak, rich/poor, useful/useless, clean/dirty, etc.

Conversely, on the level of the sexed body, libido is engaged in a becoming-woman. More precisely, the becoming-woman serves as a point of reference, and eventually as a screen for other types of becoming (example: becoming-child in Schumann, becoming-animal in Kafka, becoming-vegetable in Novalis, becoming-mineral in Beckett).

Becoming-woman can play this intermediary role, this role as mediator vis-à-vis other sexed becomings, because it is not too far removed from the binarism of phallic power. In order to understand the homosexual, we tell ourselves that it is sort of "like a woman." And a number of homosexuals themselves join in this somewhat normalizing game. The pair feminine/passive, masculine/active therefore remains a point of reference made obligatory by power in order to permit it to situate, localize, territorialize, control intensities of desire. Outside of this exclusive bi-pole, no salvation: or else it's the plunge into the nonsensical, to the prison, to the asylum, to psychoanalysis, etc. Deviance, various forms of marginalism are themselves coded to work as safety valves. Women, in short, are the only official trustee of a becoming-sexed body. A man who detaches himself from the phallic types inherent in all power formations will enter such a becoming-woman according to diverse possible modalities. It is only on this condition, moreover, that he will be able to become animal, cosmos, letter, color, music.

Homosexuality, by the very nature of things, cannot be dissociated from a becoming-woman—even non-Oedipal, nonpersonological homosexuality. The same holds true for infantile sexuality, psychotic sexuality, poetic sexuality (for instance: the coincidence, in Allen Ginsberg's work, of a fundamental poetic mutation together with a sexual mutation). In a more general way, every "dissident" organization of libido must therefore be directly linked to a becoming-feminine body, as an escape route from the repressive *socius*, as a possible access to a "minimum" of sexed becoming, and as the last buoy vis-à-vis the established order. I emphasize this last point because the becoming-feminine body shouldn't be thought of as belonging to the woman category found in the couple, the family, etc. Such a category only exists in a specific social field that defines it. There is no such thing as woman per se, no maternal pole, no eternal feminine ... The man/woman opposition serves as a foundation to the social order, before class and caste conflicts intervene. Conversely, whatever shatters norms, whatever breaks from the established order, is related to homosexuality or a becoming-animal or a becoming-woman, etc. Every semiotization in rupture implies a sexualization in rupture. Thus, to my mind, we shouldn't ask which writers are homosexual, but rather, what it is about a great writer—even if he is in fact heterosexual—that is homosexual.

I think it's important to destroy "big" notions like woman, homosexual ... Things are never that simple. When they're reduced to black-white, male-female categories, there's an ulterior motive, a binary-reductionist operation meant to subjugate them. For example, you cannot qualify a love univocally. Love in Proust is never specifically homosexual. It always has a schizoid, paranoid component, a becoming-plant, a becoming-woman, a becoming-music.

Orgasm is another overblown notion whose ravages are incalculable. Dominant sexual morality requires of the woman a quasi-hysterical identification of her orgasm with the man's, an expression of symmetry, a submission to his phallic power. The woman *owes* her orgasm to the man. In "refusing" him, she assumes the guilt. So many stupid dramas are based on this theme. And the sentential attitude of psychoanalysts and sexologists on this point doesn't really help. In fact, it frequently happens that women who, for some reason or other, are frozen with male partners achieve orgasm easily by masturbating or having sex with another woman. But the scandal would be much worse if everything is out in the open. Let's consider a final example, the prostitute movement. Everyone, or just about, at first yelled "Hurrah, prostitutes are right to rebel. But wait, you should separate the good from the bad. Prostitutes, OK, but pimps, people don't want to hear about them." And so, prostitutes were told that they should defend themselves, that they're being exploited, etc. All that is absurd. Before explaining anything whatsoever, one should first try to understand what goes on between a whore and her pimp. There's the whore-pimp-money triangle. But there also is a whole micropolitics of desire, extremely complex, which is played out between each pole in this triangle and various characters like the John and the cop. Prostitutes surely have very interesting things to teach us about these questions. And, instead of persecuting them, it would be better to subsidize them, as they do in research laboratories. I'm convinced, personally, that in studying all this micropolitics of prostitution, one might shed some new light on whole areas of conjugal and familial micropolitics—the money relations between husband and wife, parents and children, and ultimately, the psychoanalyst and his patient. (We should also recall what the anarchists of the turn of the century wrote on the subject.)

IV

CINEMACHINES

16

CINEMA OF DESIRE

The history of desire is inseparable from the history of its repression. Maybe one day a historian will try to write a history of "cinemas of desire" (the way one tells an audience who express their sentiments too excitedly to "stop their cinema"). But, at the very least, he would have to begin this history with classical antiquity! It could start with the opening of the first big theater of international renown, a theater for captive cinephiles: Plato's cave. It would have to describe the 2000 years or so of the Catholic church's monopoly of production and distribution, as well as the abortive attempts of dissident societies of production, such as the Cathar cinema of the 12th century, or the Jansenist cinema of the 17th, up to the triumph of the baroque monopoly. There would be color film in it: with 10th century stained-glass windows would be the silent cinema of the "bepowdered" and the Pierrots. A special place should be reserved for the big schools that transformed the economy of desire on a long-term basis, like that of courtly love, with its four hundred troubadours who managed to "launch" a new form of love and a new kind of woman. It would have to appreciate the devastating effects of the great consortia of romanticism and their promotion of an infantilization of love, while awaiting the saturation of the market by psychoanalytical racketeering with its standard shorts for miniaturized screens: the little cinema of transference, Oedipus, and castration.

Power can only be maintained insofar as it relies on the semi-ologies of signification: "No one can ignore the law." This implies that no one can ignore the meaning of words. Linguists like Oswald Ducrot insist on the fact that language is not simply an instrument of communication, but also an instrument of power.[1] The law, as the culmination of sexual, ethnic, and class struggles, etc., crystallizes in language. The "reality" imposed by the powers-that-be is conveyed by a dominant semiology. Therefore, one should not go from a prin-cipled opposition between pleasure and reality, between a principle of desire and a principle of reality, but rather, from a *principle of dominant reality* and a *principle of licit pleasure*. Desire is forced to maintain itself, as well as can be expected, in this space between reality and pleasure, this frontier that power jealously controls with the help of innumerable frontier guards: in the family, at school, in the barracks, at the workshop, in psychiatric hospitals and, of course, at the movies.

Thus, desire is so ruthlessly hunted down that it usually ends up renouncing its objects and investing itself and its guardians on these boundaries. The capitalist eros will turn into a passion for the boundary, it becomes the cop. While bumping on the all-too-explicit signs of the libido, it will take its pleasure from their hateful contemplation. "Look at this filth." It will become the gaze, the forbidden spectacle, the transgression, "without really getting into it." All the morals of asceticism and sublimation consist, in fact, of capturing the libido in order to identify and contain it within this system of limits. I don't mean, here, to oppose centralism with spon-taneism, or the disciplines necessary for organizing the collectivity with the turbulence of the "natural" impulses; nor is it a matter of reducing this question to a simple case of morality or ideological strategy of dominant powers in order to better control the exploited ... The dualities morality/instinct, culture/nature, order/disorder, master/slave, centrality/democracy, etc., appear to us to be insufficient as a way of accounting for this eroticization of the limits, at least in its contemporary evolution.

The development of productive forces in industrialized societies (it is true both for capitalism and bureaucratic socialism) involves an increasing liberation of the energy of desire. The capitalist system does not function simply by putting a flux of slaves to work. It depends on modelling individuals according to its preferences and, for this purpose, to propose and impose models of desire: it puts models of childhood, fatherhood, motherhood, and love in circulation. It launches these models the same way the automobile industry launches a new line of cars. The important thing is that these models always remain compatible with the axiomatic of capital: the object of love should always be an exclusive object participating in the system of private ownership. The fundamental equation is: enjoyment = possession. Individuals are modelled to adapt, like a cog, to the capitalist machine. At the heart of their desire and in the exercise of their pleasure, they have to find private ownership. They have to invest it with ideality: "production for production's sake." They can only desire the objects that the market production proposes to them; they must not only submit to the hierarchy, but even more, love it as such. To conjure up the dangers of class struggle, capitalism has tried hard to introduce a bourgeois owner into the heart of each worker. It is the prerequisite of his integration. Traditional models that attached the worker to his job, to his quarter, to his moral values, indeed to his religion (even if it be socialism) have all collapsed. The paternalistic model of the boss is no longer compatible with production, no more than that of the *pater familias* with the education of children. One now needs a deterritorialized worker, someone who does not freeze into professional experience, but who follows the progress of technology, indeed, who develops a certain creativity, a certain participation. Moreover, one needs a consumer who adapts to the evolution of the market.

For this reason, the problem raised is the transformation of traditional relations of production and other relations—familial, conjugal, educational, etc ... But if one relaxes the brakes too abruptly, then it is the machines of desire that risk flying off the handle, and breaking not only through the outdated frontiers but even the new ones the system wants to establish. The relations of production, formation, and reproduction oscillate between immobilist temptations and archaic fixations. The capitalist "solution" consists in pushing models that are at once adapted to its imperatives of standardization—i.e., that dismantle traditional territorialities—and that reconstitute an artificial security; in other words, that modernize the archaisms and inject artificial ones. In conditions such as these, from the angle of production, the worker will be deterritorialized; from the angle of relations of production, formation, and reproduction, he will be reterritorialized.

Cinema, television, and the press have become fundamental instruments of forming and imposing a dominant reality and dominant significations. Beyond being means of communication, of transmitting information, they are instruments of power. They not only handle messages, but, above all, libidinal energy. The themes of cinema—its models, its genres, its professional castes, its mandarins, its stars—are, whether they want to be or not, at the service of power. And not only insofar as they depend directly on the financial power machine, but first and foremost, because they participate in the elaboration and transmission of subjective models. Presently, the media, for the most part, functions in the service of repression. But they could become instruments of liberation of great importance. Commercial cinema, for example, entertains a latent racism in its Westerns; it can prevent the production of films about events like those of May '68 in France; but the Super-8 and the videotape recorder could be turned into means of writing that are much more direct and much more effective than discourses, pamphlets, and brochures. As such they could contribute greatly to foiling the tyranny of the *savoir-écrire* that weighs not only on the bourgeois hierarchy but which operates also among the ranks of what is traditionally called the worker movement.

Beyond the signifier, beyond the illusion of a permanent reality. It's not a speculative option, but an affirmation: all reality is dated, historically, and socially situated. The order of the real has nothing to do with destiny; one can change it. Let us consider three modern currents of thought, vehicles of three systems of signification: totalitarian systems, psychoanalysis, and structuralism. In each case, there is a certain keystone on which the organization of the dominant reality converges. A signifier dominates every statement of a totalitarian power, a leader, a church, or God. By right, all desire must converge upon it. No one can remain with impunity across "the line" or outside the church. But this type of libidinal economy centered on a transcendent object no longer corresponds exactly to the necessities of modern production, and it tends to be replaced by a more flexible system in developed capitalist countries. In order to form a worker, one must start in the cradle, discipline his Oedipal development within the family, follow him to school, to sports, to the cinema, and all the way to the juke-box.

Psychoanalysis, while borrowing its own model from this traditional type of libidinal economy, has refined and "molecularized" it. It has put to task new types of less obvious objects—objects that anyone can buy, so to speak. These objects are supposed to overcode all the *énoncés* of desire: the phallus and the partial objects—breast, shit, etc ... From then on, the despotism of the signifier no longer tends to concentrate on a leader or a God and to express itself on the massive scale of an empire or a church, but on that of the family itself reduced to a state of triangularity. The struggle between the sexes, generations, and social classes has been reduced to the scale of the family and the self. The machine of familial power, rectified by psychoanalysis, functions by means of two primary parts: the symbolic phallus and castration, instruments of the alienation of woman and child. One recalls the tyrannical interrogation of Little Hans by his father under the supervision of Professor Freud. But before that, the mother's resistance must be subdued, compelling her to submit to psychoanalytical dogma. In fact, it never crosses her mind to object to her son's coming to join her in bed whenever he wants. The mother becoming the agent of phallic power, the attack on childhood is concentrated on the question of masturbation. One does not accuse him directly of masturbating; one imposes upon him the good, "castrating" explanation with regard to this question. One forces him to incorporate a particular system of signification: "What you desire—we know this better than you—is to sleep with your mother and to kill your father."

The importance of submitting the child to the Oedipian code—and this at an early age—does not result from a structural or signifying effect, separate from history or society. It depends on capitalism's inability to find other ways of providing the family with an artificial consistency. In archaic societies, the child was relatively free in his movements until his initiation. But in a capitalist society, initiation begins with the pacifier: the mother-child relationship tends to be more and more strictly controlled by psychologists, psychoanalysts, educators, etc. In its older formulation, power was maintained as a paradigmatic series—father-boss-king, etc., culminating in a discernible, incarnate, and institutionalized God. In its present formulation, incarnation is deterritorialized and decentered. It is everywhere and nowhere, and it depends on family models to arrange a refuge for it. But in their turn, the diverse psychoanalytic models of Oedipal triangulation appear too territorialized with regard to parental images and partial objects. Much more abstract, much more mathematical models of the unconscious have to be proposed.

Structuralism in psychoanalysis—as in other domains—can be thought of as an attempt to substitute a nameless God for the God of the church and the family. It proposes a transcendent model of subjectivity and desire that would be independent of history and real social struggle. From that moment, the conflict of ideas tends to be displaced anew. It leaves the psychoanalytical terrain of the family and the self for that of the semiotic and its applications in mass media. I cannot undertake here a critical analysis of structuralism; I only want to point out that, to my mind, such a critique should start by questioning the syncretic conception of the diverse modes of encoding. It seems to me indispensable, first of all, to avoid absorbing "natural" encodings, such as the genetic code, into human semiologies. One entertains the illusion that the "natural" order as well as that of the social arrangements (like structures of kinship) would be structured "like languages." Thus, one confuses the modes of encoding that I call *asemiotic*—like music, painting, mathematics, etc.—with those of speech and writing. Second, it seems necessary to distinguish between the presignifying semiologies—for example, of archaic societies, the insane, and children—and fully signifying semiologies of modern societies that are all over-coded in the writing of social and economic laws. In primitive societies, one expresses oneself as much by speech as by gestures, dances, rituals, or signs marked on the body. In industrialized societies, this richness of expression is attenuated; all *énoncés* have to be translatable to the language that encodes dominant meanings.

It is also important to expose and insist on the independence of an asignifying semiotics. It is this, in fact, that will allow us to understand what permits cinema to escape the semiologies of meaning and to participate in the collective arrangements of desire.[2]

If structuralism refuses to consider this independence, there can be no question of leaving the domain of signification—i.e., the signifier-signified duality. It tries, moreover, to systematically inject meaning into all signifying regimes that tend to escape it. (It will invent "relational significations" for science or, for the cinema, the unities of "iconomatic" significations, etc.) In putting the signifier and the signifying chains in the forefront, it substantiates the idea of keeping the contents at a secondary level. But, in fact, it secretly transfers the normalizing power of language onto the signifier. Hence, in masking the possible creativity of asignifying semiotic machines, structuralism plays into an order tied down to dominant significations.

When it is exploited by capitalist and bureaucratic socialist powers to mold the collective imaginary, cinema topples over to the side of meaning. Yet, its own effectiveness continues to depend on its presignifying symbolic components as well as its asignifying ones: linkages, internal movements of visual images, colors, sounds, rhythms, gestures, speech, etc. But unlike the speech and writing that, for hundreds, indeed, thousands of years, has remained pretty much the same as a means of expression, cinema has, in a few decades, never ceased to enrich its technique. In this way, to catch up with these effects, the powers-that-be have tried to increase the control they exercise upon it. The more it enlarges its scale of aesthetic intensities, the more the systems of control and censure have tried to subjugate it to signifying semiologies.

As an asignifying semiotic, how does cinema go beyond the structure of signifying semiologies? Christian Metz explains it better than I can; he shows that cinema is not a specialized language and that its *matter of content*[3] is undefined: "the breadth of its semantic fabric is a consequence of two distinct causes whose effects are cumulative. On the one hand, cinema encompasses a code—language, in the talkies—whose presence itself would be enough to authorize semantic information of the most varied type. Second, other elements of the filmic text, for example, images, are themselves languages whose matter of content has no precise boundaries."[4] Its matter of content extends so much more effectively beyond traditional encodings, since the semiotic alloy that composes its matter of expression is itself open to multiple systems of external intensities.

Its matters of expression are not fixed. They go in different directions. Christian Metz enumerates some of them, emphasizing that each has an intrinsic system of pertinent features:

1) the phonic fabric of expression, that refers to spoken language (signifying semiology);

2) the sonorous but nonphonic fabric that refers to instrumental music (asignifying semiotic);

3) the visual and colored fabric that refers to painting (mixed, symbolic, and asignifying semiotic);

4) the noncolored, visual fabric that refers to black and white photography (mixed, symbolic, and asignifying semiotic);

5) the gestures and movements of the human body, etc. (symbolic semiologies).

Umberto Eco had already pointed out that cinema does not bend to a system of double articulation, and that this had even led him to try to find a third articulation. But, doubtless, it is preferable to follow Metz who believes that cinema escapes all systems of double articulation, and, in my opinion, all elementary systems of significative encoding. The meanings in cinema are not directly encoded in a machine of intersecting syntagmatic and paradigmatic axes—they always come to it, secondarily, from external constraints that model it. If silent film, for example, had succeeded in expressing the intensities of desire in relation to the social field in a way that was much more immediate and authentic than that of the talkies, it was not because it was less expressive, but *because the signifying script had not yet taken possession of the image* and because, in these conditions, capitalism had not yet seized all the advantages it could take from it. The successive inventions of the talkies, of color, of television, etc., insofar as they enriched the possibilities of expressing desire, have led capitalism to take possession of cinema, and to use it as a privileged instrument of social control.

It is interesting, in this respect, to consider the extent to which television has not only not absorbed cinema, but has even subjected itself to the formula of commercial film, whose power, for this very reason, has never been so strong. In these conditions, the stakes of liberalizing pornographic film seem secondary to me. One remains here at the level of a sort of "negotiation" with the contents that do not really threaten the established powers. On the contrary, these powers find it expedient to release the ballast on a terrain that does not threaten the foundations of established order. It would be completely different if the masses were at liberty to make the kind of film they wanted, whether pornographic or not. The miniaturization of material could become a determining factor in such an evolution.[5] The creation of private television channels by cable should be a decisive test; in fact, nothing guarantees us that what will develop, from the standpoint of the economy of desire, will not be even more reactionary than what is broadcast by national television. Whatever it is, it seems to me that all that tends toward limiting micropolitical struggles of desire to an eros cut off from all context is a trap. And this doesn't just hold true for the cinema.

The capitalist eros, we said, is always invested on the limit between a licit pleasure and a codified interdiction. It proliferates alongside the law; it makes itself the accomplice of what is forbidden; it channels the libido to the forbidden object that it only touches on superficially. This economy of transgression polarizes the desiring-production in a game of mirrors that cut it from all access to the real and catches it in phantasmic representations. In this way, desiring-production never ceases to be separated from social production. Fantasized desire and the capitalist real which convert desire to "useful" work involve, apparently, two different types of arrangements. In fact, they involve two politics of desire that are absolutely complementary: a politics of reenclosure on the person, the self, the appropriation of the other, hierarchy, exploitation, etc., and a politics of passive acceptance of the world such as it is.

Against the notions of eros and eroticism, I would like to oppose those of desire and desiring-energy. Desire is not, like eros, tied down with the body, the person, and the law; it is no more dependent on the shameful body—with its hidden organs and its incestuous taboo—than to a fascination with and to myths about the nude body, the all powerful phallus, and sublimation. Desire is constituted *before* the crystallization of the body and the organs, *before* the division of the sexes, *before* the separation between the familiarized self and the social field. It is enough to observe children, the insane, and the primitive without prejudice in order to understand that desire can make love with humans as well as with flowers, machines, or celebrations. It does not respect the ritual games of the war *between* the sexes: *it is not sexual*, it is transsexual. The struggle for the phallus, the threat of an imaginary castration, no more than the opposition between genitality and pregenitality, normality and perversion, fundamentally concern it. Nothing essential leads to the subjugation of the child, the woman, or the homosexual. In a word, it is not centered on dominant significations and values: it participates in open, asignifying semiotics, available for better or worse. Nothing depends here on destiny, but on collective arrangements in action.

In conclusion, I must say of the cinema that it can be both the machine of eros, i.e., the interiorization of repression, and the machine of liberated desire. An action in favor of the liberty of expression should therefore not be centered a priori on erotic cinema, but on what I will call a cinema of desire. The real trap is the separation between erotic themes and social themes; all themes are at once social and transsexual. There is no political cinema on the one hand and an erotic cinema on the other. Cinema is political whatever its subject; each time it represents a man, a woman, a child, or an animal, it takes sides in the micro class struggle that concerns the reproduction of models of desire. The real repression of cinema is not centered on erotic images; it aims above all at imposing a respect for dominant representations and models used by the power to control and channel the desire of the masses. In every production, in every sequence, in every frame, a choice is made between a conservative economy of desire and a revolutionary breakthrough. The more a film is conceived and produced according to the relations of production, or modelled on capitalist enterprise, the more chance there is of participating in the libidinal economy of the system. Yet no theory can furnish the keys to a correct orientation in this domain. One can make a film having life in a convent as its theme that puts the revolutionary libido in motion; one can make a film in defense of revolution that is fascist from the point of view of the economy of desire. In the last resort, what will be determinant in the political and aesthetic plane is not the words and the contents of ideas, but essentially asignifying messages that escape dominant semiologies.

17

CINEMA FOU

Félix Guattari: What seems interesting to me with regard to this film, *Badlands* [1973, by Terence Malick], is that it shows us a story of *amour fou*, which is precisely what the critics did not see. I think that this makes people nervous. There are color elements, of blue, that are really agonizing throughout. It is a film about mad love and people refuse to accept these two dimensions of love and madness in combination. If there weren't all the murders, everything that makes one compare the film to *Billy the Kid*, *The Wild Bunch*, *Bonnie and Clyde*, etc., this would be an avant-garde film and it wouldn't get shown anywhere. In fact, the story is only there to support a schizophrenic journey. At every turn, we are on the edge of madness. It is this constant crossing of borders that seems perfectly conveyed to me. What the critics retained, in short, was the idea that this guy gets unhinged by dint of imitating James Dean. But things don't happen like that at all. The first thing that one has to realize is that the boy, Kit, should never be separated from the girl, Holly. They make up a sort of double arrangement. Certain behaviors of Holly belong to the schizo-process of Kit, although she herself is not schizophrenic. Conversely, certain behaviors of Kit belong to the completely avenge, normal world of Holly. Hence, it's absolutely impossible to separate the normal and the pathological. What is paradoxical is that the entire film is built around the idea that the guy is not really mad. The proof is that he goes to the electric chair. And yet, his madness, the fact that he has a screw loose, etc., is constantly alluded to. For her part, Holly is presented as a steady girl. For example, she says: "I'll never let myself get carried away with another daredevil again." Second negation after madness: love. We are shown a love story which is totally beyond stereotypes, a kind of extraordinary schizo love. For example, when Kit has just lulled Holly's father, she says to him, "Don't worry," and gives him a small slap that is both nagging and reassuring. Or again when they flick for the first time, Kit pretends to smash his hand, a typical schizo act. She tells him: "You're making fun of me, you don't care how I feel." But his indifference is only apparent; one senses he is so sure of his love that it never occurs to him to doubt her. It is only at the end of the film, when she ends up leaving him, that there is this very beautiful scene in which he angrily threatens to shoot her. But finally, he makes an imaginary rendezvous with her knowing full well he'll not see her again.

There are two ways of considering the world of schizo-desire: the infrapersonal level of desiring-machines—how the world is organized with systems of intensity of colors, impressions, appearances—and the suprapersonal level, in direct contact with the *socius*.

I picked out several elements in these two categories. The moment when he hits a can of food in the street, the moment when he's in love, and the moment when he listens to seashells and sees Holly coming as a white form. All this remains sort of "normal." But there is also the moment when he shoots at the fish, or shoots at the balloon, or shoots at the tires, and a series of completely bizarre behaviors such as the theme of the stones that one finds throughout the film. There are also explicitly crazy acts, acts of agony: when he kills Holly's father and puts his body in the basement, he takes up a toaster that reappears several times in the film; when he puts Cato's body in a cool place and begins turning round and round in a sort of military march with completely discordant gestures; and finally, when he makes a record and then burns it.

There are also scenes of schizo humor. At one moment he says: "We could have stopped the train by putting the car in front." And then there is this incredible scene when he locks up the two guys who come into Cato's house by accident. He shoots twice and says: "You think I got 'em? I don't want to know." Another high point of the film, in my opinion, is when, refering to the owner of a villa whom he has shut up with a deaf person, he says: "They were lucky, these two." At that point one realizes that, in fact, he remembers every detail, that he is not at all confused.

Another very important theme is the loss of objects. It begins in the closed off family circle, and then assumes a cosmic perspective when some objects float toward the sky in a balloon, when he buries other objects in the ground so that they can be found a few hundred years later. When things begin to go badly for him, Kit looks at other objects that he has kept in a suitcase and says to someone: "You can take them." He keeps a children's book. At the end of the film, he gives away his pencil, his pen, etc. It is like an expanding universe. It goes in every direction, this really is a schizo thing. All the coordinates, all the values explode all over the place. This starts with the fire which is a kind of schizo *jouissance* as well, a desire for annihilation.

Now, let us take some examples in the domain I called the suprapersonal level, in direct contact with the *socius*. The characters, for example, make reflections of the kind: "You see, we've made waves, the two of us." It is clear that what they are aiming at, then, is the stupidity of society, the stupidity of the police. It is the whole James Dean dimension, the whole paranoid dimension. He dumps on us all the trash about bounty hunters, the Commies, the atomic bomb ... Same thing when he reconstructs a camp, like one in Vietnam, when he speaks in the cassette recorder: one must follow the elders, etc. Completely reactionary ...

Libération: *You say "he is schizo," you say "he is reactionary."*

Schizo or paranoid, its of little importance; he is reactionary as soon as he enters the field of dominant significations. At the level of intensities, where you don't know if you are man, woman, plant, or whatever, you stand directly in relations of desire, the relations of love with Holly. One no longer knows who is who, or who speaks to whom. Everything becomes an interrelational fabric—the eyes, the machines, the gestures. At the level of asignifying connections that escape the everyday world, one identifies something, one says to oneself: "Here is a funny thing; yes, well, I didn't see it," and then one goes on to something else. At the level where significations solidify—"I am a cop; I am a man; you are a woman, hence you do not drive; you are a cop, I shoot you face-to-face; you are a bounty hunter, I shoot you from behind"—there are double-entry tables that serve to classify all people and roles. At this moment he is completely reactionary. He organizes his whole life in exact symmetry with the girl's father; he is as much of a bastard as the girl's father or the police. The schizo is an individual who can be in direct contact with the unconscious in the social field, but who can also function in a paranoid mode, openly seeing through the stupidity of the police: "You are so proud to have arrested me, you think you're heroes." He understands immediately. He is in the unconscious of others. He deciphers American society. Because in reality, he does not take himself at all for James Dean. It is the police, in fact ...

Yes, twice he is compared to James Dean. It is the girl at the beginning who says: "I liked him because he made me think of James Dean." It is the cops in the end, after having arrested him, who say: "You are like James Dean."

Yes, his favorite hero is I don't remember who.

He wants to be Nat King Cole. It is not at all the same as James Dean.

He wants to sing. That is the world of crystallized people. They are grimacing, like TV stars. But as soon as you go beyond that, then it is a marine or airy world, a world of intensities. One goes there because the air is purer; it is the sand, the colors, the caresses. They say (the critics) that he treats her like an animal. That's wrong, it's an absolutely marvellous love story.

There's another aspect of the film we have to talk about, the political aspect. The young cop who arrests him acts exactly like him.

Exactly. He arrests him, then he shoots at him just to be mean, to scare him.

It's the same type of stupidity. At a given moment, society becomes completely crazy. Because they are on the run, sheriffs accompany the kids to school; troops guard the central bank because there are rumors that they were going to attack it. Holly says: "It's as if we were Russians." It's a critique of American society.

In *Night of the Living Dead* there was the same mass phenomenon. Good Americans all go out with their guns and end up shooting this poor black guy who had nothing to do with anything.

At first, one doesn't have to see this guy as being crazy.

He is no more crazy at the beginning than at the end, or he is crazy all the time, it's just the way you look at it. *Amour fou* is madness no matter what. He says: "Me, I can lay all the girls, I have no problem, but you are something else"; or he says: "Besides, fucking, fucking, who cares? Yeah, yeah, it was very good." He doesn't give a shit for stories about fucking. No, it is really the story of a great love. A love that goes right through people. The father's on his back? Good, well, he shoots him. Too bad, he shouldn't have been there!

It's not like that, you're rigging the story a little. At the beginning, this guy is normal.

Absolutely not normal.

He's a poor bum, a garbage collector, and he is not so proud of it. Besides, when the girl asks him what he does, he says: "I'm afraid to get up early in the morning, so I work as a garbage collector," and then afterwards he's fired from his garbage job and works on a farm. He accepts the first job the employment agency offers him; he's the kind of guy who'll take anything, not a rebel in any way. He goes out with a girl and the father doesn't want him to go out with her because she shouldn't go out with a guy of his social class. Already there, society blunders. The father prevents him from seeing the girl. They see each other anyway. Then the father kills the girl's dog to punish her. This is the first act of madness in the film. It is the father who commits it. That's what the guy is up against. So what does he do, he goes to see the father and says to him: "Sir, I've a lot of respect for your daughter. I don't see why you won't let me see her, and if one day she no longer wants to see me, I'll let her go, I promise you, etc.," and the father tells him to piss off. Then, at that point, he goes to see the girl. No one is home, he ends up entering the house, but really by chance …

No, not at all. He says: "I figured everything out."

He thinks the girl is there.

He is armed, and he says, "I figured everything out." It triggers a kind of infernal machine of which he is the prisoner. It ends up going badly, but he already had figured it might go badly, because of taking the risk of entering the girl's house, of packing up and leaving and all that …

They all have guns in this film. That's where I really see the thing about American madness. There isn't a single guy who isn't armed. If he kills the father, it's in self-defense, because the father says to him: "You entered my house. I'm handing you over to the police for armed robbery." It's twenty years; he's got to kill the father.

I'm sorry, I don't agree with you. Let's be precise. He's as crazy at the beginning as at the end, neither more nor less. Madness coincides with the schizo journey, with *amour fou*. From the moment he sees the girl, a machine of *amour fou* is triggered. He manages to get fired from his job. He wants to see her again, but because she tells him, "I don't hang out with garbage collectors," he comes back with a proper job.

He doesn't improve. He goes to work and his boss tells him, "You're fired!"

Yes, but—you understand—it's one thing if the general framework unleashes behaviors of panic, of agony, of typical madness. It's a way of making clear what is already apparent from the beginning. Remember how he behaves at the beginning: "You want shoes? A dollar! You want to eat the dead dog? Give me a cigarette?" He says this to the guy with whom he picks garbage. Is all this nothing? Is it normal? All this is of no consequence. Remember, all of a sudden, he leaves: "Oh, shit. I've worked enough for today," etc. He is crazy all the time, if one looks closely. And Holly certainly knows it. Before agreeing to leave with him, she says to herself: "I love him, but he's totally crazy! How he treats me, he's weird."

Yes, she often says it. She says it to the rich guy; she says it to the girl he's going to kill ...

At the beginning, all this is of no consequence because nobody's bothering him. When passion and repression come along, it's a catastrophe, it's as if he had been put in an asylum. You take a guy who is a bit mad, you put him in an asylum, either you or me, and he becomes completely crazy!

We are shown the kind of society that makes this guy totally crazy. He's crazy and he makes the society crazy, and at the same time, he's the perfect cop, he is respectful of the established order.

There, I'm sorry, one must avoid a major misinterpretation. A paranoiac is not necessarily a reactionary.

Why is a paranoiac not a reactionary?

Because a guy who starts talking to you about Hitler, Joan of Arc, or whoever, he borrows, let's say, semiotic elements in the social field. He is no more reactionary than a kid who says: "I'll pull the head off my little brother," or "I'll kill mum," or who will do anything to annoy you. One cannot say that he is reactionary. The paranoiac-libido is so entangled in its molecular elements with the schizo-libido that it makes no sense to divide people into good or bad, reactionary or progressive. Kids in neighborhood gangs who wear Hitlerian insignia on their backs are not fascists; fascists are White Suprematists, they are structured organisms. It's a fact that representations of the *socius*, reactionary representations, are conveyed both in one and in the other. You find unconscious, reactionary elements of the *socius* in your dreams. Sometimes you also have disgusting dreams. You look for what is most rotten in the *socius*, but what you select are semiotic chains that are all put together outside. This does not mean that you are a fascist or that the dream is fascist, it proves nothing.

There is their madness, when one presses them. The father is not dead and the girl says: "Let's call the doctor." Then he says: "No, forget it." She says: "Yes, and I'll tell 'em what happened"—implying, of course, that if one tells what happened, nothing will happen, because when the others find out the way things happened, they'll realize he isn't guilty. And he replies: "That won't do," i.e., in any case they won't believe it. It's the system; it doesn't quite fit your interpretation.

Yes, but I was careful to say at the beginning …

… that the story was only there to make you accept the rest …

… because there is something that doesn't fit. Kit, after all, is a guy who's pretty together. In various circumstances, he shows that he's an excellent organizer. He panics at the scene of the first murder—that of the father—because he'd planned everything in order to leave with the girl. He took a gun, but hadn't foreseen that it might turn out like that. But then later he thinks things out in detail. There is always a bit of improvisation, but as far as the essential is concerned, nothing is left to chance. It is there that, in my opinion, the film blunders. The way the character has been defined, it's not at all obvious that he would end up shooting guys around like this, systematically. The second time with Cato is still understandable, because he is scandalized that Cato talks nonsense to him (the story of gold pieces buried in the fields, etc.). He is terribly angry, a shot is fired as happened with Holly's father. He is infuriated by all the bullshit. The other murders seem really forced to fit the story.

You don't say it's a film about a schizo. You say it's a schizo film.

It's a schizo film. I think critics don't tolerate things like this. They have to put this somewhere.

There is an interview with the author.

An interview? Where?

Here, in Positif, *I don't think he mentions the word "schizo" even once.*

There isn't a sentence where he says the guy is crazy? He doesn't realize it himself?

I don't think so. He says: "I thought of him and the girl as the sort of children you find in fairy tales; you see them in Huckleberry Finn, Swiss Family Robinson, *and* Treasure Island. *They're lost in nature, they only know how to react to what is inside themselves. They do not communicate with the external world, they do not understand what others feel. Which doesn't mean they have no emotions, or that they are insensitive."*

Yes, it's really stupid, it's terrible.

(He takes *Positif* and glances through it.)

This interview is really revolting. Yuk! It makes me puke!

18

THE POOR MAN'S COUCH

Psychoanalysts are always a little suspicious of film, or rather, they have always been attracted to other forms of expression. But the reverse is not true. The covert advances of film into psychoanalysis have been innumerable, beginning with Mr. Goldwyn's proposition to Freud: $100,000 to put the famous loves on screen. This asymmetry is due, no doubt, not only to matters of respectability; it is tied, even more fundamentally, to the fact that psychoanalysis understands nothing of the unconscious processes involved in cinema. Psychoanalysis has sometimes tried to seize on the formal analogies between dream and film—for René Laforgue, cinema is a sort of collective dream; for René Lebovici, a dream to make spectators dream. Psychoanalysis has tried to absorb filmic syntagms into the primary processes, but it has never figured out its specificity and for a good reason: a normalization of the social imaginary that is irreducible to familialist and Oedipal models, even on those occasions when it puts itself deliberately at their service. Psychoanalysis now inflates itself in vain with linguistics and mathematics; yet it also continues trotting out the same generalities about the individual and the family, while film is bound up with the whole social field and with history. Something important happens in cinema where fantastic libidinal charges are invested—for example, those clustered around certain complexes that constitute the racist Western, Nazism, and the Resistance, the "American way of life," etc. Sophocles no longer holds his own in all this. Film has become a gigantic machine for modelling the social libido, while psychoanalysis will forever remain a small cottage industry reserved for selected elites.

One goes to the cinema to suspend the usual modes of communication for a while. All the constitutive elements of this situation lead to this suspension. Whatever alienating character the content or form of expression of a film may have, it aims fundamentally at reproducing a certain type of behavior that, for lack of a better term, I will call cinematographic performance.[1] Because film is capable of mobilizing the libido on this type of performance, it can be used to serve what Mikel Dufrenne has called a "house unconscious."[2]

Considered from the standpoint of unconscious repression, the cinematographic performance and the psychoanalytical performance ("the analytical act") perhaps deserve to be compared. For too long, belle époque psychoanalysis has persuaded us it was liberating the instincts by giving them a language; in fact, it never intended loosening the vice of the dominant discourse except insofar as it reckoned on achieving even greater success than ordinary repression had ever done: to control, to discipline, to adapt people to the norms of a certain type of society. In the end, the discourse that is proffered in the analytical session is no more "liberated" than that served up in movie theaters. The so-called liberty of free association is only an illusion that masks a certain program, a secret modelization of statements (énoncés). As on the film screen, it is understood in analysis that no semiotic production of desire should have any effect on reality. The little playhouse of analysis and the mass analysis of film both proscribe the passage to action, to "acting out." Psychoanalysts, and even, in a way, filmmakers, would like to be considered as special beings beyond time and space: pure creators, neutral, apolitical, irresponsible ... and in a sense, they may be right, they hardly have a hold on the process of control of which they are the agent. The grid of the psychoanalytical reading belongs today as much to the analyst as to the analysand. It is tailor made for all and sundry—"hey, you made a Freudian slip"—it integrates itself with intersubjective strategies and even perceptive codes: one proffers symbolic interpretations like threats, one "sees" the phallus, the returns to the maternal breast, etc. The interpretation is so obvious that the best, the most assured strategy, for an alerted psychoanalyst, continues to be silence, a systematically sanctioned silence: pure analytical *écoute*, floating attention. In truth, the emptiness of the *écoute* answers here to a desire emptied of all content, to a desire for nothing, to a radical powerlessness, and it is not surprising, under such conditions, that the castration complex has become the constant curative reference, the punctuation of every sequence, the cursor that perpetually brings desire back to the bottom line. The psychoanalyst, like the filmmaker, is "carried" by his subject. What one expects from both is the confection of a certain type of drug that, though technologically more sophisticated than the ordinary joint or pipe, nonetheless functions by transforming the mode of subjectivity of those who use it: one captures the energy of desire in order to turn it against itself, to anaesthetize it, to cut it off from the external world in such a way that it ceases to threaten the organization and values of the dominant social system. Yet, the psychoanalytic drug and the cinematographic drug are not the same; overall, they have the same objectives, but the micropolitics of desire they involve and the semiotic arrangements they rely on are completely different.

One could assume that these criticisms only aim at a certain type of psychoanalysis and are not concerned with the present structuralist current, insofar as it no longer affirms the reliance of interpretation on paradigms of content—as was the case with the classic theory of parental complexes—but rather on an interplay of universal signifiers, independent of any meanings they may carry. But can one believe structuralist psychoanalysis when they claim to have renounced shaping and translating the production of desire? The unconscious of orthodox Freudians was organized in complexes that crystallized the libido on heterogeneous elements: biological, familial, social, ethical, etc. The Oedipal complex, for example, apart from its real or imaginary traumatic components, was founded on the division of the sexes and age groups. One would think it was a matter, then, of objective bases in relation to which the libido had to express and finalize itself, with the consequence that, even today, questioning the "evidence" appears completely inappropriate to some. And yet, everyone knows about numerous situations in which the libido refuses these so-called *objective bases*, where it eschews the division of the sexes, where it ignores prohibitions linked to the separation of age groups, where it mixes people together, as if for the sake of it, where it tends to systematically avoid exclusive oppositions of subjective and objective, self and other. Orthodox psychoanalysts believe that it is only a matter of perverse, marginal, or pathological situations requiring interpretation and adaptation. Lacanian structuralism was originally founded in reaction to these "abuses," to this naïve realism, particularly regarding questions about narcissism and psychosis. It intended to radically break with a curative practice uniquely centered on reshaping the self. But in denaturalizing the unconscious, in liberating these objects from an all-too-constraining psychogenesis, in structuring them "like a language,"[3] it hasn't succeeded in breaking its personological moorings or opening up to the social field, to cosmic and semiological flows of all kinds. One no longer submits these productions of desire to the whole battery of junk room complexes, yet one still claims to interpret each connection through the unique logic of the signifier. One has renounced summary interpretations of content ("the umbrella means ...") and the stages of development (the famous "returns" to oral, anal stages, etc.). It is no longer a question of the father and the mother. Now one talks about the "name of the father," the phallus, and the great Other of the symbolic castration, yet without getting one step nearer to the *micropolitics of desire* on which is founded, in each particular situation, the social differentiation of the sexes, the alienation of the child. As far as we are concerned, the struggles of desire should not just be circumscribed in the domain of the signifier—even in the case of a "pure" signifying neurosis, like obsessional neurosis. They always overflow into somatic, social, and economic domains, etc. And unless one believes the signifier is found in everything and anything, one may as well admit that the role of the unconscious has been singularly restrained in order to consider it only from the angle of the signifying chains it activates. "The unconscious is structured like a language," Lacan tells us. Certainly. But by whom? By the family, the school, the barracks, the factory, the cinema, and, in special cases, by psychiatry and psychoanalysis. When one has fixed it, succeeded in crushing the polyvocity of its semiotic modes of expression, bound it to a certain type of semiological machine, then yes, it ends up being structured like a language. It remains fairly docile. It starts speaking the language of the dominant system, which is, moreover, not everyday language, but a special, sublimated, psychoanalyzed language. Not only has desire come to accept its alienation within the signifying chains, but it keeps demanding more and more signifier. It no longer wants to have anything to do with the rest of the world and its modes of semiotization. Any troubling problem will find there, if not its solution, at least a comforting suspension in the interplay of the signifier. Under such conditions, what becomes, for example, of the age-old alienation of women by men? For the signifier, as it is conceived by linguists, only neutral and innocent traces such as the opposition of masculine/feminine, and for the psychoanalysts, the mirages that play around the presence/absence of the phallus. In fact, for each type of linguistic performance, for each "degree of grammaticality" of an *énoncé*, there is a corresponding formation of power. The structure of the signifier is never completely reducible to pure mathematical logic; it is always partly bound by diverse, repressive social machines. Only then can a theory of universals, both in linguistics and economics, in anthropology and psychoanalysis, be an obstacle to any real exploration of the unconscious, i.e., *all kinds* of semiotic constellations, connections of flows, power relations and constraints that constitute the arrangements of desire.

Structuralist psychoanalysis doesn't have much more to teach us about the unconscious mechanisms mobilized by film at the level of its *syntagmatic organization* any more than orthodox psychoanalysis has at the level of its *semantic contents*. On the contrary, film could perhaps help us to better understand the *pragmatic of unconscious investments* in the social field. In fact, the unconscious does not manifest itself in cinema in the same way it does on the couch: it partially escapes the dictatorship of the signifier, it is not reducible to a fact of language, it no longer respects, as the psychoanalytical transfer continued to do, the classic locutor-auditor dichotomy of meaningful communication. A question arises as to whether it is simply bracketed or whether there is any opportunity for reexamining the entirety of relations between discourse and communication. Communication between a discernible locutor and auditor is perhaps only a particular case, an extreme case, of the discursive exercise. The effects of desubjectivation and deindividuation produced by the *énoncé* in cinema or in such arrangements as drugs, dreaming, passion, creation, delirium, etc., are perhaps not as exceptional as one would think in relation to the general case that "normal" intersubjective communication and "rational" consciousness of the subject object relationship is supposed to be. It's the idea of a transcendent subject of enunciation that is being questioned here, as well as the opposition between discourse and language (*langue*) or, even more, the dependence of diverse types of semiotic performance in relation to a so-called universal semiological competence. The self-conscious subject should be considered a particular "option," a sort of normal madness. It is illusory to believe there exists only *one* subject—an autonomous subject, centered on one individual. One never has to do with a multiplicity of subjective and semiotic modes of which film, in particular, can show how they are orchestrated, "machinated," and infinitely manipulated. But if it is true that the machinic expansion, the exaltation of the cinematographic unconscious, does not protect it—far from it—from contamination by the significations of power, the fact remains that, with it, things do not happen in the same way as with psychoanalysis or with even better-policed artistic techniques. And this all depends on the fact that it manifests itself through semiotic arrangements irreducible to a syntagmatic concatenation that would discipline it mechanically, structure it according to a rigorously formalized pattern of expression and content. Its montage of asignifying semiotic chains of intensities, movements, and multiplicities fundamentally tends to free it from the signifying grid that intervenes only at a second stage, through the filmic syntagmatic that fixes genres, crystallizes characters and behaviorial stereotypes homogeneous to the dominant semantic field.[4]

This "excess" of the matters of expression over the content certainly limits a possible comparison between cinema and psychoanalysis with respect to repressing the unconscious. Both fundamentally lead to the same politics, but the stakes and the means they resort to are quite different. The psychoanalyst's clientele acquiesces to the whole enterprise of semiotic reduction, while cinema must permanently stay attuned to the social imaginary's mutations just to "stay in the race." It also has to mobilize a real industry, a multiplicity of institutions and powers capable of getting the better of the unconscious proliferation it threatens to unleash. Spoken language itself does not function in film the same way it does in psychoanalysis; it isn't the law, it constitutes but one way among others, a single instrument at the core of a complex semiotic orchestration. The semiotic components of film glide by each other without ever fixing or stabilizing themselves in a deep syntax of latent contents or in the transformational system that ends up with, on the face of it, the manifest content. Relational, emotive, sexual significations—I would prefer to say intensities—are constantly transported there by heterogeneous "traits of the matter of expression" (to borrow a formula that Christian Metz himself borrowed from Hjelmslev). The codes intertwine without one ever succeeding in dominating the others; one passes, in a continual back and forth, from perceptive codes to denotative, musical, connotative, rhetorical, technological, economic, sociological codes, etc …

Commercial cinema is nothing else but a simple, inexpensive drug. Its unconscious action is profound. More perhaps than that of psychoanalysis. First of all at the level of the session. Cinematographic performance affects subjectivity. It affects the personological individuation of enunciation and develops a very particular mode of conscience. Without the support of the other's existence, subjectivation tends to become hallucinatory; it no longer concentrates on *one* subject, but explodes on a multiplicity of poles even when it fixes itself on one character. Strictly speaking, it doesn't even concern a subject of enunciation in the usual sense—what is emitted by these poles is not simply a discourse, but intensities of all kinds, constellations of features of faciality, crystallizations of affects … It reaches the point where one no longer knows who is speaking or who is who.

The roles are much better defined in psychoanalysis, and the subjective transitivity much better controlled. In fact, one doesn't stop using the *discourse of the analyst*: one says what one thinks someone would like to hear, one alienates oneself by wanting to be worthy of the listener. In cinema, one no longer speaks; *it* speaks in one's place: the cinematographic industry uses the kind of speech it imagines one wants to hear.[5]

A machine treats you like a machine, and the essential thing is not what it says, but the sort of vertigo of abolition that the fact of being "machinized" provides for you. With people dissolving and things passing unwitnessed, one abandons oneself to a guilt-free world. While on the couch one pays to have a witness (preferably someone distinguished, someone of clearly higher standing than oneself) invest and control your most intimate thoughts and sentiments, at the movies one pays to be invaded by subjective arrangements with blurry contours in order to give in to adventures that, in principle, have no lasting effects. "In principle," because the modelization resulting from this cheap sort of vertigo is not without tell-tale traces: the unconscious finds itself populated by cowboys and indians, cops and robbers, Belmondos and Monroes ... It's like tobacco or cocaine; one cannot trace its effects (even if that were possible) unless one is already completely hooked.

But wasn't the psychoanalytical cure instituted precisely to avoid such promiscuity? Wasn't the function of interpretation and transfer to saturate and select the good and the bad in the unconscious? Isn't it the point that the patient be guided, helped by a safety net? Certainly. But in reality this net is more alienating than any other system of subjectivity-control. Upon leaving the movie house, one has to wake up and quietly put on one's own film reel (the entire social reality is devoted to it), while the psychoanalytic session, becoming interminable, overflows into the rest of life. Going to the movies, as one says, is an entertainment, while the analytical cure—and it is true even for neurotics—tends to be a sort of social promotion: it is accompanied by the sentiment that in the end one will be a specialist of the unconscious—a specialist, moreover, as bothersome for the whole entourage as any other specialists whatsoever, beginning with those of film.

Alienation by psychoanalysis depends on the fact that the particular mode of subjectivation that it produces is organized around a subject-for-an-other, a personological subject, over-adapted, overindebted to the signifying practices of the system. The cinematographic projection, for its part, deterritorializes the perceptual and deictic coordinates.[6] The semiotic taste buds of the unconscious haven't even been titillated before the film, as a manufactured work, starts conditioning them to the semiologic paste of the system. The unconscious, as soon as it is exposed, becomes like an occupied territory. Cinema, in the end, has taken the place of ancient liturgies. Its function is to renovate, adapt, and assimilate the ancient gods of bourgeois familialism. The religion it serves borrows the language of "normal" communication that one finds in the family, at school, or at work. Even when it seems to give the "normal" character, a man, woman, or child a chance to speak, it is always, in reality, a reconstitution, a puppet, a zombie-model, an "invader" who is ready to be grafted onto the unconscious in order to dominate it. One doesn't go to the cinema with one's ego, one's childhood memories, the way one goes to a psychoanalyst. One accepts in advance that it robs us of our identity, our past and our future. Its derisive miracle is to turn us, for a few moments, into orphans: single, amnesiac, unconscious, and eternal. When, upon leaving, we take up our "daily" reflexes again, when we find the faces of our loved ones closed in on themselves again, we may be tempted to prolong the impression produced by the film, if it has touched us. It is even possible for a film to upset our whole existence. In truth, a film that could shake itself free of its function of adaptational drugging could have unimaginable liberating effects, effects on an entirely different scale from those produced by hooks or literary trends. This is due to the fact that cinema intervenes directly in our relations with the external world. And even if this exterior is contaminated by dominant representations, a minimal aperture could result from this intervention. Psychoanalysis suffocates us—with considerable luxury, it is true—it shuts off our relation to the external world in what is most singular, most unpredictable, by projecting the cinema of interiority onto it. Whatever its stereotypes, its conformisms, cinema is overflowing with the richness of its expressive means. In this regard, everyone knows how the work of film is prolonged, sometimes directly, in that of the dream (I have shown that this interaction was all the stronger the weaker the film seemed to be).

Commercial cinema is undeniably familialist, Oedipian, and reactionary. But it is not intrinsically so, the way psychoanalysis is. It is so "on top of everything else." Its "mission" is not to adapt people to outdated and archaic elitist Freudian models, but to those implied by mass production. Even, it should be stressed, when they reconstitute archetypes of the traditional family. While its "analytic" means are richer, more dangerous, because more fascinating than those of psychoanalysis, they are, in fact, more precarious and more full of promise. And if one can imagine another film praxis being constituted in the future, a cinema of combat attacking dominant values in the present state of things, one can hardly see how a revolutionary psychoanalysis could possibly emerge.

In fact, the psychoanalytic unconscious (or the literary unconscious, since they derive one from the other) is always a secondhand unconscious. The discourse of analysis is shaped by analytical myths: individual myths themselves have to adapt to the framework of these reference-myths. Cinematic myths do not have at their disposal such a metamythic system, and the gamut of semiological means they do mobilize directly connects with the spectator's processes of semiotization. In a word, the language of cinema and audio-visual media is alive, while that of psychoanalysis has, for a long time now, spoken a dead language. One can expect the best or the worst from cinema. From psychoanalysis, nothing but a soothing yet hopeless purring. In the worst commercial circumstances, good films can still be produced, films that modify the arrangements of desire, that "change life," while, for quite some time now, there have been no worthwhile psychoanalytic sessions, discoveries, books.

19

NOT SO MAD

Cinématographie: *What do you make of the new interest that the media, and particularly film, bring to the problem of madness?*

Félix Guattari: I don't think that this interest is completely new. Numerous films in the history of cinema have tackled this "problem." But the audience of these films, perhaps, has expanded. For example, the audience for *Asylum* has been substantial and has indirectly revealed an antipsychiatric current. The same was already true of *Family Life.*

Where does this expanded audience come from, and what does the public want?

There are perhaps two sets of phenomena. First, a certain taste for a morbid aspect—not of madness, but of what one thinks of as madness: this is part of the same "modelling" system, the "popular" taste that one finds in detective or certain porno flicks. So, from this angle, nothing new. But one can also put forth the hypothesis that society is presently being racked by a whole series of "molecular" disturbances that are not yet visible on a large scale; it is shaped by transformations that effect basic institutional systems—schools, prisons, couples, women, immigrants, the mentally ill, homosexuals … Long before certain spectacular uprisings occurred as in the university in 1968 or in prisons, a whole underground was operating, a whole new sensibility was searching for itself. I get the impression that the general crisis in psychiatry, before it expressed itself on a large scale, started to shape opinions at all levels. It was in this context that filmmakers began to get interested in it.

What do you think of the fact that Fous a délier [Not So Mad] *came out when the second round of meetings of the International Anti-Psychiatry Network were being held?*

The "Bastille Day" team came asking us what sort of film we would like to have shown during these international meetings. The film of the Parma and Bellochio teams corresponded so well to the whole orientation of the Network that it served in some ways as an introduction for us. What's it all about? Until now, criticisms of psychiatry had come from madness "professionals": from psychiatrists, nurses, or, less often, ex-patients. But often the language of these "specialists" was incomprehensible to the public at large, and sometimes, it must be said, it was counterdependent upon the system itself. What is extraordinary about *Fous a délier* is that it is the people involved who really get the opportunity to speak. Its success is a credit to the "cinema of combat." I even think they expressed themselves better here than they could have done using some other mode of communication. I don't know how the Bellochio team succeeded in working so well with the different groups that speak in *Fous a délier*: children, educators, psychiatrists, militant groups; they always give the best of themselves. It's a small miracle; for once one does not have the feeling one is being presented with another "documentary"; people speak here in a way one is not used to hearing.

How is such a result possible?

I don't know. But there is obviously a whole new technology that is being experimented with, and this at all levels of production. Members of the Bellochio team explained, for example, that each sequence, each shot, was collectively discussed during the editing. It's up to the film people to answer your question. But it seems to me that what was achieved in this film goes far beyond the problems of psychiatry. Until now, cinema of mass distribution, or commercial cinema, has functioned like an enterprise of mystification, of enlistment, that consists in making people absorb, willingly or by force, dominant representations. But here, all of a sudden, one has the impression it is just the reverse, that a cinema of the masses can become a form of expression and struggle that is even more effective than discourses, meetings, pamphlets …

After having seen Fous a délier *I wonder if it isn't abnormal to want to return such patients to work, since it is work, in fact, that alienates.*

You are right. In France today, certain organizations attempt to "readapt by work" (according to American methods of conditioning) the mentally retarded, the insane, the handicapped. At Sainte-Anne's Hospital, "scientific" methods of conditioning are also experimented with. There is a major danger here: to think that work as such can be therapeutic is absurd. What is at issue in *Fous a délier* is completely different. The workers of Parma express themselves very clearly on this point: they don't believe that work is the issue, but the fact that all these marginal types have the chance to become people like everyone else. It is not the work that allows them to be this way, it is the relations they succeed in establishing with the workers. It is the human warmth of these relations that is so well conveyed in the film.

Does cinema appear to you to be a minor art?

Yes, if one specifies that a "minor" art is an art that serves people who constitute a minority, and that it is not at all pejorative. A major art is an art at the service of power. Hence, I wonder if a certain number of films like *Fous a deliér*, *Ce gamin-là*, *Coup pour coup*, *La Ville bidon*, *Paul's Story*, *Asylum* do not announce a new era in the history of cinema. A minor cinema for minorities, in one form or another, and for the rest of us, too: we all participate in one of these minorities, more or less. Perhaps now a potential public exists that could encroach on the terrain of cinematographic distribution controlled by the big industry. Some spectacular successes have shown that the public wants more than what it is habitually presented with. Perhaps a large proportion of the public would be attracted to a new cinema, but only on condition that filmmakers manage to get away from an elitist style, a language either completely cut off from the public, or completely demagogical.

V

SCHIZO-CULTURE
IN NEW YORK

20

MOLECULAR REVOLUTIONS

There are a number of things I would like to share and discuss with you now, but I get the feeling that I could talk about absolutely anything—my private life, how I vote—except desire or revolution. They would seem truly obscene here at Columbia University.*

It has reached the point where I wonder if one wouldn't really have to be a member of the CIA in order to undertake such a thing.[1] There is something like a CIA virus here that seems to have contaminated many people and that keeps reoccuring at different times, and I can't help asking myself whether I haven't caught the bug.

If one could get beyond these walls or though this muffling that constitutes a sort of wall of sound within the university, I think one might begin to recognize that the world crisis is accelerating at a considerable pace. Am I simply caught up in an accelerating schizo-process? For some years now we have been experiencing a process comparable to that of 1929—a full range of regional conflicts, of local political confrontations, of economic crises. There are no extreme, salient characters of a Hitler or Mussolini magnitude on the political scene right now, yet extermination camps do exist. The entire country of Bangladesh is such a camp; thousands, tens of thousands of people are dying there, or on the verge of it, because they are locked in a particular economic situation, which results from

---

* Guattari is addressing here the Schizo-Culture Conference organized by Semiotext(e) in November 1975 at Columbia University.

a specific governmental policy, and no alternatives exist except being exterminated. I do believe that a whole series of factors are leading to an absolute crisis at all levels of social organization throughout the world. This situation should call for revolutionary solutions, but nothing, no one, no organization is prepared to deal with it and its imperatives. The obscene thesis I wish to defend before you now is this: all these organizations—Bolshevik, Marxist-Leninist, Communist, Spontaneist (in one form or another), Social Democratic—are missing an essential aspect of this revolutionary struggle and its development.

There are two ways of rejecting the revolution. The first is to refuse to see it where it exists; the second is to see it where it manifestly will not occur. These are, in a nutshell, the reformist and the dogmatic pathways. Indeed, a revolution of great amplitude is developing today, but at the molecular or microscopic level.

I believe that this molecular revolution can only develop in a parallel way with the general, political crisis. Some people say that the social turmoil in the United States during the 1960s, or in France in '68, was a spontaneist event—transitory, marginal—and that such a utopian revolution leads nowhere. But in my opinion, important things began happening only *after* that revolution, which perhaps was the last revolution in the old style. Molecular revolution develops in relatively unknown areas. Gilles Deleuze was just telling us[2] there isn't much to try to understand. We see students rebelling, playing at the barricades. We see teenagers changing life in the high schools. We see prisoners setting half the French prisons on fire. We see the President of the French Republic shaking hands with the prisoners. Women's revolts are moving in all sorts of directions, at many levels: against inherited politics, on the problem of abortion, on the question of prostitution. We see the struggles of immigrants or ethnic minorities, the struggle of homosexuals, of drug users, of mental patients. We even find previously unimaginable social categories being mobilized in France, for example some judges ...

When we put this all together on the table, side by side, we may ask: what does all this have in common? Can we use all this to start a revolution? Does this have anything to do, for example, with what is going on right now in Portugal, where officers of the colonial army are playing the Cohn Bendits?[3] We can certainly dismiss these phenomena as marginal, try to recoup them as excess force, which is precisely the attitude most of the groupuscules have; or—and this is my hypothesis—we can assume that the molecular revolution of which I spoke is located and developing here in an irreversible manner and that each time these movements fail because the old forms and structures of organization take power, holding the rhizomatic element of desire in a system of arborescent power. Therefore, the main question for me is a radical change of attitude with regard to political problems. On the one hand, there are the "serious" things one sees in the papers, on television—the questions of power in the parties, the unions, the groupuscules. On the other hand, there are the little things, the things of private life: the militant's wife who stays at home to look after the children, the petty bureaucrat making deals in the corridors of Congress—these are at the root of most political schisms and assume a programmatic aspect, but are invariably linked to the phenomena of bureaucratic investment and the special caste that runs these organizations.

I believe that revolutionary movements, whatever they may be, do not change their orientation because of ideology. Ideology does not weigh very heavily compared to the libidinal trafficking that effectively goes on among all these organizations. It all comes to the same thing: either political objectives are the echo of all kinds of struggles, and are associated with an analysis of the phenomena of desire and of the social unconscious within the present organizations, or else the bureaucratic impasses and recuperations will necessarily recur, the desire of the masses and of interest groups will go through representatives, and result from a representation.

We all have experienced these kinds of militant initiatives. We should be able to understand why things work that way, why desire is being delegated to representatives and bureaucrats of all kinds, why revolutionary desire is turned into organizational microfascism.

Certainly there must be a more powerful investment that comes to replace revolutionary desire. My explanation, provisionally, arises from the fact that capitalist power is not only exercised in the economic domain and through the subjugation of class, nor is it exercised only through police, foremen, teachers, and professors, but also on another front which I would call the *semiotic subjugation* of all individuals. Children begin learning about capitalism in the cradle, before they have access to speech. They learn to perceive capitalist objects and relations on television, through the family, in the nursery. If they somehow manage to escape semiotic subjugation, then specialized institutions are there to take care of them: psychology, psychoanalysis, to name but two.

Capitalism cannot successfully put together its work force unless it proceeds through a series of semiotic subjugations. The difficult thing—and one that raises a basic theoretical problem—is how to conceive the articulation and unification of struggles on all these fronts: the front of traditional political and social struggle; the liberation of oppressed ethnic groups and regions; linguistic struggles; struggles for a better neighborhood, for a more communal way of life; struggles to change family life or whatever takes the place of it; struggles to change modes of subjugation that recur in couples, whether heterosexual or homosexual. I put all these struggles under the term "microfascist," although I don't particularly like it. I use it simply because it startles and annoys people. There is a microfascism of one's own body, of one's organs, the kind of bulimia that leads to anorexia, a perceptual bulimia that blinds one to the value of things, except for their exchange value, their use value, to the expense of the values of desire.

This raises an important theoretical question, a question that, for me, Deleuze, and several others, has changed somewhat lately. We thought the most formidable enemy was psychoanalysis because it reduced all forms of desire to a particular formation, the family. But there is another danger, of which psychoanalysis is but one point of application: it is the reduction of all modes of semiotization. What I call *semiotization* is what happens with perception, with movement in space, with singing, dancing, mimicry, caressing, contact, everything that concerns the body. All these modes of semiotization are being reduced to the dominant language, the language of power which coordinates its syntactic regulation with speech production in its totality. What one learns at school or in the university, is not essentially a content or data, but a behavioral model adapted to certain social castes.

What you require of your students before all else when you make them take an exam is a certain style of semiotic moulding, a certain initiation to the given castes. This initiation is all the more brutal in the context of manual formation, with the training of workers. Exams, the movement from position to position in factory work, always depend on whether one is Black, Puerto Rican, or raised in a well-to-do neighborhood, whether one has the right accent, is a man or woman. There are signs of recognition, signs of power that operate during instructional formation, and they are veritable rites of initiation. I have taken the example of the university, I could easily have taken examples from many other formations of power.

Dominant power extends the semiotic subjugation of individuals unless the struggle is pursued on every front, particularly those of power formations. Most people don't even notice this semiotic subjugation; it's as though they do not want to believe it exists, yet this is what political organizations with all their bureaucrats are about; this is what contributes to create, engender, and maintain all forms of recuperation.

There is something that interests me very much in the United States. It has been happening for a number of years, notably with the Beat generation, and is probably due to the very acuteness of the problems concerning the semiotics of the body, of perception. This is much less true in Europe where one is tied down to a certain intellectualist conception of relations and of the unconscious. The various rationalizations or justifications that are given here for reintroducing a semiotics of the body interest me less. Some involve Zen Buddhism, or various forms of technology, like the Tai Chi that was being done just now on the stage ... It seems to me that something is being sought there in some sort of blind way. Blindness takes multiple forms. In France, for example, we have networks of gurus in psychoanalytic societies; we even have a personality like Reverend Moon heading an important psychoanalytic organization. But psychoanalysis only involves a particular set of people. In the United States, apparently, the virus of psychoanalysis has been more or less averted, but I sometimes wonder if its hierarchical systems aren't reproduced in the systems of gurus, the systems for representing desire.

The problem is this: one cannot strive toward a political objective without identifying as well all the microfascisms, all the modes of semiotic subjugation of power that reproduce themselves through that struggle, and no myth of a return to spontaneity or to nature will change anything. However naïvely one assumes to be innocent in this regard, whether in relation to our children, our partner, or our students (for professors), I believe this innocence is equivalent to guilt and engenders guilt. The question is neither of innocence or guilt but of finding the microfascism one harbors in oneself, particularly when one does not see it. The last thing I would want to bring up here, of course, is that it can receive an individual solution. It can only be dealt with a new type of *arrangement of enunciation*. One example of these arrangements of enunciation—an impossible, truly awful arrangement from the vantage point of the arrangements of desire—is that of this room itself, with some individual raised above everyone else, with a prepared discussion which would make it impossible for anyone really to start a discussion. Yesterday I proposed changing the whole format, the whole type of work we are doing here, and to my great surprise, I realized that everyone wanted the conference to remain as it was. Some people even asked for their money back, although no one here was being paid to speak.[4]

At various times there were attempts to produce this kind of dialogue. The only people who came forward to try and start a dialogue—completely phony, but full of real desire—were those who falsely accused us of being CIA agents.

As one invests in the libidinal economy of the micropolitics of desire, of microfascism, so must one precisely identify the alliances and possibilities that exist concretely at the level of political struggles and which are completely different in nature. I once told Jean Jacques Lebel, regarding his workshop on Portugal, that the judgment one makes concerning the attitude of the Portuguese Communist Party is necessarily different from Spinola's and his own, and yet the mechanisms of bureaucratization and the ignorance about the desire of the masses are comparable in both cases.

Another example. In France we have some groups, gangs of people who wear swastikas on their backs and who walk around covered with all sorts of fascist insignia. Yet one should not confuse their microfascism with the fascism of political groups like Occident, etc. To the extent that one fights microfascism at the molecular level, one can also prevent it from happening at the level of large political groups. If one believes that each one of us is immunized against microfascist contamination, against semiotic contamination by capitalism, then we can surely expect to see unbridled forms of macrofascism well up.

21

DESIRE IS POWER, POWER IS DESIRE

Answers to the Schizo-Culture Conference

Félix Guattari: After a systematic attack (at least I think so) on psychoanalysis, Gilles Deleuze and I began asking ourselves about the linguistic and semiotic conceptions underlying formations of power in psychoanalysis, in the university, and in general.

A sort of generalized suppression of what I call the *semiotic components of expression* takes place in a certain type of writing, such that even when people speak, they speak as if they were writing. At the same time, the rules of their speech not only depend on a certain syntax, but on a certain *law of writing*.

Unlike primitive societies, our society doesn't think much of speech—only writing, writing that is signed, attested. Subjugation in capitalist societies is basically a semiotic subjugation linked to writing. Those who escape writing give up any hope of survival. They end up in specialized institutions. Whether at work or in any other area of life, one must always make sure that the semiotic modes one uses relate to a phenomenon of the law of writing. If I make a gesture, it must relate to a text that says: "Is it appropriate to make this gesture at this point?" If my gesture is incoherent, there will be, as in a computer, some written or digitalized device that will say: "This person may be mad, or drugged, perhaps we should call the police, or maybe he is a poet: that individual belongs to a certain society and should be referred to a written text." I think, therefore, that the problem posed in this colloquium—

whether to read certain texts or not—is basically a problem of the formation of power that goes beyond the university.

Question: *Doesn't this relate to what Antonin Artaud said about the written text?*

Absolutely. Artaud understood theater and cinema in their multiplicity of semiotic components. Most of the time a film is based on a written text, a script, and the plastic and aural elements are referred to, and alienated from, the text.

Isn't it more a question here of linearity rather than of writing, strictly speaking?

Certainly, or what could be called digitalization, putting everything into digits.

Is the problem of linearity specific to capitalism, or is there a form of writing specific to capital?

Yes, I believe so. The whole evolution of systems of enunciation tends toward the individuation of enunciation and toward the degeneration of collective arrangements of enunciation. In other words, one moves toward a situation where the entirety of complex systems of expression—as in dance, tattoo, mime, etc.—is abandoned for an individuation that implies the position of a speaker and an auditor, such that the only thing that remains of a communication is the transmission of information quantified in "bits." Yet, in another arrangement, the essence of communication is a communication of *desire*. A child who plays, or a lover who courts someone, does not transmit information, he creates a richly expressive situation in which a whole series of semiotic components are involved.

Capitalism refuses to take these components into consideration; what it wants is: 1) people to express themselves in a way that confirms the division of labor; 2) desire to be only expressed in a way that the system can recoup, or only if it is linearized, quantified in systems of production. A number of people here have remarked that linearization is the best way of transmitting data for a given purpose, even in genetic systems. For example, consider what happens in a primitive society when a purchase is made. The purchase is often a body linked to interminable discussions; it is more often like a donation, even though it is presented as an exchange. Today, shopping ideally demands that the salesperson behaves like a computer. Even if the salesperson is someone affable, and displays all the iconic components of seduction, she nonetheless seduces according to a precise code. Her skirt must be a certain length, her smile artificial, etc. The best way for capitalism to insure semiotic subjugation is to encode desire in a linear way. Whether in a factory or a bank, capitalism does not want people who bring the totality of what they are, with their desire and their problems. One doesn't ask them to desire, to be in love, or to be depressed; one asks them to do the work. They must suppress what they feel, what they are, their entire perceptive semiotics, all their problems. To work in capitalist society implies isolating the usable quantity of semiotization which has a precise relation to a law of writing.

That's questioning capitalism in an extremely broad sense.

Clearly, one must also include bureaucratic socialism.

To take up the question of linearity again, what consequence follows, according to you, from the critique and rejection of the Oedipal triangle in Lacan? What is the impact of such a critique in terms of revolutionary action; not just as critical exegesis, but as intellectual praxis?

To me, the Lacanian definition of the unconscious seems particularly pertinent if one remembers that it forgets the unconscious of the capitalist socialist bureaucratic social field. What, in fact, does Lacan say? He says that the unconscious is structured like a language and that a signifier represents the subject for another signifier. One gains access to the unconscious through representation, the symbolic order, the articulation of persons in the symbolic order, through the triangle and castration. In fact, and this is really what it's all about, desire can only exist insofar as it is represented, as it passes through representatives. Otherwise, one falls into the black night of incestuous indifferentiation of drives, etc. For the whole question lies here; if one follows Lacan closely to the end, what does he ultimately say? You accede to desire by the signifier and by castration, and the desire to which you accede is an impossible desire.

I think that Lacan is completely right in terms of the unconscious of the capitalist social field, for as soon as someone represents our desire, as soon as the mother represents the desire of the child, as soon as the teacher represents the desire of the students, as soon as the orator represents the desire of the audience, or the leader, the desire of the followers, or ourselves in our ambition to be something for someone who represents our desire (I've got to be "macho," or else what will she think of me), then there is no more desire. I think the position of the subject and the object in the unconscious is one that continually implies not a metaphysical, general subject, but a particular subject, a type of particular object in a definite socioeconomic field. Desire as such escapes the subject as well as the object, and in particular the series of so-called partial objects. Partial objects of Psychoanalysis only appear in a repressive field. For those who remember Freud's monograph *The Little Hans*, the anal partial object appears when all the other objects have been forbidden, the little girl next door or crossing the street, going for a walk, sleeping with the mother, or masturbating—then, when everything has become impossible, the phobic object appears, the phobic subject appears.

Systems of signification are always linked with formations of power and each time the formations of power intervene in order to provide the significations and the significative behaviors, the goal is always to hierarchize them, to organize and make them compatible with a central formation of power, which is that of the state, of capitalist power mediated by the existence of a national language, the national language being the machine of a system of general law that is differentiated into as many particular languages as will specify the particular positions of each one. The national language is the instrument of translatability which specifies each person's way of speaking. An immigrant does not speak the same way as a teacher, as a woman, as a manager, etc., but in any case each is profiled against a system of general translatability. I do not believe one should separate functions of transmission, of communication, of language, or the functions of the power of law. It is the same type of instrument that institutes a law of syntax, that institutes an economic law, a law of exchange, a law of labor division and alienation, of extortion, of surplus value.

And yet I am so talkative myself that I don't see how one could accuse me of denying language and power. It would be absurd to go to war against power in general. On the contrary, certain types of politics of power, certain types of arrangements of power, certain uses of language, notably national languages, are normalized in the context of a historical situation, which implies the seizure of power by a certain linguistic caste, the destruction of dialects, the rejection of special languages of all kinds—professional as well as infantile or feminine (see Robin Lakoff's study)—I think that is what happens. It would be absurd to oppose desire and power. Desire is power; power is desire. What is at issue is what type of politics is pursued with regard to different linguistic arrangements that exist. Because—and this seems essential to me—capitalist and socialist-bureaucratic power infiltrate and intervene in all modes of individual semiotization today, they proceeds more through semiotic subjugation than through direct subjugation by the police, or by explicit use of physical pressure. Capitalist power injects a micro-fascism into all the attitudes of the individuals, into their relation to perception, to the body, to children, to sexual partners, etc. If a struggle can be led against the capitalist system, it can only be done, in my opinion, through combining a struggle—with visible, external objectives—against the power of the bourgeoisie, against its institutions and systems of exploitation, with a thorough under-standing of all the semiotic infiltrations on which capital is based. Consequently, each time one detects an area of struggle against bureaucracy in the organizations against reformist politics, etc., one must also see just how much we ourselves are contaminated by, are carriers of, this microfascism

Everything is done, everything organized in what I will call the *individuation of the enunciation*, so that one is prevented from taking up such work, so that an individual is always coiled up in himself, his family, his sexuality, so that such work of liberation is made impossible. Thus, this process of fusing a revolutionary political struggle with analysis is only conceivable on condition that another instrument be forged. In our terminology (i.e., with Gilles Deleuze), this instrument is called a collective arrangement of enunciation. This doesn't mean it's necessarily a group: a *collective arrangement of enunciation* can bring both people and individuals into play—but also machines, organs. This can be a microscopic endeavor, like that of certain characters we find in novels (I am thinking of Beckett's *Molloy*); it can be transcendental meditation or a group work. But the collective arrangement of enunciation is not a solution by the group. It is simply an attempt to create opportunities of conjunction between different semiotic components in order that they not be systematically broken, linearized, separated.

In the previous talk, the person who was "discoursing" came to me and said: "If I spoke a long time, all at once, it was because I felt inhibited, because I could not speak." We did not function as a collective arrangement of enunciation; I didn't manage to relate my own inhibition about hearing him with his inhibition about speaking. It always comes back to the idea that if you abandon the discourse of reason, you fall into the black night of passions, of murder, and the dissolution of all social life. But I think the discourse of reason is the pathology, the morbid discourse par excellence. Simply look at what happens in the world, because it is the discourse of reason that is in power everywhere.

In your collective arrangement of enunciation, how do you prevent the reimposition of linearity and syntax?

It would also be absurd to want to suppress the information, the redundancies, the suggestions, the images all the powers-that-be want to suppress. The question, then, is not semiotic, or linguistic, or psychoanalytic—it is political. It consists in asking oneself where the emphasis is put—on the politics of significative redundancy or on the multiple connections of an entirely different nature.

You have to be more precise. You speak of semiotics, of information, of collective arrangements of enunciation, i.e., of linguistics, and then you displace your argumentation from the linguistic or psychological system to that of politics. I no longer follow you.

Each time it is the same thing. Let's take a concrete example: teaching writing in school. The question is often posed in a different, global method. Society being made as it is, even in a completely liberated school, one can hardly imagine refusing to teach children how to write or to recognize linguistic traffic signs. What matters is whether one uses this semiotic apprenticeship to bring together Power and the semiotic subjugation of the individual, or if one does something else. What school does is not to transmit information, but to impose a semiotic modeling on the body. And that is political. One must start modeling people in a way that ensures their semiotic receptiveness to the system if one wants them to accept the alienations of the bureaucratic capitalist-socialist system. Otherwise they would not be able to work in factories or offices; they would have to be sent away to asylums, or universities.

Do you completely reject the system of knowledge elaborated by Lacan through linguistics and Psychoanalysis?

Completely. I believe Lacan described the unconscious in a capitalist system, in the socialist-bureaucratic system. This constitutes the very ideal of Psychoanalysis.

But is it valid as a system for describing this system?

Certainly. Psychoanalytic societies (and this is why we pay them dearly) represent an ideal, a certain model that can have great importance for the other domains of power—in the university and elsewhere—because they represent a way of making sure desire is invested in the signifier and only the signifier, in pure listening, even the silent listening of the analyst. It is the ideal of semiotic subjugation pushed to its highest expression.

According to Nietzsche, one assumes or goes beyond one's own weaknesses in adjusting oneself to them, in refining them. Yet Nietzsche is a reactionary. Is it possible for someone who is a radical to propose going further into psychoanalytic discourse and industrial discourse?

First of all, I am no Nietzschean. Second, I do not think of going beyond my weaknesses. Third, I am soaked to my neck in psychoanalysis and in the university, and I do not see what I could bring to this domain. All the more so since I do not believe that anything can be changed by a transmission of information between speaker and listener. This is not, then, even a problem of ideological striving or of striving for truth, as one could have understood it here. It is simply this: either there will be other types of arrangement of enunciation in which the person will be a small element juxtaposed to something else (beginning with me), or there will be nothing. And worse than nothing: the development of fascism in continuous linear fashion is taking place in many countries, and there you have it.

22

GANGS IN NEW YORK

Marginality is the vantage point which illuminates the points of rupture within social structures and the beginnings of a new problematic in the field of the collective desiring-economy. It is a matter of analyzing marginality, not as a psychopathological manifestation, but as the most vibrant and mobile part of human collectivities in their attempts to find responses to the changes in social and material structures.

But the notion of marginality itself remains extremely ambiguous. In fact, it always implies the idea of a hidden dependence on a society which claims to be normal. Marginality calls for recentering and recuperation. We would like to oppose it to the idea of *minority*. A minority may choose to be definitively minoritarian. For example, militant homosexuals in the United States are minoritarians who refuse to be marginalized. In the same way, we may consider that black and Puerto Rican gangs in the United States are no more marginal than the blacks and Puerto Ricans in the districts of the large cities which they sometimes almost entirely control. What we are dealing with here is a new phenomenon which indicates new directions. A current simplification consists in saying that these types of gangs simply deploy self-defense mechanisms and that their existence only results from the fact that political power, the parties, and the unions *still* have not found a response to this problem. (It is in the hope of finding such a response that the governor of California, Ronald Reagan, tried to establish a colossal research center meant to study the means of curbing violence. It ended up going in the same direction as the film *A Clockwork Orange*, and hardly in a less caricatural way.)

It is a fact that given the phenomena of decomposition experienced by very large cities in the United States, urbanization and "urbanity," if they ever did, cease to go hand in hand. The function of the city as a "melting pot" gives rise, when the urban texture is cancerous, to an acceleration of racial segregation, and a reinforcement of particularisms service to such extent that circulating from one district to another becomes impossible. (The police only enter exceptionally into certain districts in New York.)

Rather than considering such phenomena as collective responses improvised because of a lack (a lack of shelter, for example), we should study them as a blind social experiment on a huge scale. In a more or less significant manner, social minorities explore the problems raised by the economy of desire in the urban field. This exploration does not offer forms or models, and it does not provide a remedy to something that would be pathological; it indicates the direction of new modalities of the organization of collective subjectivity.

Let us consider a typical example: that of South Bronx in New York. Bands of youths sometimes involving several thousand individuals control an entire part of this city. They had given themselves a very rigid, very hierarchized, and even traditionalist organization. Women are organized in parallel gangs but remain completely subjected to the male gangs. These gangs participate, on the one hand, in a fascist desiring-economy, and, on the other, in what some of their leaders themselves call a primitive socialism (*grassroots*). Let us note the signs of an interesting evolution. In certain Puerto Rican gangs in New York, where young women were traditionally subjugated to male leaders, more autonomous feminine structures of organization now appear which do not reproduce the same types of hierarchy; these women say that, unlike the males, they do not feel the need for such a structuration. It is possible that there was another type of organization of power which appeared, one which began to disengage from the mythology tied to the phallic cult of the leader.

A whole series of questions can be posed following this:

1) how has this happened? Notably on the *level* of racial segregation,

2) why have the movements of emancipation been made to become implicitly an accomplice to this segregation?

3) why have the national revolutionary movements (Black Panthers, Black Muslims, Young Lords, etc.) remained out of touch with these thousands of gangs who control, block-by-block, a considerable portion of these large American cities?

A certain culture, specific to the most deprived masses, a certain model of life, and a certain sense of human dignity exists among these gangs, and they could also be credited with many social interventions providing answers to problems which no kind of state power has been able to tackle with. Thus, it sufficed that a team of doctors worked together with these gangs in the South Bronx for a truly original organization of mental hygiene to be put together.

In particular, let us highlight one of the most original experiments with the drug problem, that also happened in the South Bronx. Two years ago, in the middle of racial struggles, the Lincoln Hospital was occupied by revolutionary militants and then evacuated after a few weeks. But an entire floor of the hospital continued to be occupied and has never stopped being occupied since then by ex-addicts who took over by themselves the organization of detox services. This kind of self-management of hospital services would deserve being examined in some detail. Let us simply relate several facts:

1) The majority of the staff is made of old addicts.

2) The doctors never have direct access, not only to the patients, but even to the service.

3) The center has its own police, and a status quo has been established with the police of the state of New York.

4) After fighting the Center for a long time, the state of New York finally accepted to subsidize it.

5) A very special use of methadone has been made. Here it is no longer used as an intensive treatment for several days, as in traditional treatment, but its administration lasts for years and constitutes a sort of artificial drug that definitively subjects ex-addicts to "medical power."

But perhaps what is most interesting is the conjunction of gang activity with this self-management service. It has led not only to focusing on a system of effective treatment (addicts come staggering on their own to the Center), but has also to elaborate solutions to a more general problem, that of drug trafficking. In fact, gangs took things into their own hands, in truth quite ruthlessly, through persuasion, or sometimes physically, in order to eliminate "pushers" (dealers). Some black gangs and movements have become conscious of the manipulation of the State's power through the dissemination of drugs. (This became obvious to them when they discovered that a load of drugs, seized by New York police, had been replaced by flour and resold by the police on a colossal scale.)

But the pacific examples remain the exception. Violence and fear, often stimulated by the police, prevail within these gangs. One couldn't say that such an "experiment" offers a model for the "quality of life" to us. Typically, more systematic attempts at organization are combated by the authorities, in particular the relations which are beginning to be instituted between different gangs, even between different races (Blacks and Puerto Ricans, Chicanos, etc.), and the relations between local gangs and nationally organized movements.

The gang phenomenon, in its full extent and in its current style, only dates back several years. Previously, the ensemble of black movements was drowned out by a wave of white drugs which had reached up to the highest ranks. Yet it is not at the level of national movements that the beginnings of a response to the problem of drugs has been found, but at the level of those gangs who in addition considered these movements as too elitist, whereas they remain in close proximity with the masses.

Several teachers and social workers have begun working with these gangs. One teacher and a French filmmaker have created a film with some of them. The authorities have barely tolerated such initiatives; they have sought to co-opt them for police purposes. It is nevertheless possible that the Alternative Network to Psychiatry in Europe will get to revive these attempts.

Bibliography

DELEUZE/GUATTARI ON ANTI-OEDIPUS

1. "Capitalism: A Very Special Delirium." Translated by David L. Sweet. Discussion with Gilles Deleuze and Felix Guattari. In *C'est Demain la Veille,* M.-A. Burnier, ed. (Paris, Editions du Seuil), 1973.—Ed's title

2. "Capitalism and Schizophrenia." Translated by Jarred Becker from the Italian. Interview with Vittorio Marchetti and Caroline Larne, *Tempi Moderni,* no. 12 (1972).

3. "In Flux." Translated by Jeanine Herman. Discussion on *Anti-Oedipus* between Deleuze/Guattari and Maurice Nadeau, et al., *La Quinzaine Littéraire* 143, June 16–30 (1972). "Deleuze et Guattari s'expliquent ..."—Ed's title.

4. "Balance-Sheet for Desiring-Machines." Translated by Robert Hurley. Appendix to 2nd ed. of *Anti-Oedipe.* Paris: Minuit (1972).

BEYOND ANALYSIS

5. "Guerrilla in Psychiatry: Franco Basaglia." Translated by Gary Genesco. First published in *Quinzaine littéraire,* n° 94, mai (1970). Reprinted in Félix Guattari, *Psychanalyse et transversalité.* Maspero (1972), rééd. La Découverte (2003) p. 263.

6. "Laing Divided." Translated by Bernard Schütze. *La Quinzaine Littéraire,* Jan. 1 (1972).

7. "Mary Barnes's Trip." Translated by Ruth Ohayon. *Le Nouvel Observateur,* May 28 (1973). First published in *Semiotext(e),* "Anti-Oedipus" issue, vol. 2, no. 2. (1977).

8. "The Best Capitalist Drug." Translated by Janis Forman. Interview with Arno Munster, *Frankfurter Rundschau,* January 17 (1973). First published as "Psycho-analysis and Schizoanalysis," Semiotext(e), "Anti-Oedipus" issue, vol. 2, no. 2 (1977). Reprinted as "La Fin des fetichismes," in Félix Guattari, *La Révolution moléculaire.* Paris: UGE (1977).

9. "Everybody Wants to be a Fascist." Translated by Suzanne Fletcher and Catherine Benamou. Lecture delivered in Milan for Colloquium "Psycho-analysis and Politics," December 1973. Published in *Psychanalyse et politique*. Paris: Le Seuil (1974). First published in *Semiotext(e)*, "Anti-Oedipus" issue, vol. 2, no. 2 (1977).

10. "La Borde: A Clinic Unlike Any Other." Translated by David L. Sweet. First published in *La Quinzaine Littéraire*, no. 250 (1977).

11. "Beyond the Psychoanalytical Unconscious." Translated by Chet Wiener. Lecture written in 1977 and delivered in Mexico City in October 1981. Published in *Reseaux-Systemes-Agencements* 7, 1983 and in *Les Années d'Hiver, 1980–85*. Paris: Barrault, 1986.

MINOR POLITICS

12. "To Have Done with the Massacre of the Body." Translated by Jarred Becker. Unsigned essay published in the censored 1973 *Recherches* issue, "Three Billion Perverts: Great Encyclopedia of Homosexualities." None of the pieces were signed, but this one may be attributed to Felix Guattari.

13. "Three Billion Perverts on the Stand." Translated by Sophie Thomas. (1973) from *La Révolution moléculaire*, op. cit.

14. "I Have Even Met Happy Drag Queens." Translated by Rachel McCormas and Stamos Metzidakiswas.First published in *Libération*, April 3 (1975), and in the "Polysexuality" issue of *Semiotext(e)*. Vol. IV, no 1, 1981, Francois Peraldi, ed. Reprinted in *La Révolution moléculaire*, op. cit.

15. "Becoming-Woman." Translated by Rachel McComas and Stamos Metzidakis. Fragment of an interview with Christian Descamps first published in *La Quinzaine Litteraire*, August (1975), and in the "Polysexuality" issue of *Semiotext(e)*. Vol. IV, no 1, 1981, Francois Peraldi, ed. Reprinted in *La Révolution moléculaire*, op. cit.

CINEMACHINES

16. "Cinema of Desire." Translated by David L. Sweet. Paper delivered in Bologna, Italy, at a conference on Eroticism and Cinema in December, 1973. First published in *La Révolution moléculaire*, op. cit. First translated as "Cinematic Desiring Machines," *Critical Theory* 3 (7), August 3–9 (1988).

17. "Cinema Fou." Translated by David L. Sweet. Interview with Delfeuil du Ton on Terence Malick's *Badlands* first published in *Libération*, July 17 (1975). Reprinted in *La Révolution moléculaire*, op. cit.

18. "The Poor Man's Couch." Translated by Gianna Quach. First published in *Communications* 23 (1975).

19. "Not So Mad." Translated by Gianna Quach. First published in *Cinematographie* 18. April (1976). Interview with Jean-Noël Keller. Reprinted in *La Révolution moléculaire*, op. cit.

SCHIZO-CULTURE IN NEW YORK

20. Molecular Revolutions. Translated by David L. Sweet. Transcript of Guattari's improvised address to the Schizo-Culture Conference organized by Semiotext(e) in November, 1975 at Columbia University in New York. Not yet published in French. The Schizo-Culture Conference was the first encounter in the United States between post-'68 French theorists (Michel Foucault, Felix Guattari, Gilles Deleuze, Jean-Francois Lyotard), R.D. Laing, the New York art world (John Cage, William Burroughs, Richard Foreman) and the "radical" academic constituency (Ti-Grace Atkinson, Joel Kovel, etc.). Guattari's address was cut short by followers of Atkinson, who spoke right after him on the podium, and Foucault was accused publicly by agents provocateurs of being paid by the CIA. For two days about two thousand people attended the various workshops, lectures, discussions on psychiatry, madness, political repression, etc.

21. "Desire is Power, Power is Desire." Translated by David L. Sweet. Guattari's response to the Schizo-Culture Conference, November, 1975. Not yet published in French.

22. "Gangs in New York." Translated by Taylor Adkins. Fragment of a research project (1974). Frist published in *La Révolution moléculaire*, op. cit.

Notes

Introduction by François Dosse

1. Félix Guattari, conversation with Robert Maggiori, *Libération*, June 28-29, 1980 ("I am an Idea Thief," in *Soft Subversions*. Translated by Chet Wiener. New York: Semiotext(e) (1996), p. 37.

2. Félix Guattari, letter to Gilles Deleuze, IMEC archives, June 1, 1969.

3. FGERI: Federation of Study groups and Institutional Research created in 1965 by Guattari.

4. Félix Guattari, letter to Gilles Deleuze, IMEC archives, June 1, 1969.

5. Expression used among militant organizations to describe the actual bureaucratization of decisions.—Ed.

6. *Ibid.*

7. The CERFI is a research group in the social sciences created by Félix Guattari in the mid-'60s: Center of Studies, Research and Institutional Formation.

8. See Stéphane Nadaud, *The Anti-Oedipus Papers*. Translated by Kalina Gotman, New York: Semiotext(e) (1996).

9. Arlette Donati, conversation with Eve Cloarec, IMEC archives, October 25, 1984.

10. Félix Guattari, "In Flux," *infra*, p. 69.

11. Gilles Deleuze, "In Flux," *infra*, p. 73.

12. Stéphane Nadaud, *The Anti-Oedipus papers*, op. cit., p. 12.

13. Gilles Deleuze, letter to Kuniichi Uno, October 25, 1982, reprinted in *Two Regimes of Madness*. Translated by Ames Hodges and Michael Taormina, New York: Semiotext(e) (2006).

14. *Ibid.*

15. *Ibid.*

16. *Ibid.*

17. Gilles Deleuze, "Nomad Thought" (1972), reprinted in *Desert Islands and Other Texts (1953–1974)*. Translated by Michael Taormina, New York: Semiotext(e) (2003).

18. Gilles Deleuze and Félix Guattari: "Balance-Sheet Program for Desiring Machines," *Infra*, p. 90–115.

19. See "La Borde: a Clinic Unlike Any Other," *Infra*, p. 176–194.

20. Félix Guattari, *La Révolution moléculaire*. Paris: Recherches (1977).

21. *Potere Operario* dates back to 1969, and self-dissolved in 1973. This influential organization was led, among others, by Toni Negri, Oreste Scalzone, Franco Piperno, Nanni Balestrini, and Sergio Bologna. *Lotta Continua*, born around the same time, also self-liquidated some time later, in November of 1976.

22. *Radiotelevisione Italiana.*—Trans.

23. La Scala is a famous opera house in Milan. It generally opens its season in December.—Trans.

24. Fabrizio Calvi, *Italie 77: Le "Mouvement."* In *Les Intellectuels*. Paris: Seuil (1974), p. 34.

25. Félix Guattari, "Preface," A/Traverso Collective, *Radio Alice, radio libre*, ed. Jean-Pierre Delarge (1977), p. 6.

26. Besides Guattari, participants in the CINEL were the jurist Gérard Soulier, the painter Gérard Fromanger, Yann Moulier-Boutant, Eric Alliez, Jean-Pierre Faye, Jean Chesneaux, Gilles Deleuze, among others ...

27. Cf. Félix Guattari, "La Borde: a Clinic Unlike Any Other," *Infra*, p. 176–194.

28. Félix Guattari, "Guerrilla in Psychiatry: Franco Basaglia." Translated by Gary Genesco. First published in *Quinzaine littéraire*, n° 94, mai (1970). Reprinted in Félix Guattari, *Psychanalyse et transversalité*. Maspero (1972), rééd. La Découverte (2003) p. 263. *Infra*, p. 121.

29. R.D. Laing, *The Politics of Experience*. Harmondsworth: Penguin (1967); David Cooper, *Psychiatry and Anti-Psychiatry*. Paladin (1967).

30. *Recherches*, no. 7, "Enfance aliénée I," September 1967; *Recherches*, no. 8, "Enfance aliénée II," December 1968.

31. Félix Guattari, "Mary Barnes's Trip,'" *Infra*, p. 120–140.

32. *Ibid.*

33. Cf. Mony Elkaïm, *Réseau-Alternative à la psychiatrie. Collectif international* 10/18 (1977).

34. This group includes the GOP, the Workers and Peasants' Left, notably with Marc Huergon, Alain Rist, Alain Lipietz, Alain Desjardin, and Gérard Peurière.

35. Félix Guattari, "Une autre vision du futur," *Le Monde*, February 15, 1992.

36. Félix Guattari, "Vers une nouvelle démocratie écologique," July 1992, IMEC archives.

37. *Ibid.*

38. Félix Guattari, *Three Ecologies*. Translated by Paul Sutton and Ian Pindar, London: Continuum (2008).

39. *Ibid.*

40. Cf. Félix Guattari, "Pratiques écosophiques et restauration de la cite subjective," *Chimères*, no. 17 (Autumn, 1992).

41. Félix Guattari, *Three Ecologies*, op. cit.

42. Félix Guattari, *Chaosmosis: An Ethico-Aesthetic Paradigm*. Translated by Paul Bains and Julian Pefanis, Bloomington: University of Indiana Press (1995).

43. *Ibid.*

44. Daniel Stern, *The Interpersonal World of the Infant: A View from Psychoanalysis and Development*. New York: Basic Books (1985).

45. Félix Guattari, *Cartographies schizoanalytiques*, Paris: Galilée (1989).

46. *Ibid.*, pp. 49–50.

47. Pierre Lévy, *Les Technologies de l'intelligence*. Paris: La Découverte (1990).

48. Félix Guattari, "Réinventer la politique," *Le Monde*, March 8, 1990.

49. Félix Guattari, "Les nouveaux mondes du capitalisme," *Libération*, December 22, 1987.

50. Félix Guattari, "Pour une refondation des pratiques sociales," *Le Monde diplomatique*, October 1992.

51. *Ibid.*

52. *Ibid.*

53. Félix Guattari, "Regression de l'ordre international," conversation, *Globe*, February 1991.

54. Félix Guattari, "Le courage d'une politique," *Lettre d'information de Génération Ecologie*, no. 6, January 28, 1991.

55. Gilles Deleuze and René Schérer, "La guerre immonde," *Libération*, March 4 1991. Cf. Gilles Deleuze, in *Two Regimes of Madness*, op. cit.

56. *Ibid.*

57. *Ibid.*

58. Paul Virilio, "Le concept de guerre," typographical transcript of a dialogue with Guattari, August 4, 1992, IMEC archives.

59. Félix Guattari, *ibid.*, May 1992.

60. Paul Virilio, conversation with Virginie Linhart.

2. Capitalism and Schizophrenia

1. Silvano Arieti, *Interpretation of Schizophrenia*. New York: Basic Books (1955).

3. In Flux

1. "*Machin*," in French, is used to designate an undefined object, a "thing." Like the flux, a machine remains ordinary and undefined—a thing. Deleuze and Guattari also use the verbs "*machiner*" and the substantive "*machination*" to suggest plotting or conniving, or simply putting things together.—Ed.

4. Balance-Sheet for "Desiring-Machines"

1. Géza Róheim, *Psychoanalysis and Anthropology*, International Universities Press (1968).

2. Pierre Auger, *L'Homme microscopique*, Paris: Flammarion (1951), p. 138.

3. The allusion here is to Sade's perversely rational pamphlet of 1795, "Français, encore un effort si vous voulez etre republicains ..." (incorporated in *La Philosophie dans le boudoir*) in which he turns postenlightenment principles into an argument for the total eradication of the Church, a bare minimum of laws, an end to the bourgeois family, and a perpetual revolution in manners and morals.—Trans.

4. Michel de M'Uzan, in *La Sexualité perverse*. Paris: Payot (1972), pp. 34–37. Translated in the "Polysexuality" issue of *Semiotext(e)*. Vol. IV, no 1, 1981, Francois Peraldi, ed.

5. With regard to machinic continuity and discontinuity, cf. André Leroi Gourhan, *Milieu et techniques*. Albin Michel (1945), pp. 366sp.

6. It is again Róheim who clearly reveals the Oedipus projection-representation linkage.

7. Marcel Moré, *Le très curieux Jules Verne*. Paris, Gallimard, 1960; and *Nouvelles explorations de Jules Verne*. Paris, Gallimard, 1963.

8. Roger Dadoun, "Les ombilics du rêve," in *L'espace du rêve*. Paris: folio essais, Gallimard (1972).

9. Dolfi Trost, *Vision dans le cristal*. Bucharest: Les Éditions de l'Oubli (1945). *Visible et invisible*. Éditions Arcanes (1953). *Librement mécanique*. Le Minotaure (1955). Gherasim Luca, *Le Vampire passif*. Bucharest: Les Éditions de l'Oubli (1945).

10. Mouvement pour la Libération de la Femme, one of the groups active in the women's liberation movement in France.—Trans.

11. Serge Leclaire, "La réalité du désir," in *Sexualité humaine*. Aubier (1971).

12. With regard to the aleatory, the "mad vector," and their political applications, cf. Pierre Vendryes's books, *Vie et probabilité*, Paris: Albin Michel (1945); *La probabilité en histoire*, Paris: Albin Michel (1952), and *Determinisme et autonomie*, Paris: Armand Colin (1956). Regarding a "prowl machine" of the Brownoid type, cf. Guy Hocquenghem, *Le Désir homosexuel*. Ed. Universitaires (1972).

13. Ivan Illich, "Retooling Society," *Le Nouvel Observateur*, Sept. 11, 1972 (regarding largeness and smallness in the machine, cf. Gilbert Simondon, *Du mode d'existence des objets techniques*, Méot (1958), pp. 132 133).

14. David Robinson, "Buster Keaton," *Revue du Cinéma* (this book contains a study of Keaton's machines).

15. With regard to this other biological schema based on the types of organization, cf. "Afterword" to the Second German Edition of *Capital* (International Publishers, pp. 17–19).

16. "Every rupture produced by the intrusion of a machine phenomenon will be found to be conjoined to what we shall call a system of anti production, a specific representative mode of the structure ... Antiproduction will be, among other things, what has been entered in the register of relations of production."

17. Regarding the role of machines in Futurism and Dadaism, cf. Noémi Blumenkranz, *L'Esthétique de la machine* (Société d'esthétique), "La Spirale" (*Revue d'esthétique*, 1971).

5. Guerrilla in Psychiatry: Franco Basaglia

1. Edgar Faure was named Minister of [National] Education immediately following the events of May 1968.

2. Cf. R.D. Laing, *The Politics of Experience*. Harmondsworth: Penguin (1967), and *Recherches*, "Special enfance aliénée," II (Dec. 1968); David Cooper, *Anti-Psychiatry*. Paladin (1967).

6. Laing Divided

I. "L'avenir d'une utopie," *Net* 42 (1972).

2. Cirque Rurbain d'Animation, d'Action, d'Agitation Koultourelle (Urban Animation Circus for Cultural Action and Agitation).

3. David Cooper, *Psychiatry and Anti-Psychiatry*, op. cit.

4. Hochmann, *Pour une psychiatrie communautaire*. [*For a Communal Psychiatry*] Paris: Le Seuil (1971).

5. R.D. Laing, *The Politics of Experience*, op. cit.

7. Mary Barnes's "Trip"

1. David Cooper, *Psychiatry and Anti-Psychiatry*, op. cit.

2. Not to be compared, however, with the Italian repression, which destroyed less "provoking" attempts, and above all the German repression, truly barbaric, presently inflicted against members of the SPK in Heidelberg.

3. 'Behaviorism'; turn of the century theory which reduces psychology to the study of behavior, defined as the interaction between outside stimuli and the subject responses. Present neobehaviorism tends to reduce all human problems to those of communication, putting aside socio political problems of power at all levels.

4. Contradictory double constraint established on the level of the communications between a subject and his family, which perturbs him completely.

5. Her exhibitions in Great Britain and abroad guaranteed her a certain reputation. A lot could be said about this kind of recuperation, in the style of "art brut," which amounts to promoting a mad artist ... like a music hall star, for the good of the producers of this kind of show. The essence of mad art is to be above and beyond the notions of oeuvre or the authorial function.

8. The Best Capitalist Drug

I. Their second part is *A Thousand Plateaus: Capitalism and Schizophrenia*. Translated by Brian Massumi. Minneapolis: University of Minnesota Press (1987).

2. *Seriality*: The repetitive and empty mode of existence of a group.—Ed.

3. Cf. Gilles Deleuze and Felix Guattari, *Kafka: Toward a Minor Literature*. Minneapolis: University of Minnesota Press (1986).

4. See "La Borde: A Clinic Unlike Any Other."—Ed.

5. The Movement of March 22 was instrumental in bringing about the May '68 "revolution" in France.—Ed.

9. Everybody Wants to be a Fascist

1. There was a homogeneous attitude on the part of the capitalist. Krupp, at first hostile towards Hitler, only rallied to him after the course was set ...

2. One of contemporary capitalism's major concerns is the search for forms of totalitarianism tailored to the countries of the Third World.

10. La Borde: A Clinic Unlike Any Other

1. See "Three Billion Perverts on the Stand" in this volume.

11. Beyond the Psychoanalytical Unconscious

1. In communication theory, "noise" is one element of anticommunication, like "static."—Ed.

13. Three Billion Perverts on the Stand

1. The March issue of *Recherches*, "Three Billion Perverts: An Encyclopedia of Homosexualities," had been seized, and Felix Guattari, as the publications director, was fined 600 francs for affronting public decency. No. 12 of *Recherches* was judged to constitute a "detailed display of turpitude and sexual deviation," the "libidinous exhibition of a minority of perverts." All copies of the issue were ordered to be destroyed.

15. Becoming-Woman

1. Renée Nelli, *Les Troubadours*. Paris: Desdée de Brouwer (1960–66).

16. Cinema of Desire

1. J. L. Austin, *How to Do Things With Words*. Oxford: Clarendon Press (1962).

2. One must address in detail the role of asignifying components vis-à-vis analogical ones: the fact, in particular, that the functioning as machines of deterritorialized signs "breaks" the effects of signification and interpretation, thwarts the system of

dominant redundancies, accelerates the most "innovative," "constructivist," "rhizomatic" components.

3. Cf. Louis Hjelmslev, *Essais linguistiques*. Paris: Minuit (1971), and *Prolégomènes a une théorie du language*. Paris: Minuit (1971).

4. Christian Metz, *Language and Cinema*. The Hague: Mouton (1974); *Film Language, A Semiotic of the Cinema*. New York: Oxford University Press (1974).

5. The recent development of free radios on miniaturized FM transmitters would seem to confirm this tendency.

18. The Poor Man's Couch

1. One could speak here of "film viewing-acts" in symmetry with the "speech-acts" studied by John Searle.

2. "One offers you beautiful images, but in order to entice you: at the same time that you believe that you are having a treat, you absorb the ideology necessary to the reproduction of the relations of production. One dissimulates historical reality for you, one camouflages it under similitude of convention that is not just tolerable, but fascinating: so much so that you no longer even need to dream, nor have the right to do so, because your dreams could be nonconformist: one gives you the kind of packaged dream that disturbs nothing: tailormade fantasies, an agreeable phantasmagoria that puts you in tune with your unconscious, for it is understood that your consconcious must be given its due, from the time when you are knowledgeable enough to draw upon it and beg for it. Cinema today puts at your disposal a house unconscious perfectly ideologized." Mikel Dufrene in *Cinema, Theory and Reading*. Paris: Klincksieck (1973).

3. With his theory of the little object *a*, Lacan came to treat partial objects as logico-mathematic entities ("There is a mathème of psychoanalysis").

4. One should take up again the analysis of Bettini and Cosseni, who distinguished the notion of iconicity from that of analogism: the filmic syntagmatic, in some way, "analogizes" the icons which are transported by the unconscious. See "La sémiologie des moyens de communications audio-visuals," *Cinema*. Paris: Klincksieck (1973).

5. The psychoanalyst is somewhat in the position of the spectator at the cinema: he assists in the unfolding of a montage that one fabricates especially for him.

6. With television, the effect of deterritorialization seams attenuated, but perhaps it is still more underhanded: one bathes in a minimum of light, the machine is before you, like an amicable interlocutor, it's a family affair; in the Pullman car, one visits the abyssal profundities of the unconscious, then one switches to advertising and the

news. The aggression is, in fact, even more violent than anywhere else; one bends unconsciously to the sociopolitical coordinates, to a type of moralization without which capitalist industrialized societies probably could not function.

20. Molecular Revolutions

1. Attracted by world-wide media coverage, agent provocateurs, presumably from Larouche's Labor Committee, tried a few times to disrupt the Conference by publicly accusing R.D. Laing and Michel Foucault of being paid by the CIA. See *Foucault Live*. New York: Semiotext(e) (1995).—Ed.

2. Gilles Deleuze spoke in French in the afternoon about trees and rhizomes while drawing graphs on the blackboard, an idea later developed in "Rhizomes." See *On The line*. New York: Semiotext(e) (1983).—Ed.

3. Daniel Cohn-Bendit, called "Danny the Red," was the most outspoken leader of the May '68 uprising.—Ed.

4. The previous day Guattari had suggested replacing the formal lecture format with short summeries followed by discussions, and the audience split in two over this proposal in the middle of Joel Kovel's Paper. Half of the audience remained in the main hall, while the rest moved with Guattari to a smaller room where Foucault had his paper on "Infant Sexuality" read in English. It is at that point that a provocateur accused Foucault of being a CIA agent. It should be noted that the Conference was not sponsored by Columbia University and that registration fees for the Conference were entirely used to pay for the lecture rooms at Teacher's College.—Ed.

Index

as text without signifier, 78; and the university, 87–88; (D&G's) writing arrangement for, 9–12

Antiproduction, 71, 109, 113, 305 n.16; discourse of, 65; structures of, 71

Antipsychiatry, 7, 19–21, 57, 121–122, 124, 126–127, 129, 131, 134, 184, 186, 268; mass-mediatized character of, 186

Anxiety, 49, 122, 137

Archaic societies, 182, 240–241

Arieti, Silvano, 61–63, 304 n.1

Art, 72, 192–193, 174; fluctuations of, 47; minor vs. major, 271; of real distinction, 104–105. *See also* Artists

Artaud, Antonin, 53, 125, 164, 283; *Heliogabalus*, 82; and mental illness, 65–66

Artistic: creation, 41, 147, 216; production, 145

Artists, 152, 229, 306 n.5; and machines, 105–106, 108. *See also* Art

Asceticism, 9, 40, 138, 196, 236

Asignification, 173–174, 241–243, 245–246, 250, 263, 307

Assemblage, 10–11

Association, 102–104

Asylum, 268

Asylums, 129, 170, 217, 289; families demand reopening of, 185; closed vs. open, 50

Auger, Pierre (*L'Homme microscopique*), 93, 304 n.2

Autonomists, 7

Autopoiesis, 28

Avant-garde, 42, 45, 60, 72, 170, 228, 247

Badlands (Malick), 247–256

Barbarians, 84–85

Barbarism, 85–86

Barnes, Mary, 21, 129–140 *passim*, 184; biography of, 131; as boss of Kingsley Hall, 138; brother of, 133; extreme case of, 131–132; familialist neurosis of, 133–134; as famous painter, 135; and regressive familialism, 140; as superstar of Kingsley Hall, 130

Basaglia, Franco, 119–123 *passim*; 165, 196–197, 199; Guattari's critique of, 20; and radical Italy, 20

Bassi, 172

Bateson, Gregory, 127

Bauer, Felice, 151

Beckett, Samuel, 8, 229, 287

Becoming, 201

Becoming-woman, 225–226, 228–231, 235

Behavior, 195; film and reproduction of, 258; imparted by school & university, 279; obsessive, 59

Bellochio, Marco (*Fous à délier*), 186, 269–270

Berardi, Franco (Bifo), 16–18

Berke, Jospeh, 130–138 *passim*

Berlinguer, Enrico, 13, 18

Bibliophilia, 60

Bicycle, 107

Bifo, 16–18

Billy the Kid, 247

Biologists, 63

Biology, 53

Black movements, 295

Black Panthers, 293

Body, 51, 53, 63, 67, 74, 78, 85, 138, 160, 172, 175, 181, 194, 207–214 *passim*, 225–226, 229–230, 241, 243, 245, 280; liberation of, 213; microfascism of, 278; and representation, 225; school imposes semiotic modeling on, 289; and semiotization, 279; sexed, 229;

CRAAAK, 125, 306 n.2

Creation, 28, 182, 203, 262; artistic, 41, 147, 216

Creativity, 192, 195, 200, 203, 216, 237, 242

Criminality: as dynamite carrier, 142

CRS (French riot police), 40

Crusades, 47, 51

Culture: as beginning point of schizophrenic delirium, 58. *See also* Counter-culture movement

Cultural divisions: calling into question of, 59

Dada, 104, 114–115, 305 n.17

Dadoun, Roger, 101

Daddy-cop, 137

Dancer-Danger (Ray), 91

Davis, Angela, 51

Death, 43, 86–87, 91, 98, 113, 137, 150, 168–169, 175, 207–209, 211; drive, 105; instinct, 98, 152, 166, 168, 200; machinic vs. regressive, 105

Debt: primacy of genealogy of, 85

Deleuze, Gilles, 26, 28; and *Anti-Oedipus*, 83–89 *passim*; and becoming, 201; and collective arrangements of enunciation, 287; and desire, 279; and molecular revolution, 276; and power formations, 282; and rejection of Iraq war, 30; and semiotization, 279; (Guattari's) writing with, 7–12, 20, 174

Delirium, 101, 165, 262; and desiring-machines, 95; fascist and revolutionary elements of, 58; Freud's despise for, 145; as misunderstood by psycho-analysis, 74; political-historical-cultural content of, 57–58; underneath all reason, 36; very special, inherent to regime of money, 37

Democracies, 156, 161, 167, 170

Desire, 36–46 *passim*, 53–54, 64–65, 78, 82, 87, 90–115 *passim*, 127, 133–134, 137, 146–148, 152-153, 162-163, 169, 172–179, 197, 275; analysis required of, 115, 277; and *Anti-Oedipus*, 74–75; atomic energy of, 164; and books, 75; and capitalism, 284; capitalism imposes models of, 237; collective formations of, 203; and communication, 283–284; connectors and repressors of, 98; constituted before crystallization of body & organs, 245; as constituted by man-machine relation, 72; constitutive arrangements of, 262, 281; deterritoriality of, 148, 159–160; economy of, 40–41, 132, 171, 200, 203, 235, 244, 246, 292; effecting changes in economy of, 132; vs. eros-body-person-law-organs-phallus, 245; energy of fascism at heart of, 171; and film, 241, 267; foolish search for raw, 137; historical dimensions of, 36, 155, 163, 235; history incessantly shaped by, 71; hunted down, 236; ideological oppositions mask conflicts of, 39; liberation of, 42–43, 70, 151, 164; possibility of liberated, 41, 43, 245; for liberation moves beyond limits of person, 210; difficulty of systematic liberation of, 70; liquidation of, on scale of society as a whole, 70; and machines, 90, 163; machines of, and relation with social machines, 74, 88, 162, 203; molecular machinizing, 109; microfascism blinds value of, 278; micropolitics of, 156, 158, 173, 231, 259, 261, 281; micropolitical theory of, 154–156, 158, 164–165, 166, 173, 175; negative vs. positive conception of, 80; and objects, 78–80, 239; personalistic wisdom and repression of, 128; political trial of, 224; two politics of, 245; is power, 286; held by power, 277; organization of power as unity of, 38; and private-life-profit-society, 144; production of, 144; productive & revolutionary essence of, 82; extermination of, by psychoanalytic interpretation, 83, 88; emptied by psychoanalytic écoute, 259; as misunderstood by psychoanalysis, 74, 80; and representation, 285; repression of, 142, 235; reproductive of established domination or neutralized, 208; revolution of, 72; revolutionizing, 213; schizo, 248; and schizophrenics, 41; situation of, 71–72; social chemistry of, 163; and sterilized labor movement, 142; as strange thing beneath reasons of society, 111–112; struggles of, 170, 226, 244, 261; subjected to rules of reproduction of capitalism, 210; subjugated by dictatorship of capitalist totalitarian organization, 207; and technology, 108; as texture of society, 41; totalitarian adapting of, 171; totalitarian seizing of, 163; transcendent model of, 241; as understood by reference to production, 54, 71. *See also* Antidesire; Collective—desire; Liberation—of desire; Masses—desire of; Regimes; Repression—desire for

Desiring: economy, 141–142, 291–292; energy, 151, 245; flow, 152

Desiring machines, 14, 53–54, 72, 74, 77, 90–115 *passim*, 144, 159, 248; and artists, 108; as defined by connections, 96; and institutional madness, 72; as molecular micromachines in the great molar social machines, 74; multiplicity of, 159; as multiplicity of distinct elements, 112–113; as nonorganic system of the body, 74; profoundly de-Oedipalizing, 105; reduced excess of, 64; schizophrenic process of, 72; sexual dimensions of, 113; and social technical machines, 106–108, 115; as internal limit of social/technical machines, 112; as split by dominant system, 144; totalitarian, 168

Desiring: machinism, 165; mutation, 150; power, 40; process, 151; production, 54, 71, 83, 101, 144, 147, 175, 216, 244; will, 40

Despotic: organization, 107; relations, 107

Despotism, 72, 85, 156, 239

Deterritorialization, 45, 86, 94, 97, 100–101, 104, 115, 150, 152, 175, 203, 308 n.6

Dialectical materialism, 141

Dialogue: retaliation against maneuvers of, 70

Difference: question of true, 80–81; and repetition, 150

Dimitrov, 46

Disciplines, 59, 89, 236; division of, 60

Discourse: and *Anti-Oedipus*, 75; everyone stuck to, of analyst, 264; psychoanalytic and industrial, 290; of reason, 288; repression on level of, 65

Dissociation, 102–103

Distinction, 104–105, 112

Divided Self (Laing), 125

Doctor-patient relations, 179, 191

Double bind, 127, 132, 185

Drag, 225, 227

Ideology, 37–38, 40, 49–50, 64, 75, 87, 114–115, 126, 142, 153, 277, 308 n.2

Illich, Ivan, 107

Imaginary, 52.58, 80–81, 90, 92–93, 96, 99, 106, 115, 136–137, 147, 149, 181, 199–201, 203, 242, 245, 248, 257, 260, 263

Imagination, 56, 91, 95

Incorporeal universes, 199, 202

Individuals, 57, 60, 66, 77, 140, 167, 172, 232, 246; act in ways against their interest, 195; and antifascism, 166; capitalist overcoding of, 151; capitalism depends on modeling of, 237; as cripples under capitalist totalitarian subjugation, 207; and desire for repression, 146; familialized, 137; microfascism injected into attitudes of, 287; notion of, overturned for liberation of body, 210; of primitive societies, 52; repressive power of superego over, 156; semiotic subjugation of, 278, 289; serialized, 159; subjective positions of, 182; and subjectivity production, 193–194; theory of discontent of, 126; transforming relations between, 15

Individuation, 155, 160, 262, 283, 287; de-, 262–263

Industrial societies, 29, 170, 160, 182, 237

Industries: computerization of, 26, 186

Information, 24, 107, 172, 180, 194, 219, 238, 242, 283, 288–290

Institutional analysis, 182–183. *See also* Analysis

Institutional Psychotherapy. *See* Psychotherapy

Integrated World Capitalsim. *See* World Integrated Capitalism

Intensification, 62–63

Intensity, 27, 62–64, 98, 101, 104, 134, 138, 199, 212, 229, 242–243, 248, 250–251, 263–264

International Network of Alternatives to Psychiatry, 21–22, 186, 269, 295

Interpretation, 54, 61, 67, 72, 76, 83, 85, 101–102, 134–140, 185, 191–192, 196, 200–201, 254–255, 259–260, 265, 304, 307 n.2; as criterion of psychoanalytic method, 134; as extermination of desire, 83

Interpretative: delusion, 132, 135; machine, 136; reduction, 134

Iron curtain: ontological, 27; opportunity lost after fall of, 189;

Irreversibility, 193

Italian Autonomists, 7

Italy: molecular revolution of, 12–19

Jackson, 47

Jaspers, Karl, 65

Jervis, Giovanni, 184

Jones, Maxwell, 21, 120–121, 129

Joyce, James, 26

Justice, 14, 17, 42–43, 223

Kafka, Franz, 100–101, 149, 151, 229

Keaton, Buster, 95, 104, 115; as great artist of desiring-machines, 108; *The Navigator*, 108

Kennedy Act, 185

Kern, Anne-Brigitte, 24

Kingsley Hall, 21, 126, 129–140 *passim*, 184; Barnes and publicity of, 130–131; beginning of antipsychiatry at, 129–130; familialist interpretation as favorite game of, 140; vs. La Borde, 21; and Laing's attempt to destroy psychiatry, 132–133; and psychoanalytic shortcomings, 134–140; schizophrenia and familialism at, 133–134

Kinsey Report, 215

Knots (Laing), 125, 128, 132, 137

Knowledge: destruction of specialization of, 107; transmission of, and problem of entire society, 143

Kojève, Alexandre, 87

Kursbuch Number 28, 143

Labor, 217; division of, 164, 202, 284, 286; movement, 141–142. *See also* British labor movement

La Borde Clinic, 7, 9, 12, 19, 21, 152,176–194 *passim*, 247; baroque treatment at, 181; engagement of global issues at, 183; vs. Kingsley Hall, 21; as model, 193; and a new relation w/ the world, 180; police search at, 222; reformism of, 153; and revolutionary organization of staff-patient relations, 177–182; therapeutic mixture of people at, 187

Lacan, Jacques, 20, 57, 78–79, 81, 127–128, 154, 184, 192, 261, 284–285, 289; and unconscious structured like language, 199, 261, 285

Lacanian: pretension, 191; structuralism, 260; theory, 154; unconscious, 285

Laforgue, René, 257

Lahire, Bernard, 29

Laing, R.D., 20–21, 65, 121, 124–132, 134, 172, 184–186; and antipsychiatry at Kingsley Hall, 129–133, 136; criticism of, 185; as deviant psychiatrist, 124; and familialism, 127; importance of, in context of new movements, 124; and personalistic nexus, 127; public fascina-

tion with books of, 125. *See also Divided Self; Knots; Mental Equilibrium; Politics of Experience; Self and Others*

Lakoff, Robin, 286

Lalonde, Brice, 24

Language, 79, 191, 173; alive in media, 267; dominant, and semiotization, 279; of film for minorities, 271; film irre-ducible to, 262; film images as, 242; fluctuations of, 47; as instrument of power, 236; military, 64–65; national, 286; normalizing power of, 242; opening of, by subject groups, 161; and power, 261, 279, 286; purification of, for media, 219; at service of bour-geois familialism, 266; vs. speech, 262; transformations in, 64; unconscious structured 'like,' 199, 241, 260–261, 285. *See also* Dialogue; Discourse; Political militants—language of; Psychiatrists—language of; Psychoanalysts—language of; Schizophrenics—language; Speech; Texts; Writing

Law, 236, 286

Law 180 (Italy), 185–186

Lebel, J.J., 113, 281

Lebovici, René, 257

Leclaire, Serge, 12, 79–80, 83, 88, 103, 112; (*Sexualite humaine*) 305 n.11

Left, 13–14, 23–24, 37–40, 74–75, 115, 148, 178, 185, 303 n.34; Italian, 13–18; Laing as voice of, 126; -ist élan, 40; -ist movements, 141; -ist organizations, 70, 167

Leger, 97

Leibniz, Gottfried, 112

Lenin, 130, 141

Leninism, 13–15, 71, 87, 276

Leroi-Gourhan, Andre (*Milieu et technique*), 304 n.5

Levi-Strauss, Claude (*The Interpretation of Schizophrenia*), 61

Lévy, Pierre, 27

Liberation, 14, 30, 42, 49, 69, 88, 119, 152, 175, 189, 208, 210, 212–213, 218, 225, 237, 238, 278, 287; of desire, 43, 70, 130, 151, 164; women's, 145, 213, 218

Libidinal: economy, 150, 172, 239, 246, 281; energy, 152, 165, 238; investments, 108; unconscious, 36, 113

Libido, 37, 51, 79, 88–89, 101, 113, 138, 142, 154–155, 171–172, 203, 211, 229–230, 236, 244, 246, 254, 258, 260

Lincoln Hospital, 293

Linearity, 283–284, 288

Linguistics, 58, 257, 262, 288–289

Lipietz, Alain, 23

Literary: imagination, 91; machine, 61, 100

Literature, 82, 100, 224

Loach, Kenneth (*Family Life*), 184

Logic: blindness of individuals frozen in, 68; of real desire, 72

Logos: vs. pathos, 73

Luca, Gherasim (*Le Vampire passif*), 101–102, 305 n.9

Lucretius, 76

Machine(s), 40, 46, 54, 79, 81–82, 90–115 *passim*, 129, 264–265; and affect, 98; and artists, 105–106, 108; as conceived in direct relation with social body, 110–111; connection of, with revolutionary possibilities, 61; consequences of new understanding of, 111–115; continuity of totalitarian, 161–164; created by autistic patient, 67; (Deleuze & Guattari's) definition of, 74, 91–92, 111; of desire, 155; as destruction of Oedipus, 99; as determined by bio-evolutive schema, 92, 109–110; and dreams, 101–102; as flooded by screen memory, 100; influence of Lévy's work, 27; and man, 72, 74, 91–95, 106; meaninglessness of, 76; of production, 144; productive transhuman chain of, 164; our relationship with, 106; and representation, 97–98; small vs. large, 107; and state apparatus, 43; and structure, 104; and tool(s), 92–95, 109–111; two powers of, 96; unconscious, 79; World War I as meeting ground of four great attitudes on, 166. *See also* Desiring machines; War-machines

Machinic: agency, 93, 97; innovation, 108; phyla, 92–93, 96, 102, 111, 192; recurrence, 97; systems, 183, 198; unconscious, 197–202; uselessness, 107

Machinism: as beyond mechanics of technology and organization of organism, 74; humanist anti-, 115

Madness, 77, 123, 163, 167, 171, 173, 175–176, 188, 196, 217; break through/collapse of, 66; changed view on, 125, 180; and connection with family, 57; depsychiatrization of, 22; and distinction from desiring machines, 72; expression of and access to, 56; Freud & Lacan and dealing with, today, 128; public interest in, 125, 268; unchanged public status of, 184. *See also* Oedipal madness

Malinowsky, 200

185; problems posed by, 188; singularities and psychic virtualities of, 190. *See also* Insane; Patients; Psychiatric population; Schizophrenics

Meta-modelization, 192–193

Methodology, 76

Metropolitan Indians (Italy), 15

Metz, Christian, 242–243, 264, 307 n.4

Microfascism, 278, 280–281, 287

Micropolitics, 22, 154–156, 158, 166, 173–175, 202–203, 231, 259, 261, 281

Middle East, 174. *See also* Near East

Militancy: as freedom from fantasies of dominant order, 72

Militant practice: and representation, 157

Militants, 14–15, 17, 23–24, 39–41, 64, 70–71, 148, 153, 157, 186, 226, 293; complicity of, 70; Guattari as, 178, 221; homosexual, 216, 228, 291; language of political, 64; revolutionary, 293; struggle, 72, 119; theatre, 225; unconscious and mentally ill, 186

Military: discourse of, 65

Minds: no universal structure of, 150

Minguzzi, Franco, 119, 184

Minority, 169–170, 216–218, 229, 271, 276, 291–292

Mirabelles, 225–227

Misery, 143, 203, 211, 223

MLF, 103, 218, 305 n.10

Modelization, 192–193

Moholy-Nagy, László, 114

Molecular revolution, 275–281 *passim*; created by Gramsci, 12; in Italy, 12–19; as permanent reinvention, 182; and political crisis, 276. *See also* Revolutions

Mommy-Daddy, 58, 66, 88, 96, 134

Money, 36–37, 73, 110, 112–113, 132–133, 153, 231, 281

Montesano, Gianmarco, 17

More, Marcel (*Le très curieux Jules Verne*), 99, 304 n.7

Mouvement pour la Libération de la Femme (MLF), 103, 218, 304 n. 10

Movement of March 22, 153, 306 n.5

Multiplicities, 72, 78–79, 263

Music, 174, 201, 230, 241, 243

Mussolini, Benito, 46, 275

Mutations, 14, 24, 29, 96, 114, 150, 162, 165, 230, 263

M'Uzan, Michel de (*La Sexualité perverse*), 95, 304 n.4

Nadal, Jean, 94

Nadaud, Stephan, 10, 301 n.8

Narcissism, 98, 200, 260

Narcissistic: exercises, 99; passion, 134

Nature: and machine, 74; and machinic uselessness, 107; and man, 92. *See also* Naturist tendency

Naturist tendency, 48. *See also* Nature

Nazi: eros, 151; party, 162

Nazism, 71, 163, 165–167, 257

Near East, 48. See also Middle East

Necessitation, 193

Negri, Tony, 17, 302 n.21

Neighborhoods, 43, 278–279; as segmented by psychiatry, 50. *See also* Urban issues

Nelli, Renée, 228

Neo-Marxist method, 156–157

Nerval, Gérard de, 66

Neurosis, 27, 56, 72, 128, 133, 138, 163, 191, 196–197, 261

Nietzsche, Friedrich, 36, 289; and mental illness, 65–66

facilities, 189; medication negotiated with, 122, 191, 293–294; and problem of society, 143–144; and schizoanalysis, 149; and talk about politics, 88; as victims of mediocrity, 190; and work, 270. *See also* Insane; La Borde Clinic—and revolutionary organization of staff-patient relations; Mentally ill; Psychiatric population; Schizophrenics

Pedagogy, 182–183, 193, 223

Person, 81, 127, 138–139; and anti-production, 71

Personality, 181

Phallic: cult, 293; power, 156, 228–229, 231, 240

Phallocentrism, 145

Phallus, 103, 213, 239–240, 245, 259–261

Phantasy, 100; as residue of desiring-machines, 90; vs. programming, 95

Pharmaceutical treatment, 63

Photography, 100, 149–151, 243

Picabia, Francis, 95, 97–98

Pietrantonio, 173

Pividal, Raphael, 88

Pleasure: vs. desire, 154; and revolution don't mix, 154–155

Police, 14, 17, 19, 40–41, 88, 121–122, 161–162, 165, 167, 169–170, 219, 221–222, 224, 249–250, 253, 263, 278, 282, 287, 292, 294–295. *See also* Cops

Political: action, 15, 17, 149, 210; confrontations, 275; economy, 113, 171; machines, 61; militants, 64; objectives, 280; organizations, 46, 48, 59, 279; parties, 25, 70; problems, 277; responsibility, 59; struggles, 146–147, 156, 159, 164, 244, 281, 287. *See also* Analysis—political

Politicians, 16, 18, 45, 59–60, 64–65, 142; discourse of, 65; explosions that elude comprehension of, 82; ignore desiring economy, 142; kidnappings of, 16; nonreceptiveness of, 70

Politics: all actors in, ought to make themselves schizophrenic, 59; as beginning point of schizophrenic delirium, 58; as context for struggle with traditional psychoanalysis, 147; and desire, 155; ecological movements and restoration of, 23–25; and mental patients, 88–89; of oppression, 19, 108; and organization of individuals, 39; of power, 286; of psychiatric hospitals, 49; of significative redundancy, 288. *See also* Analysis—political; Micropolitics

Politics of Experience (Laing), 125

Pompidou, Georges, 184

Popular justice, 42

Popular struggle, 70

Potere Operario, 15–16

Power, 13, 15, 45, 49, 70–72, 76, 86–88, 92, 130, 151, 156, 158, 287, 293; absurdity of general war against, 286; based on codification-segregation-stratification, 226; capitalist organization of, 44; as concentrated for administrators, 188; is desire, 286; epistemology as veil of organization of, 76; formations of, 282, 286; importance of organization of, 37–39; and language, 261, 279, 286; machines of, 167, 170, 174; molecular, 164; political-economic concentration of, 107; questions of, 277; relations, 126, 195, 202, 262; via semiotic subjugation, 278; and signification, 236, 279

normalization of socius, 202; at La Borde Clinic, 152–153; and leftist movements, 141–142, 148; as manager of semiotic subjugation, 278; vs. micropolitics of desire, 154–156; Oedipal/repressive descriptions furnished by, 63, 90, 145; and models independent of history and struggle, 241; negative theology of, 80; original defect of, 191; original task of, 195; and the partial object, 79–80; power and ideals of, 289; radical reform and credibility of, 196; and repression of homosexuality, 228; and revolutionary movement-madness-artistic creation, 147; ridiculous familialism of, 88; vs. schizoanalysis, 103; speech in, 264; structuralism in, 241–242, 259–267 *passim*; suffocates the singular, 266; and system of signification, 239; (D&G's) two reproaches against, 74; as untouched by criticism until now, 75; various forms of, 172– 173. *See also* Oedipal psychoanalysis

Psychoanalysm, 132, 134

Psychoanalysts: crush contents of unconscious, 51; fake security of, 155; and general mother-fathers, 150; Guattari as, 152; language of, 64; piety of, 80; reactionary behavior of, 135, 140; remain unchallenged, 192; as saboteurs of desire, 98, 137; and schizoanalysis, 149; and social issues, 142; systematic silence of, 259; and unconscious, 196

Psychoanalytic: breast-feeding, 90; discourse, 8, 290; euthanasia, 105; machine, 54, 61; method, 134; models, 155, 198, 240; movement, 142, 145; pleasure,

155; prejudices, 216; struggle, 147; strategy, 259

Psychologists, 50, 189–190, 240

Psychology, 306 n.3; analytical, 82; machinic unconscious exceeds realm of, 197 ; as manager of semiotic subjugation, 278

Psycho-pharmacology, 122, 191

Psychosis, 27, 55–56, 64, 126, 128, 145, 176, 181, 185, 191, 196–197, 260

Psychotherapy, 19, 22, 49, 57, 67, 120, 125–127, 176, 183

Psychotics, 56, 177, 185, 229

Public service: reconception of, 15, 189

Puritanism, 21, 130

Questioning: labor of, stopped up by repression on level of discourse, 65

Race: mad ravings about, 57–58; struggles, 293

Racism: delirious-fascist, 166; fascism in, 171; and schizophrenic delirium, 58; and segregative attitudes, 188

Radek, 167

Radio, 16–17, 94, 218, 302 n.25, 308 n.5

Radio Alice, 16–17

Radio Popolare, 16

Ray, Man (*Dancer-Danger*), 91

Reagan, Ronald, 292

Reality: and representation, 160; technical, 110; totalitarian, 80

Reason: as region of irrationality, 35–36

Recherches, 20, 124, 183, 218–222

Recurrence, 91–92, 95, 97, 104

Red Brigades, 16

References: becoming-woman as, for other becomings, 229; castration as constant curative, 259; historical, of deliriums,

Ricci, 173

Right, 77, 141, 145

Rimbaud, Arthur, 58

Robin, Jacques, 24

Roheim, Gesa (*Psychoanalysis and Anthro-pology*), 92, 304 n.1, 304 n.6

Rolland, Roman, 82

Rotelli, Franco, 187

Roussel, Raymond: and mental illness, 65–66

Russian Social Democratic Party, 45, 276

Sabourin, Danièle, 124

Sade, Marquis de, 304 n.3

Saint Albans Hospital, 189

Sartre, Jean-Paul, 27, 128, 149, 180

Savages, 84–86

Scarecrow, The, 95

Schérer, René, 30, 183, 303 n.55

Schizo, 41, 47, 82, 98, 101, 105, 133, 152, 247–250, 253–254, 256

Schizoanalysis, 27, 67, 77, 82, 84, 103, 143, 147, 149–150, 152, 193, 197, 199–200; development of, 67; dissociation as principle of, 103; imperatives of, 193; and revolutionary struggle, 153. *See also* Machinic unconscious

Schizoanalyst, 150

Schizoanalytic: cartographies, 27; struggle, 147

Schizo-desire: two ways of considering, 248

Schizo-process, 133, 152, 247, 275

Schizoid flows, revolutionary, 115

Schizophrenia: access to, 56; dissociation as characteristic of, 103; etiology of, 127; as experience of intensification, 63; Guattari vs. Freud on, 145; as limit of society, 84; and question of logic of sensible qualities, 62; as refusal of

system of logic, 61; as regime of desiring-machine, 109; two elements of, 65. *See also* Capitalism—and schizophrenia

Schizophrenics, 73, 82–83, 85, 87, 164, 173; and analysts, 151; autistic, 66; capacity of, to range across fields, 59; collapse, 66; and delirium about race and racism and politics, 57–58; illusory image of, 59; language, 58, 61–64; lightning-like focus of, 67–68; machine, 73; as threat to social order, 152. *See also* Insane; Mentally ill; Patients; Psychiatric population; Desiring-machines—schizophrenic process of

Schleicher, General von, 165

Schools, 21, 38, 43, 170, 182, 196, 201, 211, 235, 268, 276, 279, 289

Schreber, 57–58, 89, 145, 152

Schwitter, 105–106

Science: aspirations of, as industry for normalization of socius, 202; calling into question divisions of, 59; deepening of, 60

Scientific: description, 192; paradigm, 191

Scientific thought, 61

Scientists: discourse of, 65; Freud et al. as, 191–192

Screen memories, 100–102

Second International, 87

Secteur, 49–50, 183–184, 187, 189

Sectorization: utopian politics of, 49, 150

Self and Others (Laing), 126, 128

Semantics, 59, 63, 242, 262–263

Semiology, 173–174, 236, 241–243, 246; presignifying vs. signifying, 241

Semiotics, 135, 160–161, 164, 172–175, 199, 241–243, 245, 254–255, 258–259,

foundation of, 230; and desiring-machine, 109; and threat of schizophrenics, 152

Social production, 144, 148, 175, 244

Social rationality: eruptions that exceed, 45

Social relations, 25, 191–192, 197, 203, 221; and tool-machine, 109

Social revolution, 44, 51; as inseparable from revolution of desire, 72

Social sciences: all actors in the, ought to make themselves schizophrenic, 59; analysis of schizo language as instrument of incomparable value for, 61; calling into question divisions of, 59; question of research methods in, 215; research group started by Guattari, 301 n.7; all themes of, under scrutiny, 55

Social scientists: explosions that elude comprehension of, 59–60

Social security, 50, 153, 189

Social struggles, 142, 148, 161, 217, 241, 278

Social system, 28, 40, 46, 93, 197, 212, 259

Social technical machines, 106–108, 115. *See also* Technical social machines

Socialism, 166, 168, 237, 284, 292

Socialist: bureaucracy, 203, 285, 289; movement, 141; Party, 23–24; revolution, 70

Society: analysis as instrument for study of, 61; as if at a remove, 48; convivial, 107; desire beneath reasons of, 111–112; desire and repression in, 155; ecology and profound change of, 23; Freud's representation of, 145; full body of, 112–113; general theory of, 84–86; illusion of step-by-step transformation of, 153; and machinism, 74; madman as high priest of, 125; modern, 55; problems of contemporary, 59, 143–144; and psychosis, 126; as rational and irrational, 35; schizophrenia as limit of, 84; totality of, 41. *See also* Archaic societies; Industrial societies; Primitive societies; Repressive society

Sociological approach, 156

Sociologists, 120, 143

Socius, 84, 160, 182, 202–203, 230, 248–249, 254–255

Sophocles, 257

Space: living, 194

Specialists, 59, 71, 89, 160, 197, 265, 269

Specialization, 107

Speech, 13, 15–16, 28, 79, 241–242, 264, 278–279, 282, 308 n.1; capitalism begins before, 278; coordinated by language of power, 279; free, 219–224; vs. language, 262; primitive vs. contemporary, 282; and writing, 282

Spinoza, 112

Stalinism, 40, 156, 161, 163, 167–170

Stankiewicz, Richard, 105

State: apparatus, 14, 42–44, 46; capitalism, 59; power, 72, 293; and regulation of crowds, 169; theory of, 86; terrible burden of, 188–189

Stern, Daniel, 27

Strasser brothers, 162

Strikes, 16, 101, 139, 170

Structural logic, 147

Structuralism, 26, 85, 239, 241–242, 260; nascent critique of, 241; in psychoanalysis, 241–242, 259–267 *passim*; and system of signification, 239; stuck in domain of signification, 241–242; tied to dominant significations, 242

Structuralist analaysts, 134

Structures: official vs. alternative, 188

Struggles, 276; and analysis, 277; question of unification of, 278; against semiotic subjugation, 279. *See also* Antifascist struggle; Capitalism—struggle against; Class struggle; Classless societies—and struggle against the state; Desire— struggles of; Family—all struggles reduced to; Fascist—struggle; Militants— struggle; Object—militant struggle against reductive sense of; Political—struggles; Politics—as context for struggle with traditional psychoanalysis; Popular struggle; Psychoanalysis—and class struggle; Psychoanalytic— struggle; Race—struggles; Revolutionary —struggle; Schizoanalysis—and revolutionary struggle; Schizoanalytical struggle; Social struggles

Students, 14–15, 17, 23, 40, 143, 276, 279–280, 285; National Union of (UNEF), 182

Subject-groups, 149, 160–161; vs. power of fascism, 171. *See also* Group—subject

Subjects: castrated equilibrium of, 146; constitutive structural logic of, 147; desire strays from, 159–160; fabrication of, 182; micropolitical conflicts that emprison, 137; as sedated by best capitalist drug, 147

Subjectification, 7, 11, 23, 25–27

Subjectivation, 193, 262, 264–265; de-, 262–263

Subjective: arrangements, 182, 265; positions, 182; prostitution, 148; system, 68

Subjectivities: explosive cocktail of contemporary, 26; producing new types of, 180

Subjectivity: capitalist-totalitarian control of, 169; collective arrangements of, 193; and ethico-aesthetics, 193; expects transformation by film and psychoanalysis, 259; heterogenetic character of, 27; machinic diversity of, 197; modelization of all facets of, 183; not ready-made, 202; pleasure and individuated mode of, 155; production of, 31, 180, 192–193; and representation, 160; serialized, 182; transcendent model of, 241. *See also* Capitalist subjectivity; Group subjectivity

Subjugation, 245, 278–280, 282, 284, 287, 289

Superego, 39, 145–146, 152, 156, 163

Surrealism, 115; as enterprise of Oedipalization, 104

Symbolic: castration, 200; order, 147, 191, 285

Symbolism, 72, 113

Symptoms, 73, 101, 129, 146, 199

Syntax, 59, 198–199, 202, 263, 282, 286, 288; blindness of individuals frozen in, 68

Tatlin, Vladimir, 114

Technical machines, 28, 74, 104, 106–108, 115, 175, 203; desiring-machines as unconscious of, 111; relations of production outside of, 113; and social machines, 111

Technical objects: conditioned use-control-possession of, 109

Technical reality, 110

Technical social machines, 94–95, 112. *See also* Social technical machines

Technocracy, 48–49, 189

Technocrats, 36, 100, 143, 170, 180

Technological necessity, 107

Publisher contact:
The MIT Press
Massachusetts Institute of Technology
77 Massachusetts Avenue, Cambridge, MA 02139
mitpress.mit.edu

EU Authorised Representative:
Easy Access System Europe, Mustamäe tee 50,
10621 Tallinn, Estonia
gpsr.requests@easproject.com

Printed by Integrated Books International,
United States of America